The Design of Requirements Modelling Languages

Ivan Jureta

The Design of Requirements Modelling Languages

How to Make Formalisms for Problem Solving in Requirements Engineering

 Springer

Ivan Jureta
Département des Sciences de Gestion (B423)
Université de Namur
Namur
Belgium

ISBN 978-3-319-36973-0   ISBN 978-3-319-18821-8 (eBook)
DOI 10.1007/978-3-319-18821-8

Printed on acid-free paper

Springer International Publishing AG Switzerland is part of Springer Science+Business Media
(www.springer.com)

For Zorana ;-)

Preface

You have a requirements engineering problem to solve, if (i) you have unclear, abstract, incomplete, potentially conflicting information about expectations of various stakeholders, and about the environment in which these expectations should be met, (ii) you know that there is presently no solution which meets these expectations and (iii) you need to define and document a set of clear, concrete, sufficiently complete, coherent statements, often called requirements; so that a system is made and operated to satisfy these statements will in fact meet stakeholders' expectations.

Requirements engineering problems are ill-structured problems. Solving them is hard. You typically have to do many complex and interdependent tasks, such as elicitation, categorization, evaluation, prioritization, negotiation and prediction.

Solving a requirements engineering problem relies on intuition and creativity, but more importantly for this book, it mobilizes experiential knowledge which was shaped by your problem-solving experience. This book shows how to create artificial intelligence (AI) from that experiential problem-solving knowledge. You can see such AI as an assistant to which you can delegate some problem-solving tasks.

AI is a combination of formal languages or formalisms used to represent (make models of) problem-solving information and algorithms used to carry out transformations of, and computations on those representations. Formalisms and algorithms preserve and automate the application of that experiential problem-solving knowledge you built into them.

This book focuses on the formalisms part of AI. On the algorithm side, it shows how models made with the various formalisms can be translated, and translations fed into already well-known and general purpose algorithms.

This book was influenced by research which I carried out with John Mylopoulos and Alexander Borgida. I co-authored papers on problem solving in requirements engineering with them, as well as with Neil Ernst, Stéphane Faulkner, Anna Perini, Pierre-Yves Schobbens, Alberto Siena, Angelo Susi, and many others. They have all shaped the content of this book in various ways. This does not mean that we agree on the ideas which I present here.

March 2015   Ivan Jureta

Contents

Chapter 1
Requirements Problem Solving

This chapter clarifies what requirements problem solving is. Section 1.1 gives reasons why it is interesting to study requirements problem solving and learn how to create artificial intelligence, which automates tasks of requirements problem solving. Sections 1.2–1.4 give the characteristics of requirements problem solving, by describing the problem situations which initiate requirements problem solving, tasks done in requirements problem solving, and the solution situations sought by doing these tasks. Section 1.5 gives a synthetic definition of requirements problem solving.

1.1 Motivation

This section argues why requirements problem solving is interesting to study, and why it is relevant to generate artificial intelligence which automates tasks in requirements problem solving.

This book is about how to create artificial intelligence that helps you solve problems. If your expertise is in, or is related to these topics, then this probably brings to mind many ideas on notions such as ontologies, formal languages, algorithms, complexity, and so on. They will turn up later.

In nontechnical terms, this book is about how to define specific kinds of instructions that can be given to computers. This is interesting, because it lets you delegate some of the problem-solving work to computers, work that you need to do when solving particular kind of common, but hard problems.

Consider the following situations. You have to solve a problem to successfully get out of each. All these problems share some common characteristics and because of this, they belong to the class of so-called problems.

- A law firm has a new owner. The owner sees that the employees are delivering the same services in different ways, and believes these inconsistencies will inevitably lead to lower quality in the future. She asks you to suggest how to avoid this in the long term.

© Springer International Publishing Switzerland 2015
I. Jureta, *The Design of Requirements Modelling Languages*,
DOI 10.1007/978-3-319-18821-8_1

- A company makes software that sports coaches use to give training instructions to athletes. The owner wants every future software improvement to help reduce the time that coaches spend on repetitive tasks. You are asked how to ensure this.
- A company makes software products for telecommunications service providers. The company CEO wants all its current and future software products to have clearly defined rules and processes for customization, installation, and maintenance. He asks you to propose how to ensure this in the long term.
- A small firm designs its products and outsources manufacturing and distribution to other companies. The managing director is interested in investing in software which would help keep track of the status of new product development tasks. You are asked to suggest how to proceed.
- An electronics manufacturing company sells its products through distributors. A regional marketing director wants to improve sales decisions by collecting more merchandizing data, that is, data about product placement in distributors' points of sale. You are asked for advice on how to do this.

These situations are different. They are about *different* industries, companies, and products. They involve different people and consequently not the same expertise, experiences, or expectations. In reality, they also happened to me at different times and places, over the course of a few years.

The obvious question is:

What would you do to successfully resolve each of these situations?

The motivation for this book *does originate* in the need to answer this question. However, the book's focus is *not* to answer it. As I will mention later, there are several fields of research and practice that already provide ample material about what to do in these situations.

Instead, the book aims to answer the following question:

If you do know how to successfully resolve situations such as the above, and are often in such situations, then how can you delegate some of your problem-solving effort to computers?

There are several simple reasons to answer this question. If computers do part of the work, you have more time to apply intuition and creativity to the rest of problem solving, or for solving other problems. Others can use the same computers or more precisely software on their own, when in similar situations. Finally, the instructions that you define and the computers apply constitute a record of parts of your problem-solving knowledge, which may be a relevant source of learning for others.

1.2 Problem Situations

This section lists the characteristics of problem situations that trigger requirements problem solving.

I briefly described five situations in the preceding section. Each gave cues to there being problems, but it gave no clear, complete, precise, and coherent description of each problem. This absence of a given problem is one of the several characteristics of situations I focus on in this book. There are problems to solve in these situations.

The interesting situations, called problem situations hereafter, have the following characteristics.

1. *The problem needs to be defined. It is not given.* Instead, there is information about what someone wants and believes about the situation, the reasons and causes behind it. There is nothing that guarantees that realizing what they say they want will indeed alleviate the troubles observed in that situation.

   In absence of the exact and precise problem to solve, you have to find it out, describe it clearly, communicate it to those who expect the solution, and have them agree that solving that problem rather than another will make them happy. For example, the owner of the law firm may know what she dislikes about the current situation. But that tells you nothing about the events that led to that situation, and the actions that led to these events. The problem may be, for instance, that current instructions and incentives allowed and motivated these actions.

2. *Defining the problem requires collaboration.* A given situation may involve one or many different problems which may be independent or somehow related. There is rarely one clear problem that you can observe and describe in isolation from everything else. I emphasize that the problem is defined, and the parties involved need to agree that this is indeed the problem to solve.

   The information you may need to define the problem is not necessarily held by one individual. Problems may arise in situations or cause situations which involve people with different backgrounds, expertise, and expectations, and it may be that many of them have information you need to define the problem.

   The regional marketing director of the electronics manufacturer may want to collect some merchandizing data. It may be that only the distributor's lawyer knows if giving that data clashes with the distributor's contracts with other manufacturers.

   To find the repetitive tasks that sports coaches do, and which software should help them with it, makes it necessary to collaborate with these coaches to identify and understand such tasks, with engineers to understand the feasibility of automating these tasks, with the software product designer to prioritize which tasks the software should automate, in which release, and so on.

3. *Different people see different problems.* Different people involved in a given situation perceive the problem or problems in it differently, depending on their expertise, experience, motivations, and so on. In the same situation, a management professional may focus more on coordination between people, a lawyer on the relationships between actions and applicable legal constraints, a finance professional will look for incentive problems, and so on. Not all perspectives always matter, but it may also be that defining the problem by focusing on one of them only will lead to irrelevant solutions.

You might think the law firm owner's problem as one of leadership. An employee of the same firm may see it as an incentive problem. An information technology specialist could conclude that the situation is caused by the absence of relevant software.

1.3 Problem-Solving Tasks

This section lists the characteristics of tasks done in requirements problem solving.

What to do in a problem situation? A number of different tasks can be done. The overall aim is to move from the situation in which you recognized that there is a problem, to a situation in which the relevant parties, **stakeholders** hereafter, recognized that the problem no longer exists. All that happens between these two points is called problem solving.

There are different kinds of problem-solving tasks. They require different skills and inputs, give different outputs, and can be done at different times during problem solving. The following are typical kinds of problem-solving tasks done for problems. I cite some of the relevant research on each.

- *Elicitation* involves all tasks done in order to obtain information from people, or any other source. Collection and analysis of documentation, interviews, workshops, observation of stakeholders, or others, are some of the possible elicitation tasks [38, 55, 70].
- *Representation or modeling* involves tasks that aim to divide available information about the problem or its solutions into pieces that share similar characteristics and/or which somehow make a coherent whole, and to represent these pieces in models, which in turn are used to draw conclusions useful for deciding what to do next in problem solving [36, 84, 153].
- *Clarification* involves identifying, for example, ambiguous, vague, or otherwise unclear information and finding out more in order to repair these deficiencies, if they are deficiencies in the first place [81, 96, 105].
- *Prioritization* consists of deciding what the relative importance of various sub-problems is, so as to better use the available resources and work on dedicating more resources to the most pressing ones. It also means deciding which solution parts to implement before the others [11, 69, 88].
- *Negotiation* aims to reconcile disagreements about the problem and its solutions among the stakeholders [13, 85, 95].

There are other problem-solving tasks, and they include responsibility allocation [23, 36, 50], cost estimation [14, 17, 128], conflicts and inconsistency [68, 107, 142], comparison [96, 97, 105], satisfaction evaluation [16, 90, 105], operationalization [46, 50, 53], traceability [31, 56, 115], and change [20, 26, 146].

Almost all kinds of problem-solving tasks mentioned above are *not* specific to solving problems. Medical diagnostics involves, for example, elicitation from the patient via interview and medical devices, clarification to the patient, prioritization of symptoms and potential conditions, negotiation in case the patient disagrees with the treatment, responsibility allocation to the patient to take medication or medical personnel to administer treatment, comparison of possible treatments for the same condition, change of treatment in case it proves inadequate.

The following characteristics of problem solving for problems set them to some extent apart from other classes of complicated problems.

1. *Problem definition and solution definition are intertwined.* In simple terms, since you are defining the problem to solve, you are also defining what its solutions can be. Pushing this idea to its extreme perhaps you can convince the stakeholders that there is no problem, which is a solution. The other extreme is that you are defining an unsolvable problem within any or the given resources. Most cases are between the two, where the problem you define is influenced and influences the expectations of the stakeholders, restricts the range of possible solutions that can be considered, and the extent to which their expectations can be met.

   If, for instance, you convince the law firm owner that the problem is something intangible and abstract as employees react by being destructive to her excellent leadership style, then potential solutions narrow down to, for example, firing everyone, which would likely close the law firm given that it will become impossible to serve the same clients with untrained new employees.

2. *Problem definition identifies new (sub-)problems.* There is no guarantee that defining one problem will not lead you to find others. Defining the problem in one problem situation can lead you to another.

   In the company that makes software products for telecommunication service providers, elicitation from an employee experienced in product customization may tell you that customizations take time to define clearly with clients, and that shorter times are not feasible. Elicitation with the CEO may suggest that this should take considerably less time. The clash between the two pieces of information may be a symptom of a problem of there being few people, with little time to actually talk to clients to define customizations. It may be that clients take time to decide. Both are new problems, which may need to be solved in order to proceed to the solution of the initial problem.

3. *Problem solving rarely stops because the best solution is defined.* A solution changes the initial problem situation. Even elicitation changes it since your interaction with stakeholders can change what they understand the problem to be. Events that occur may or may not be under your or the stakeholders' influence. They can change stakeholders' understanding of the problem situation, of what worked or did not, and why you got involved in the first place.

   Change means that the best optimal solution is a moving target. Problem solving thus stops more often due to resource constraints than the willingness to seek the best solution, or more generally, to move from the problem situation to one which is more desirable.

   In the law firm, elicitation involved questions about when and what caused errors in the work with clients. These questions alone create expectations with the employees, who expected some inevitable change in the organization, be it training, changes of work processes and rules, firing, and so on. This in turn created anxiety, which contributed to errors observed in work with clients observed during problem solving. Changed work practices and rules in turn generated new anticipated problems, creating new problem situations, requiring problem solving to continue.

1.4 Solution Situations

This section lists the characteristics of solution situations when requirements problem solving stops.

A solution situation is when problem solving can stop. This can be a hard target to aim for, given that solutions to problems tend to share the following characteristics.

1. *Solutions are temporary.* Change in the environment and stakeholders' expectations will make you move from one problem situation to another, requiring moves from one solution situation to another.

   Sports coaching is not a well-defined and unchanging activity. It changes as coaches acquire new knowledge about the mechanics of the body, about the psychology of the athletes, and about the relationship of these to environmental conditions. Automating some of the tasks in sports coaching is consequently a task that can go on indefinitely, or at least for a very long time, as a perfect universal sports coaching method is a long way off, or simply does not exist.

2. *Best solutions are elusive.* Given that different people can see different problems in the same problem situation, that problems cannot be treated in isolation, and that conditions change, optimal solutions are unlikely to be easy to find, or may not exist at all. Good enough solutions have to do instead. Good enough in practice means that at least some of the most important expectations of the stakeholders are satisfied.

3. *Defining, making, and running a solution requires collaboration.* Agreeing that the solution should, for example, involve the introduction of new work rules and processes, requires designing these, training people to use them, perhaps making software that automates some, and responding to issues that arise, once the processes and rules are used. This can require expertise from management professionals, organizational psychologists, human resources specialists, business analysts, software and hardware engineers, and technical support specialists.

1.5 Requirements Problem Solving

This section gives the definition of requirements problem solving used throughout this book. The definition does not list activities done when doing requirements problem solving. Instead, it says that requirements problem solving includes all activities triggered in response to situations that satisfy specific properties. The definition lists these properties.

The characteristics of problem situation and solution situations presented in this chapter suggest that there is no known best way to do requirements problem solving. It is not known exactly which problem-solving activities need to be done, when one starts and the other stops, the exact properties their inputs and outputs should have, and the steps to take to collect the required inputs, and to produce the desired outputs.

As I will argue in Chap. 2, requirements problem solving is a kind of ill-structured problem solving, an argument which will further support observations in the paragraph above.

In conclusion, an exact and relevant list of activities that make up requirements problem solving is elusive. A definition of requirements problem solving via such a list is consequently also elusive.

My suggestion is to define requirements problem solving as all activities that people do when confronted with problem situations that satisfy specific properties or rules. These rules are not as elusive.

Definition 1.1 Requirements problem solving includes all activities done in response to situations, called problem situations, which satisfy the following conditions:

1. there is unclear, abstract, incomplete, potentially conflicting information about expectations of various stakeholders, and about the environment in which these expectations should be met,
2. there is presently no clear definition of the problem to solve, in order to satisfy these expectations, and no solution which indeed meets them, and
3. it is necessary to define and document a set of clear, concrete, sufficiently complete, coherent statements which

   a. define the problem that stakeholders agree on, and
   b. define the solution that the stakeholders agree on, such that if the solution is made and used, then it should in fact meet stakeholders' expectations and thereby solve the problem.

The resulting definition of requirements problem solving places emphasis on conditions that trigger it. It suggests that requirements problem solving includes all activities done in response to these triggers. The definition is therefore not prescriptive, suggesting what requirements problem solving should be, or when it is good or bad. Requirements engineering is an engineering discipline and field of research that prescribes which activities to do, a topic I develop in Chap. 3.

Chapter 2
Problem-Solving Automation with Artificial Intelligence

This chapter connects requirements problem solving with central ideas and terminology of problem solving and artificial intelligence. Section 2.1 clarifies what automation means in this book, and why it is interesting to automate tasks in requirements problem solving. Section 2.2 argues that requirements problem solving is one type of ill-structured problem solving, which makes it impossible to automate fully, and recalls the characteristics of ill-structured problems. Section 2.3 recalls the characteristics of well-structured problems, whose resolution can be automated, and Sect. 2.4 argues that there are well-structured subproblems that can be identified in requirements problem solving. Section 2.5 argues that there are tasks in requirements problem solving that reappear across cases, and automating them is particularly interesting. Section 2.6 connects automation of recurrent requirements problem-solving tasks to the concepts of formal language and algorithm. Section 2.7 connects these ideas to the basic terminology of artificial intelligence.

2.1 Automation

This section clarifies what automation in this book means, what its purpose is in requirements problem solving, and gives an outline of the ideas developed in the rest of the chapter.

AI's role in this book is practical. It is used to automate problem-solving tasks. I will say that a task is automated if it can be done by a computer. The specifics of the computer, its speed, memory, or other characteristics are not relevant for now.

There are machines that automate tasks without being computers, for example, a mechanical arm that closes a door. I am interested specifically in computers and not such machines, because requirements problem solving tasks involve taking and making changes to data. There is no need for the mechanical arm to have a representation of the door being open or closed, or of the door itself, and perform computations on those representations in order to accomplish closing the door. In requirements problem solving, there is a need to have data about phenomena in problem situations

© Springer International Publishing Switzerland 2015
I. Jureta, *The Design of Requirements Modelling Languages*,
DOI 10.1007/978-3-319-18821-8_2

and solution situations, and to perform computations on it. The AI for requirements problem solving may recommend through that data what to do next, but I will assume that people who read this data remain autonomous to themselves to choose the course of action.

Benefits of automation should be obvious, and I have mentioned them earlier. If a machine can do part of the problem-solving work, you can invest it in improving the quality of the solution to the current problem, or in improving your overall efficiency in problem solving (by solving more problems in the same amount of time).

Artificial intelligence is the means to automate *some* requirements problem-solving tasks. It cannot automate all of them, because it is still not clear which ones they are and how exactly to do them. Many of them rely on intuition and creativity. For example, it is not clear today how to automate elicitation via interviews, negotiation between stakeholders, or creation of relevant representations of what stakeholders say, to name some. All this might be amenable to automation using some advanced and currently unknown forms of AI, a topic which is speculative and remains outside the scope of this book.

To explain the practical role AI has in requirements problem solving, I will present and argue for the following ideas in the given order. Each has its own section in the rest of this chapter.

1. *Requirements problem solving is one of many kinds of ill-structured problem solving.* This is important, because if requirements problem solving is a kind of ill-structured problem solving, then I am right to argue that requirements problem solving cannot be fully automated.
2. *It is possible to identify tasks in requirements problem solving, in which the subproblems to solve are not ill-structured, but well-structured, in that the tasks for solving them can be automated.* In other words, although problems are ill structured as a whole, there is some structure to some of their parts, and such parts can be treated as well-structured problems.
3. *To automate the solving of a well-structured subproblem, it is necessary to have algorithms that solve it, and in turn, have rules for how to communicate with these algorithms.* You need to communicate the data about problem situations and solution situations, and the algorithms should be able to communicate back data in a way that is understandable to human problem solvers. If this is the case, then it is relevant to have specialized languages for communicating with the algorithms.
4. *AI for requirements problem solving amounts to combinations of algorithms that automate problem-solving tasks and languages for communicating with these algorithms.*

2.2 Ill-Structured Problems

This section argues that requirements problem solving as a class or type of activities falls within a broader class of activities called ill-structured problem solving. Characteristics of ill-structured problems are given, so that you can compare them with those of requirements problem-solving.

You can see this by comparing the characteristics I gave for requirements problem solving, and the characteristics of ill-structured problem solving which I give in this section. By requirements problem-solving characteristics, I mean those of problem situations, problem-solving tasks, and solution situations in Chap. 1.

There are two main reasons why it is important to be concerned if requirements problem solving is a kind of ill-structured problem solving. First, it influences the perception of how much of requirements problem solving can be automated. Second, it is relevant to know if requirements problem solving is something entirely new, unrelated to existing research and practice, or an old discussion topic.

Given the similarities between the characteristics of requirements problem solving and ill-structured problem solving, my first conclusion is that requirements problem solving cannot fully be automated. Only some parts of it can, as I will argue in Sect. 2.3. My second conclusion is that requirements problem solving is neither a fundamentally new kind of problem solving, nor targets a new class of problems. However, requirements problem solving is a hard activity to do well and it is very relevant to research how to better perform and automate requirements problem solving. At least three decades of existing research agree on this, as I will mention in Chap. 3.

The rest of this section recalls the well-known characteristics of ill-structured problem solving, specifically in engineering domains. I give these characteristics so that you can decide if you agree with my conclusions above.

To illustrate the characteristics, I borrow quotes from interviews that Jonassen et al. [79] had with engineers experienced in solving ill-structured problems.

Workplace problems are often ill-structured, including those in engineering domains, in that there is missing information, there is a need to work and coordinate with other people to get and clean up the information, there is a need to negotiate, to reach agreement, and so on.

> *"Probably the biggest challenge that we see in some of these projects is dealing with incomplete information. Invariably people will not know what the output is going to be for the product. So you do not know what kind of cooling load or heating load [is] to be expected. You do not know the specific heat is because its not listed. Or any number of design parameters that are not defined. In some cases you are making assumptions in design and you are making critical assumptions that you can do what you are wanting to do based on some piece of information or lack of information."*

Ill-structured problems include well-structured subproblems, as there may be subproblems which, if properly formulated, can be solved with existing tools and algorithms.

> *"We had to decide how big [to build] a lagoon to hold the dirt and the possible rain for the possible amount of time we were treating this soil. And we had to decide how best to treat the soil. We had to make calculations how long [it] would take to put back into the ground. As we were doing all this [we had to] decide where we would sample the soil and separate [it]. We had to figure out what we were going to find in the hole, how we would treat it so*

that we would know about the size, and what to put in the water treatment system, and how we were going to power it. So those were a few of the decisions we needed to make.

With all the data that we collected out in the field on their performance in the past years, we looked at which had the fewest cracks, which had come loose the most, which had the fewest repairs, and which were more impermeable to chlorite, to salt that gets down in them and corrodes the rebar. It was analysing the data and then also trying to confirm that with me other state DOTs that had used the same thing."

Ill-structured problems often involve many potentially conflicting goals, meaning that even when there is one seemingly clear main goal, such as "build new terminal to increase the capacity of the airport," there are subgoals, or equally important goals which can come from other stakeholders, such as "keep the number of flights constant or lower, in order to maintain or reduce noise pollution." Here is an example from a construction project, still from Jonassen et al. [79]:

"We will measure it with a variety of things. Number 1, did we meet the anticipated goals for hiring of a diverse work group. That is part of the contractual requirements as well as the participation of a variety of different kinds of enterprises. Our safety record, and of course, did we make any money on the project? [...] Our goal is always to work safely and make money. Safely and on time and make our clients happy and to get additional work from our client."

There can be many different and initially unknown ways to solve an ill-structured problem, so that the best approach is normally not known and has to be designed from scratch, or found among known alternative approaches.

The success of a solution is rarely measured by engineering standards, as it involves criteria such as satisfying the client, ontime completion, staying within the budget, as well as various legal, regulatory, and others.

"So we are pretty savvy as to understanding what the code is trying to say. You have some people in these code making bodies that you can consult to make formal interpretations and writen interpretations. So we had to make sure the bank would give us a line of credit and we had to talk to our client to see if they would pay us some up front money to start building these systems. Funding was a big concern, and we have to make sure we have legal constraints as long as we are complying with the law, and we want to make sure the client is not asking us to do something illegal. We also want to make sure that we have a contract where every party is happy, if that is possible. Make sure we get paid, and they understand what we are going to do and we understand what their expectations are."

Many constraints in problem solving are unrelated to engineering, such as cultural, political, or environmental ones.

"We are solving a whole series of things in the fact that an architect or owner wants to build a building a certain way, and he has certain needs and desires, but yet we have all these safety codes that need to be met...the state...building and Fire Department that had their whole set of requirements. And we had to make sure that those requirements also didn't pose problems. So we had a whole series of requirements one playing off against the other that we had to balance out. And there were several environmental issues up there, concerns from the U.S. Fish and Wildlife that we were going to hurt the fish."

Knowledge required to solve the problem is distributed across different people, in same or different, related or unrelated organizations, and they all have to contribute during problem solving.

"There's certainly the property owner, there's the telephone company regional manager, there's the utility company chief engineer, there's the utility company distribution engineer, there's there utility company attorney. There's the utility company's insurance company attorney. There's the homeowners, the homeowners' insurance company attorney. There's his insurance adjuster. There's a fire investigator, two fire investigators, that's about all, there's my electrical testing company technicians.

Inside our organization engineers, partners, cad drafters, graphical, computer, secretarial help. Outside our form we interfaced with the architect, the owner, the structural engineer, mechanical engineer, electrical engineer. We interfaced with all those disciplines because it is essential to have all those things working together as a package."

Problem solving requires extensive collaboration, which is not unusual, given that the problem-solving knowledge is distributed.

"We all pretty much know our roles but know that in our specialisation those people touch on certain things affect fire protection engineering and life safety.

We are all working together for a common goal, which is to make sure that we have an economically viable building and a safe building – on that is going to function the proper way. We all sit down at the conference table together and we come up with a plan and then we work very closely with the engineering disciplines so we have all the details ironed out."

Experience guides problem solving, in that they will rely on information that they can recall from the past, when they faced and did, or failed to solve similar problems and do so more, than rely on their understanding of the abstractions which the concrete problem instantiates.

"Experience some problems like [those] that have occurred in the past. Experience on those things is probably the biggest way we get them solved quickly anyway."

Unanticipated problems often arise in problem solving, as the environment and expectations may change, and more specifically budgets, regulations, client's goals, and so on.

"Also at different times we don't live in a perfect world and when buildings get put together at times people can make mistakes. Sometimes they can't be rectified and need to be ripped out and other times where it would be disastrous to do that so we develop equivalency concepts for that. The other unanticipated thing is you can get in a project and the owner can change his mind and all of a sudden the whole dynamics of the project changes."

2.3 Well-Structured Problems

This section recalls the characteristics of well-structured problems. This is relevant because the solving of well-structured problems can be automated.

A problem is well structured if there is sufficient knowledge about how exactly to describe it, what its solution is, and what exactly to do, in order to reach the solution. This is reflected in the characteristics of well-structured problems, which I recall below. They are essentially the same as those that Herbert Simon argued for, and which seem to be widely accepted in artificial intelligence research [127].

(1) Well-defined solution situation: There is a well-defined situation, called solution situation, which if observed, means that the problem is solved.

A well-defined situation means that there is a set of variables, and each obtains a value. This is also called a solution state. I use the terms "situation" and "state" interchangeably. Variables can be "product profitability," "employee satisfaction," or something that has a widely accepted definition, such as "outside temperature," or "elevation."

Clearly defined also means that there is no room for interpretation of what variables and their values stand for. For example, $x = 5$ is clearly defined only if it is known how to measure, observe, compute, or otherwise obtain the value of x in a way stakeholders agreed on.

A condition such as "product is profitable" is not clearly defined if stakeholders disagree about the exact way to measure product profitability. If, however, all agree about what exactly profitable means for that specific product (say, that if the accounting profit generated through sales of a product is above a given threshold amount of money), then it is clearly defined.

(2) Solution test: There is a test, called solution test, which can be carried out to check if the solution situation is reached. If the solution situation is, for example, that "employees are satisfied with new work processes," there has to be a procedure to apply, in order to check if this is the case. To have the procedure, you have to know how to measure "employee satisfaction," and in the absence of a universal definition (which is present if you are measuring, say, distance on land), you need an instrument for measurement, and the stakeholders have to agree on it. The instrument could be a survey questionnaire. The test, in turn, could be that you distribute the questionnaire to a sample of employees or all of them, and observe a specific pattern of responses.

(3) Language: There is a set of agreed-upon terms, and of rules for using these terms for describing the problem situation, solution situation, and intermediate situations. Such languages will be called requirements modeling languages in this book as they are used to represent or make models of information used during requirements problem solving.

Take a simple example, such as a heating a room when you are cold. The thermometer reads 20 °C, the heater is on at heating intensity 2 (out of five intensity values). What I just wrote are the terms that define three variables, for temperature, heater being on, and heating intensity. Each is clearly defined, as you know the possible values, you know which of them you can directly change values of (heater being on and heating intensity), and you know how to measure the one you cannot (temperature). The initial state of the problem is defined as the assignment of values to the variable, that is, temperature is equal to 20 °C, heater status is on, and heating intensity is 2. You decide that the solution situation is temperature being 25 °C. In an intermediate situation, you may measure that temperature is 22 °C.

In other words, there is an agreed-on language for describing the initial conditions, in which there is the problem, the intermediary conditions that you get into by problem solving, and the solution that you want to reach.

(4) Operator: There is a set of operators used to change from one situation to another. For each operator, the conditions it applies are known, that is, it is known which values variables should have in order to be able to apply the operator.

You can think of an operator as an action that can be taken when specific conditions are satisfied (that is, some variables take some values), and which changes the values of some other variables.

Continuing the heating example, an operator is you changing the heating intensity level by turning a knob on the heater. The operator applies when heater status value is on, and its effect can be that you reduce or increase heating intensity from the current, to any one of the five intensity values. Another operator may be that you can turn the heater on or off, and thus change the value of heater status variable to either of its two values.

(5) Difference tests: There are tests that can detect differences between values of variables in two situations. They are used to detect how applying operators changed the values of variables.

A difference test may consist of measuring room temperature, that is, checking the temperature, to conclude that changing heating intensity from value 2 to value 4 increases the room temperature by $6\,^\circ$C.

(6) Difference rules: There are rules defining which operators to use, to reduce differences observed with difference tests.

A difference rule may say that if the difference between the temperature in solution situation and the temperature in the current state is between 2 and $4\,^\circ$C, then apply the operator to increase heating intensity level and increase it to level 3.

2.4 Well-Structured Subproblems

This section argues that although requirements problem solving is ill-structured problem solving, it is possible to identify tasks which target subproblems having all the characteristics of well-structured problems. Such tasks in requirements problem solving can be automated.

If you wanted to approach the law firm owner's case as if it was a well-structured problem as a whole, then can you describe solution situation? What is the language to use to describe the problem situation, intermediary situations, and the solution situation? What are the variables? What are the possible values of these variables? What operators act in those situations? How would you test if you reached solution situation? The same questions arise, if you wanted to apply well-structured problem solving to all cases in Chap. 1.

The trouble with these questions and the main reason why those cases involve ill-structured problem solving is that there is no existing knowledge, in research or practice, which gives agreed-on answers. There is no standard that prescribes what to do in those cases. There is no book that guides you step-by-step from the problem situation to a satisfactory solution situation.

It is possible, however, to identify parts of the ill-structured problem for which you can answer the questions above in a satisfactory manner.

In the law firm owner's case, issues seem related to how employees deliver services. It is likely that solving them requires the help of employees. It thus seems useful to evaluate employee satisfaction at present and in the future. Their satisfaction matters, and it would be relevant not to judge it informally, but to have an evaluation procedure which they and the owner agree on.

Is making and carrying out the survey to evaluate employee satisfaction a well-structured subproblem in the law firm case?

There is no standard or scientific rule for this. The quality of a solution is ultimately evaluated by stakeholders. The solution itself is influenced by the problem that you defined during requirements problem solving.

It follows that you have three options. In one, the subproblem is well-structured because you have the knowledge required to address it as a well-structured problem. This means that you know a language, relevant operators, and so on, *and stakeholders agree that your approach is appropriate*. You would define and perform the surveys, which would require that you define the variables whose values are measured via data collected in the survey, the survey questions, and so on.

A second option is that you do not know how to solve it as a well-structured problem, and so it is an ill-structured problem for you. But you may know someone whom you can delegate it to, and for whom it is a well-structured problem.

It is important to keep in mind that the resulting well-structured problem is one of measuring employee satisfaction, not changing it. The change is not part of this subproblem.

Take another example. One of the tasks many of the sports coaches from the earlier case do is invoicing and some outsource it to their accountants. Invoicing includes producing invoices at regular intervals. There are accountants capable of doing this, and there is also software capable of doing this. It may thus be that producing invoices is a well-structured subproblem. Notice that although producing an invoice is an ill-structured problem for a coach, it is not for an accountant, or for a software designed to do it.

The third option is that the subproblem is ill-structured, when neither of the two options above are feasible.

The first two options are interesting because they mean that

"You managed to divide the ill-structured problem into parts, you can call them subproblems, or at the very least, you identified one subproblem which you, or someone you choose, is capable of solving as a well-structured problem."

Problem structuring is the task that aims to identify subproblems, and understand the relationships between them as well as their solutions. This task itself need not be a well-defined subproblem. You may never manage to have an accurate map, a description of all the subproblems, and of all their relevant relationships.

But while you recognize one or some well-defined subproblems, the rest of the initial and overall ill-structured problem need not be as well behaved. Simon described the challenge as follows [127]:

"Interrelations among the various well structured subproblems are likely to be neglected or underemphasized. Solutions to a particular subproblem are apt to be disturbed or undone at a later stage when new aspects are attended to, and the considerations leading to the original solutions forgotten or not noticed."

One of the recurrent topics in requirements problem-solving research is how to document the decomposition of the ill-structured problem into subproblems, to record their relationships, and to evaluate how solving some subproblem in one way influences the resolution of another subproblem.

2.5 Case-Specific and Recurrent Tasks

This section argues that requirements problem solving involves case-specific and recurrent tasks. It is interesting to automate recurrent tasks which target well-defined subproblems.

In the above section, I used as examples two tasks that can be relevant to perfom in two different cases. One is surveying the employees of the law firm and the other is invoicing in the sports coach software case. An important idea to keep in mind is that producing invoices and surveying are tasks specific to the problem situation. They are *case-specific* tasks.

It is interesting to develop knowledge of how to solve these subproblems as well-structured problems. If you manage to do so, perhaps you can go further and automate the solutions. The result might be relevant to companies and/or individuals who happen to encounter similar problem situations.

This book focuses instead on the automation of *recurrent tasks* in requirements problem solving, of tasks that reappear in different cases.

Problem structuring is one example of such a task. It is hard to avoid it when solving requirements problem solving, regardless of case specifics. Keeping track of subproblems and their relationships is not specific to a given problem situation, but seems necessary for any ill-defined problem, that is, whenever you do requirements problem solving. It is therefore particularly interesting to try to incorporate AI which helps with these recurrent requirements problem-solving tasks.

2.6 Languages and Algorithms

This section argues that automating a task in requirements problem solving requires defining formal languages used to represent information about problem situations, solution situations, and intermediary situations and algorithms which perform computations over these representations.

To have a computer automate a recurrent requirements problem solving task, such that the task solves a well-defined subproblem, you need to identify the subproblem, define all the components required for it to be a well-structured subproblem, and have them in a format which the computer can store, read, and perform computations on.

This book is about how to do the above. Using simpler yet technical terms, the challenge is to define languages and algorithms, which together can be used to make software to which you can delegate a recurrent task in requirements problem-solving.

I will not go so far as to show how to actually make that software. Instead, I will stop at the point where it is clear what that software would do, and how.

Languages need to be formal languages, that is, such that terms and rules for using terms of the language are precisely defined. Such languages are used to describe situations, whether they are problem situations, solution situations, or intermediary ones.

Algorithms describe procedures applied to descriptions of situations. They perform calcuations over variables that describe situations. They take some input written in the language, perform computations (value calculations, changes, additions, deletions, etc.) to these, and produce results that are, again, written with the language, and describe situations.

You can see the algorithms as combinations of operators, solution tests, difference tests, and difference rules, all used when solving a well-structured subproblem.

2.7 Artificial Intelligence

This section argues that AI for requirements problem solving amounts to combinations of a formal language and algorithms.

AI is a science on its own, and this book makes no contributions to it. Instead, I will use existing results in AI when they are useful to automate requirements problem-solving tasks.

Making AI for requirements problem solving in this book equates to the problem of making languages and algorithms that can automate specific requirements problem-solving tasks. Both the languages and algorithms are not somehow made by, or discovered by AI, but at best imperfectly reflect the knowledge of human problem solvers. The resulting AI is thus not smart in any meaningful way, but is only able to apply quickly many rules that are inspired by what an expert problem solver would otherwise do.

In the rough classification of major lines of research in AI, which Stuart Russell and Peter Norvig suggested in a classical textbook [120], AI for requirements problem solving in this book falls in the so-called "laws of thought," or logicist approach, in which the emphasis is on defining rules for how to draw a correct conclusion from some given information. The rules to apply to the given information when drawing conclusions can reflect the thinking patterns of a typical individual or of an expert.

It is consequently true that AI for requirements problem solving, as it is developed in this book, also suffers from two main limitations of the logicist approach, which Russell and Norvig summarize as follows [120]:

> *"First, it is not easy to take informal knowledge and state it in the formal terms required by logical notation, particularly when the knowledge is less than 100% certain. Second,*

there is a big difference between being able to solve a problem 'in principle' and doing so in practice. Even problems with just a few dozen facts can exhaust the computational resources of any computer unless it has some guidance as to which reasoning to try first. Although both of these obstacles apply to any attempt to build computational reasoning systems, they appeared first in the logicist tradition."

This book is intended to help solve the first issue, specifically for requirements problem solving. If you yourself have that informal knowledge relevant for solving recurrent requirements problem solving tasks, or you have access to someone who does, the book will suggest how to go from that informal knowledge to languages and algorithms.

As for the second issue, I have no better solution than to map algorithms used for requirements problem solving to well-known algorithms in AI. This book will illustrate that there is quite a lot you can automate in requirements problem solving by using a language whose sentences can be converted into graphs, and by applying algorithms for reasoning on graphs (such as searching subgraphs with some interesting properties). This will be clearer later in the book.

Chapter 3
Problem and Solution Concepts in Requirements Engineering

Requirements engineering designates both the rigorous practice of requirements problem solving and the field of research which studies this practice and ways to improve it. This chapter connects the ideas discussed in Chaps. 1 and 2 to the basic ideas and terminologies of requirements engineering. This is important because various requirements modeling languages and algorithms, that is, AI for requirements problem solving, have been proposed in requirements engineering since the origin of the field in the 1970s.

3.1 Requirements Engineering

This section suggests the following relationship between requirements problem solving and requirements engineering: The former designates the phenomenon which the latter studies and aims to influence.

Requirements engineering is a term that designates both an engineering discipline and a field of scientific research.

The engineering discipline covers various activities, such as elicitation, modeling, analysis, negotiation, and so on, which are carried out in order to define rules that a system has to satisfy when it is made and used. The rules can originate in expectations of stakeholders who invest, use, or otherwise influence and are influenced by the system, in the conditions of the system's operating environment, its regulatory environment, and so on.

It is an engineering discipline. These activities have to be done rigorously, in planned steps, using tried and tested mathematical or other tools.

Requirements engineering as a field of scientific research studies a variety of topics, such as information elicitation [38, 55, 70], categorization [36, 84, 153], vagueness and ambiguity [81, 96, 105], prioritization [11, 69, 88], negotiation [13, 85, 95], responsibility allocation [23, 36, 50], cost estimation [14, 17, 128], conflicts and inconsistency [68, 107, 142], comparison [96, 97, 105], satisfaction evaluation [16, 90, 105], operationalization [46, 50, 53], traceability [31, 56, 115], and change

© Springer International Publishing Switzerland 2015
I. Jureta, *The Design of Requirements Modelling Languages*,
DOI 10.1007/978-3-319-18821-8_3

[20, 26, 146]. Each topic is related to issues and tasks that occur during requirements problem solving.

Historical origins of requirements engineering are in software engineering, and specifically in the challenge to define and document what the system should do for its stakeholders and in its environment, without saying exactly how it will do this. The "how" usually remains outside the scope of requirements engineering and is the responsibility of those engineering, making, maintaining, and changing the system.

The notion of *system-to-be* is a term that emphasizes it is not made yet, or simply *system* is central to requirements engineering.

Due to the historical origins, system usually designates *software and hardware*. At its boundary are the people who interact with it and any other thing in the environment which the system can somehow exchange information with, influence, and be influenced by.

The phenomenon that the requirements engineering discipline and field focus on existed before either the discipline or the field was formally recognized. Requirements engineering arose in response to situations observed in systems engineering in general, of not knowing how to make sure that the system being made will in fact appropriately address the issues that motivated making it in the first place.

Requirements problem solving designates that phenomenon, namely all that people do when they have unclear, abstract, incomplete, and potentially conflicting information about expectations of various stakeholders and about the environment in which these expectations should be met; a system should be made to satisfy these expectations, and they want to define rules, such that if the system is made to satisfy these rules, then it will also satisfy the expectations in its given environment.

Requirements problem solving is present when designing new and changing existing systems. It needs to be done for any system class and domain, and regardless of the extent to which people are involved in the system, from autonomic Internet-scale clouds, to traditional desktop applications, industrial expert systems, and embedded software, all enabling anything from massive mobile application ecosystems, global supply chains, medical processes, business processes, mobile gaming, and so on. Requirements problem solving is done regardless of how the software in the system is designed and made, from a military waterfall approach to a startup's own agile dialect, and from organizations where software engineers talk directly to customers, to those where product designers, salespeople, or others mediate between requirements and code. In all these cases, there will be unsatisfied expectations and the need to make systems to satisfy them.

3.2 Problem and Solution

This section introduces definitions for the terms problem and solution, and relates them to the notions of problem situation, solution situation, and requirements problem solving.

Problem and solution are common terms. The dictionary definition of problem is that it designates "a matter or situation regarded as unwelcome or harmful and needing to be dealt with and overcome." The corresponding definition for solution is that is "a means of solving a problem or dealing with a difficult situation."[1]

This section introduces definitions for "problem" and "solution" which are specific to this book. They are simple, uncontroversial, and coherent with their dictionary definitions. The main benefit of having specific definitions is that they use the terminology introduced for requirements problem solving in Chap. 1. Secondary benefits are less obvious, and I will highlight them below.

3.2.1 Problem

I use the term "problem" to refer to *ideas* about what is observed or believed to be true in a problem situation. Problem is what you observe or think is true in the problem situation. It is *not* a record of these ideas, for example, a document where you wrote them down. It is the ideas or thoughts themselves.

It is important that a problem designates ideas, not their representations. This is because I argued earlier in Sect. 1.2 that different people can see different problems in the same situation. They may pay attention to different events, things, and individuals. They may draw different conclusions about what is and is not desirable in that situation. You may hold one set of ideas, but there is no reason others should share them.

Instead of using the terms "ideas" and "thoughts" in my definitions, it is more conventional in requirements engineering to talk of *propositions*. I consequently say that you and I may believe different *propositions* to be true of a situation, even if we are in that same situation. The term "proposition" has a specific definition in philosophy, and I follow the one from Matthew McGrath [101] in the Stanford Encyclopaedia of Philosophy:

> "Propositions [...] are the sharable objects of the attitudes and the primary bearers of truth and falsity. This stipulation rules out certain candidates for propositions, including thought- and utterance-tokens, which presumably are not sharable, and concrete events or facts, which presumably cannot be false."

Tying the above to problem situation leads me to the following simple definition for the term "problem."

Definition 3.1 *Problem*: propositions believed to be true of a problem situation.

---

[1] Both quotations come from a Google search for keywords "define:problem" and "define:solution."

3.2.2 Solution

Comments I made for the term "problem" apply for the term "solution." Solutions are ideas believed to be true of the solution situation. Hence the following definition.

Definition 3.2 *Solution*: propositions believed to be true of a solution situation.

The major difference from the common sense definition of the term "solution" is that here, "solution" is not that which brings about the solution situation. It amounts to propositions about the solution situation. As I explain in Sect. 3.3, I use the term system for that which brings about the solution situation.

3.3 System

This section introduces the term system and relates it to the terms introduced so far.

Although the historical origins of requirements engineering are in software engineering, the term "system" in contemporary requirements engineering is not restricted only to software and/or hardware. Its scope can include only limited to specific (parts of) software and hardware, or widened to include such issues as work guidelines, business processes, responsibilities, contracts, or other concerns.

As various things can be part of a system, I prefer not to define the term by saying what can be in it, or has to stay outside. It makes no difference in this book what exactly is, or is not part of a system. What matters is that the system is all that is made and used to bring about a solution.

Definition 3.3 *System*: that which is made and used in order to make solution true.

A system need not be about software or hardware. It can be a brand, a political election program, a corporate strategy, or a business process.

In all cases I discuss in this book, the system is not restricted to software and hardware. In some of the cases, software and hardware were not mentioned at all as important parts of systems which were actually used.

3.4 Model

This section introduces the terms model, problem model, solution model, and relates them to those introduced so far.

The remaining piece of the puzzle is to describe solutions, problems, and systems in such a way that we can communicate about them during requirements problem solving. This is done with models.

Definition 3.4 *Model*: representation of propositions.

This is not a conventional use of the term model in requirements engineering. Model is normally used to designate the representation of the system only. However, I need to talk about representations of solutions, problems, and systems, which lead me to several kinds of models.

Definition 3.5 *Problem model*: representation of a problem.

Definition 3.6 *Solution model*: representation of a solution.

Definition 3.7 *System model*: representation of propositions believed to be true of the system.

It is on the basis of system model that the system is implemented, updated, changed, its new releases planned, made, announced, and rolled out. The system model's scope may be limited to specific (parts of) software and/or hardware, or widened to include such issues as work guidelines, business processes, responsibilities, incentives, contracts, or other concerns.

System model can take different forms, from minimalistic to-do lists that hint at stakeholders' expectations and subsume implicit design and engineering solutions, to elaborately structured documentation on contracts with employees and suppliers, responsibilities of positions in the value chain, guidelines for employee coordination and collaboration, as well as software pseudocode.

A system is not the output that requirements engineering produces. Requirements engineering does not include, for example, the detailed engineering, development, testing, release, maintenance, and so on, of software that may be part of the system, nor can it include the training of people who should use it. In the law firm owner's case, the solution included changes in contracts with employees, in incentives, training, team building, among others. They are activities which in order to be done well require specific expertise and are delegated to those who have it.

Problem models, solution models, and system models are the output sought in requirements engineering and requirements problem solving.

3.5 Default Problem and Solution

This section presents and discusses the default problem and default solution concepts in requirements engineering.

There is a default definition of the problems that requirements engineering tries to solve when applied. There is also a default definition of the solution sought. It is important to know them because they highlight a number of assumptions made in requirements engineering.

The de facto default view in requirements engineering is that requirements problem solving is done incrementally, starting from incomplete, inconsistent, and imprecise information about the requirements and the environment, and that each design step reduces incompleteness, removes inconsistencies, and improves precision, toward the system model [15, 23, 36, 46, 48, 58, 80, 107, 119, 141, 153].

This general view of the problem-solving process, which you start with less detailed and somehow deficient information, and then increase detail and remove deficiencies, is also shared in other domains involving design, such as architecture [92, 134] and civil engineering [4].

Within that view, which requirements engineering has of requirements problem solving, what is the default definition of problems and solutions?

The most influential treatment of this question is in Pamela Zave and Michael Jackson's seminal paper "Four Dark Corners of Requirements Engineering" [153], and is echoed in discussions on the philosophy of engineering [132]. Their view is aligned with some of the most influential research in requirements engineering, which both preceded and followed said paper. This includes, for example, contributions from Boehm et al. [13, 15], van Lamsweerde et al. [36, 37, 96, 141, 142, 143], Mylopoulos et al. [23, 58, 107], Robinson et al. [119], Nuseibeh et al. [74, 107], to name some.

According to Zave and Jackson, requirements engineering is successfully completed in any concrete engineering project when the following conditions are satisfied [153]:

1. *"There is a set R of requirements. Each member of R has been validated (checked informally) as acceptable to the customer, and R as a whole has been validated as expressing all the customer's desires with respect to the software development project.*

2. *There is a set K of statements of domain knowledge. Each member of K has been validated (checked informally) as true of the environment.*

3. *There is a set S of specifications. The members of S do not constrain the environment; they are not stated in terms of any unshared actions or state components; and they do not refer to the future.*

4. *A proof shows that $K, S \vdash R$. This proof ensures that an implementation of S will satisfy the requirements.*

5. *There is a proof that S and K are consistent. This ensures that the specification is internally consistent and consistent with the environment. Note that the two proofs together imply that $S, K,$ and R are consistent with each other."*

Using the terms I introduced so far, Zave and Jackson's conditions translate as follows:

1. There is a requirements model, call it R, which stakeholders agreed on. It represents propositions that convey stakeholders' expectations.
2. There is an environment model, called K, which stakeholders agreed on. It represents propositions believed to be true of the environment in which the system will run.
3. There is a system model, call it S, which describes propositions true of the system.
4. If the propositions represented in the environment model are true, that is, the environment is as described, and the system is made and runs in that environment according to the system model, then propositions described in the requirements model will also be true.

5. If the system is made and runs according to system model, then the environment
   will remain as described in the environment model, and if the environment remains
   as described, then the system will continue to run without violating system model.

The translation emphasizes that there are *representations* of three kinds of propositions, namely requirements, domain knowledge, and system propositions. The translation also does *not* assume that any of these representations is written in classical
logic, and therefore, cannot talk about proofs. Instead, it rewrites the fourth and fifth
conditions without assuming the language used to make the representations. All these
are minor changes, and the translation preserves the central ideas. ·

Perhaps the most important observation to make about the conditions from Zave
and Jackson is that they do not talk about the structuring of the problem and solution,
and about the design of the system. In other words, there is no indication that this is ill-
structured problem solving. The conditions should be checked after the requirements,
environment, and system are clear enough, to make problem solving well structured.

Returning to the main topic of this section, the translation suggests a default
problem and solution for requirements engineering.

Definition 3.8 *Default problem*: there are

1. a set R^p of requirements propositions, which are propositions believed to be true
   of what stakeholders expect, and
2. a set K^p of environment propositions, which are propositions believed to be true
   about the environment in which the system will be used,

and it is not sufficient for the environment propositions alone to be true, in order for
requirements propositions to be true.

The default problem is that you know something about stakeholders' expectations
and about the environment in which they need to be satisfied, yet that environment
alone does not ensure that these expectations indeed are satisfied.

I write X^p for a set of propositions, and X for the set of representations of propositions, which may, but need not be related to those in X^p. The reason I dissociate
X from X^p is that it is hard to be sure that all propositions in R^p are accurately
represented by the content of R. Keep in mind that propositions in R^p are ideas,
not representations of ideas. They are hard to access, so to speak, because by being
ideas, they are "in the mind" of your own and of others. Going from R^p to R is
complicated, involves having people communicate with you during elicitation about
propositions, and thus probably means that you and someone else would produce
different R sets, from presumably the same R^p.

In contrast to the default problem, the solution is not the input, but the output
of problem solving, which comes therefore after problem structuring, and is about
models.

Definition 3.9 *Default solution*: there are

1. a requirements model R, which stakeholders agreed on, and which may represent propositions from R^p in the Default problem,
2. an environment model K, which stakeholders agreed on, and which may represent propositions form K^p in the Default problem,
3. a system model, call it S, which describes propositions true of the system,

and the system model S is such that

1. if the propositions represented in K are true, that is, the environment is as described, and the system is made and runs in that environment according to the system model, then propositions represented in the requirements model R will also be true, and
2. if the system is made and runs according to S, then the environment will remain as described in the environment model K, and if the environment remains as described in K, then the system will continue to run without violating the propositions represented in S.

Keep in mind that K in the default solution does not need to represent exactly all or any of the propositions in K^p in the default problem. Same applies to requirements propositions in R^p and the requirements model R. This is because the default problem triggers requirements problem solving, which involves problem structuring, and the information known for the original problem can be removed or replaced.

Chapter 4
Introduction to Requirements Modeling Languages

Requirements modeling languages are formal languages specialized for use in requirements problem solving. This chapter clarifies what a formal language is normally made of, and explains its role in problem solving in general. To give a clearer idea of where requirements modeling languages come from and look like, this chapter gives a rough historical overview of their design, discusses their broad similarities and differences, and presents two requirements modeling languages called i-star and Techne.

4.1 Formal Language

This section explains what a formal language is normally made of, regardless of the kinds of problems it is used for. The basic components, syntax, and semantics are explained and a trivial example of a formal language is given.

Formal languages are used for communication, same as natural languages such as English or French. An important difference between a formal language and a natural language is that every sentence in a formal language is made according to a clearly defined and finite set of rules. The definition of a formal language amounts to a number of rules, which together define what sentences of that language can look like and what they are about, that is, to what they refer.

I follow David Harel and Bernhard Rumpe [67] in seeing a formal language as made of two basic sets of rules. They are syntax rules and semantics rules, or simply, syntax and semantics. Each set can be further broken down into pieces, and this section clarifies the purpose of these pieces and how they fit together to define a formal language.

© Springer International Publishing Switzerland 2015   29
I. Jureta, *The Design of Requirements Modelling Languages*,
DOI 10.1007/978-3-319-18821-8_4

4.1.1 Syntax

Syntax rules say which symbols can appear in sentences and how these symbols are combined into sentences. Syntax is defined with two sets of rules. *Symbol rules* define all allowed symbols. *Grammar rules* define all allowed combinations of symbols.

For illustration, suppose that you want the language L to have sentences in which there are only Arabic numeral symbols. You first define the set of allowed symbols, call it S, as follows:

$$S = \{0, 1, 2, 3, 4, 5, 6, 7, 8, 9\}.$$

The above is a set of symbols, not of numbers. I still have not said what each symbol represents or stands for; I will do it later with semantics.

Suppose, then that you want all sentences of this language to include exactly 10 symbols. In other words, any sentence in L has the following format:

where each ⌣ must be replaced by any one symbol in the set S. It follows that 0019200216 is a sentence in L, but 108141 is not, and neither is $401 - 8208w28085 < k\%0258$.

To define that all sentences in L must include exactly 10 symbols from S and that there can be no white spaces between them, you can write that every sentence of L, call that generic sentence a, must have the following format:

$$a ::= xxxxxxxxx$$

where x is any member of S, that is $x \in S$. The rule above is itself written in a formal language, called Backus–Naur Form.

If you need no more symbols and no more rules on combining symbols, then the syntax of L is defined with the following rules where the first three are symbol rules and the fourth is a grammar rule:

$$L = \{a_1, a_2, \ldots\},$$
$$S = \{0, 1, 2, 3, 4, 5, 6, 7, 8, 9\},$$
$$x \in S,$$
$$a ::= xxxxxxxxx.$$

It is important to keep in mind that symbols can be anything, and it is up to you to choose them and the grammar for combining them into sentences. They do not need to look like anything in natural language. Modern musical notation is one example. You may want to use pictures as symbols, or sketches, or physical objects as long as they serve the purpose of the language you are making.

4.1.2 Semantics

Semantics are rules that define what the symbols and sentences are meant to represent, and how to determine which symbol and sentence represents what. In technical terms, semantics defines the *semantic domain* of the language and the *semantic mapping* which ties sentences to elements in the semantic domain.

Suppose I want to use the syntax defined above to represent cell phone numbers in Belgium. The semantic domain is therefore the set of all possible cell phone numbers in Belgium.

I know that any cellphone number in Belgium must have ten digits, so sentences in syntax have good length. To map these sentences to cell phone numbers, it is enough to map each symbol to a number and I can do this with the following rules:

symbol 0 represents number 0,

symbol 1 represents number 1,

symbol 2 represents number 2,

...,

symbol 9 represents number 9.

The above is the same as defining a function, called the semantic mapping function, or simply semantic mapping. Denote that function m, and let it take any symbol, and return the corresponding number, so that $m(\text{symbol } 1) = 1$, and so on.

I also know that Belgian cell phone numbers always begin with a zero. This is something that I know about the domain, and the language should reflect this. As mentioned above, the syntax of L allows any number symbol to be in the first place in the sentence. I therefore change the syntax by using the following rule instead of the previous rule for a:

$$a ::= 0xxxxxxx.$$

The reason why it is relevant to map sentences to numbers, is because of the way cell phone operators defined cell phone numbers, and their systems recognize cell phone numbers as 10-digit integer numbers.

Suppose, instead, that cell phone numbers are not numbers, but to call someone's cell phone, you have to input ten Latin alphabet letters. In that case, the semantic domain would be all 10-place words made from Latin alphabet letters. The syntax of L would no longer be appropriate since it has no unique symbol for the smallest relevant element of the semantic domain. This does not mean that Arabic numeral symbols are not good, but only that I can no longer map individual symbols to individual elements of the domain, and ensure that each element in the domain has a corresponding unique representation in syntax. This change in the semantic domain would result in changes to both syntax and semantic mapping.

Defining formal languages is usually harder than in the example above, but this is a fair start. The rest of the book will raise and discuss many language design issues. The terminology of syntax and semantics will come back every time, and it will keep being used in the same way as above.

4.2 Role in Problem Solving

This section argues that the role requirements modeling languages have in requirements problem solving and requirements engineering is based on the assumption that they influence how requirements problem solving is done, by influencing how information used during problem solving is represented, and that this in turn influences how human problem solvers think during problem solving.

Requirements modeling languages are formal languages. They differ from various other types of formal languages in that their syntax and semantics are designed to support specific tasks in requirements problem solving.

It is an implicit assumption in requirements engineering that the way information is represented during problem solving influences problem solving. That assumption is an important motivation for doing research on and teaching formal languages for requirements problem solving and requirements engineering, and on the creation of guidelines, processes, and methods for making and manipulating the resulting representations.

The assumption is very much related to research on the relationship between language and thought in linguistics and cognitive science. It is aligned with the Sapir–Whorf hypothesis [89], which is that "[s]tructural differences between language systems will, in general, be paralleled by nonlinguistic cognitive differences" and that "[t]he structure of anyone's native language strongly influences or fully determines the world-view he will acquire as he learns the language." It is related to the linguistic relativism position [51, 62], which is that [109] "use of the linguistic system [...] actually forces the speaker to make computations he or she might otherwise not make." [1]

In cognitive science, there are empirical results [34, 78, 155] supporting the claim that "external representations" or sentences of a formal language are relevant when solving complex problems. They are not only memory aids, but they also influence

---

[1]Linguistic relativism is usually related to the nativist position; the latter argues that concepts are prior to and progenitive of natural language. The two positions are usually not seen as conflicting. As Gleitman and Papafragou note [54]: "To our knowledge, none—well, very few—of those who adopt a nativist position on these matters reject as a matter of a priori conviction the possibility that there could be salience effects of language on thought. For instance, some particular natural language might formally mark a category whereas another does not; two languages might draw a category boundary at different places; two languages might differ in the computational resources they require to make manifest a particular distinction or category."

how people discover, describe, and explore problems and their solutions. Similar views were echoed in programming language design, for example, in Kenneth E. Iverson's 1979 Turing award lecture, on notation as a tool of thought [76].

4.3 Rough Historical Overview

This section gives a rough historical overview of requirements modeling languages in requirements engineering research. The section uses specialized terminology of requirements engineering to mention the main similarities and differences between these languages.

Requirements modeling languages are formal languages proposed in requirements engineering research to support various tasks in requirements problem solving. They arose in response to three intertwined questions, which remain among the central ones in the requirements engineering research field, and for at least four decades now [60]:

1. What information should be elicited from the stakeholders of the system.
2. How to represent and create models of the elicited information.
3. What kinds of computations should be performed over these models and why.

The initial response to these questions was to apply formal methods [30, 147] in requirements problem solving. Formal methods are highly developed formal languages for the specification of the properties of a system. Examples of formal methods are VDM [8], Larch [64], Z [130], B [1], and Alloy [77].

Since the 1990s, it is recognized in requirements engineering research that formal methods are not relevant as formal languages for requirements problem solving [58]. The main complaint is that they are too generic. They give no indication about the types of information to elicit or represent about the problem situation and solution situation, how to organize and represent this information in ways that can help such tasks as the negotiation and validation of requirements by stakeholders. Their syntax and semantics are not designed with requirements problem solving in mind. They have no specific features for answering recurring questions in requirements problem solving.

The contemporary view is that requirements modeling languages have the difficult task to bridge the messy steps in requirements problem solving and those when rigorous application of formal methods becomes feasible. This view is reflected in many requirements modeling languages as they include concepts and rules for translating their models, or some parts thereof, into models in formal methods.

The first formal language that was considered a requirements modeling language is RMF [59]. It is "a notation for requirements modeling which combines object-orientation and organization, with an assertional sublanguage used to specify constraints and deductive rules" [58].

An idea in RMF, which still remains important today, is that a requirements modeling language should explain how its sentences can be translated into sentences of a formal logic, such as classical first-order logic, or a specialized variant such as linear temporal first-order logic. This ensures that algorithms that can be applied to sentences of such logics can be applied, after translation, to sentences in a requirements modeling language. It also means that representations made with the requirements modeling language can be translated into those of a formal method, as long as the formal method has a translation to the same formal logic as the requirements modeling language.

The semantic domain of RMF distinguished between propositions about entities and about activities. This may be generic and consequently versatile, but it is also still generic. For example, it may be relevant to know which of the given activities are more important than the others or which are more desirable, as this may influence deciding which activities to include and exclude from a solution.

The distinction between entities and activities in the semantic domain of RMF was judged limited [58] and responses to limitations went in two directions.

One direction in requirements modeling languages such as KAOS and i-star, is to have more categories and relations predefined in the semantic domain, and to keep that set of categories and relations fixed. This means, for example, that if the language has no category or relation that you can use to indicate that some situation is more desirable than another one, or that an activity is more important, then you cannot show this in models made with this language. The language does not have rules for how to add new categories and relations to it, so that you can, for example, add a new relation and use it to show that a situation shown in a model is more desirable than another situation shown in the same model. To compensate for this, the languages in this approach often include many categories and relations judged relevant for requirements problem solving in general.

The other direction was adopted in the formal language Telos [104] and consists of leaving the concepts and relations in the semantic domain undefined. The language includes tools to define the categories and relations in the semantic domain. This second approach is more versatile, but its abstraction makes it difficult to provide methodological guidance that can be given when a fixed set of concepts is known and manipulated every time the language is used. Although Telos could be used for requirements problem solving, it has rarely assumed that role.

KAOS remains an important requirements modeling language. "The overall approach taken in KAOS has three components: (i) a conceptual model for acquiring and structuring requirements models, with an associated acquisition language, (ii) a set of strategies for elaborating requirements models in this framework, and (iii) an automated assistant to provide guidance in the acquisition process according to such strategies" [36]. The conceptual model of KAOS defines the categories and relations that make up the semantic domain. There are objects, operations, agents, goals, obstacles, requisites, scenarios, and relations such as specialization, refinement, conflict, operationalization, concern, and so on. There are rules in KAOS for translating its models into sentences of linear temporal logic.

KAOS introduced many important new ideas in the design of requirements modeling languages. It introduced the concept of "goal" to requirements modeling languages and used it to represent stakeholders' expectations, which the system and stakeholders should work together to achieve. KAOS gave the template for the definition of new requirements modeling languages by showing how to closely fit the language and the guidelines for using it. The language also allowed one to have models that are written only in a visual notation and simple templates, and to rewrite parts of models in linear temporal logic only if it was relevant in the specific case of requirements problem solving. This role of linear temporal logic in KAOS made it possible to see KAOS as a language that comes before and naturally precedes the application of formal methods, at least those that also use linear temporal logic. One could use KAOS for requirements problem solving, and once the solution is found, take relevant parts of the KAOS model of that solution, and carry them over into a detailed system model made with linear temporal logic.

i-star is a language that distinguishes itself from those mentioned above both in its design and its focus. In terms of design, its initial definition did not come with rules for translating its models in sentences of a formal logic or formal method. The focus of i-star is on helping the engineers and stakeholders understand the interdependencies of actors within and in relation to a system, their individual and joint goals, tasks, available or necessary resources, and the roles they occupy.

A model in i-star aims to be a snapshot of the intentional states (what they want, assume, know, and so on) of actors in a situation, along with what roles they adopt, and how they depend on each other for the satisfaction of individual and joint goals, the performance of tasks, and use of resources. The system or its components are considered as actors, alongside human individuals and groups.

i-star is a lightweight language relative to KAOS. This should make it easier to learn. This was recognized as a critical feature, given that requirements be validated by stakeholders who cannot be expected to manipulate artifacts produced with formal methods and formal logics.

i-star was used as the requirements modeling language component of Tropos [23], a methodology for information systems engineering. Once i-star models of the system within its organizational environment are made, Tropos suggests how to proceed toward models of data and behavior, useful for detailed engineering of the system. Formal Tropos [50] continued the tradition of mapping models to first-order logic sentences, by mapping i-star models to sentences of linear temporal logic. This connected i-star to formal methods, in an analogous way as KAOS is related to formal methods.

Techne [80] was a more recent development in requirements engineering research. It highlighted and promoted three ideas for the design of requirements modeling languages. One is that each requirements modeling language comes with its own assumptions about what requirements problem solving involves, and what the problems and solutions should look like. However, it might be the first language which explicitly defined the generic problem it is used to solve, and gave formal properties that a model has to satisfy, in order to include a solution to a given problem. The second idea is that there can be different candidate solutions to the same problem, and that it is important for a language to have tools to indicate which of these solutions is more desirable than others, and to compute which of them is the most desirable, or roughly speaking, "the best." The third idea is that it is possible to have a language with a relatively simple semantic domain, and be able to represent in its models many things that were normally thought to require more categories and relations in the semantic domain of a language.

Another interesting characteristic of Techne is that it is perceived as an "abstract" requirements modeling language intended to be used as the starting point for the definition of new requirements modeling languages. Languages made from Techne are bound to be quite different from RMF, KAOS, and i-star. Techne is not object-oriented and does not incorporate the specialization relation. Elements of the semantic domain in Techne are propositions. Techne supports neither the definition of temporal constraints, nor task sequencing, nor can it distinguish between domain assumptions which are facts (say, laws of nature) from those that are open to debate. Emphasis is on straightforward knowledge representation and its use toward the identification of candidate solutions.

Techne and i-star, for example, differ in several respects. i-star cannot represent conflict, preferences, or mandatory and optional requirements. Alternative decompositions of a goal in i-star are compared in terms of their contributions to softgoals. Techne keeps softgoals, but due to the vagueness of softgoal instances [82, 84] it requires that they are approximated, meaning "refined" by other non-softgoals, among which preference relations can be added to indicate which ones satisfy the softgoal in more desirable ways than others. Techne includes no concepts pertaining to actors and roles.

Paolo Giorgini et al. [53] recognized the need to formalize representations of goals identified during requirements problem solving. The aim is to evaluate which goals will be satisfied and how much. Their goal models are AND/OR graphs in which nodes are goals and a number of relations are provided to indicate if the interaction is positive or negative (how the satisfaction of a goal influences the satisfaction of the other goal related to it), as well as to specify the strength of the interaction. Techne uses preferences to indicate in the relative degrees of satisfaction, while quantitative estimates of satisfaction levels are not used.

Techne's handling of inconsistency is similar in aim to Anthony Hunter and Bashar Nuseibeh's in LQCL. They are interested in reasoning on inconsistent models and "keeping track of deductions made during reasoning, and deciding what actions to perform in the presence of inconsistencies" [74, pp. 363–364], while avoiding drawing trivial conclusions from inconsistent models. A Techne model keeps track of all the deductions made, and inconsistencies (conflicts) are clearly shown. A significant difference is that their work is based on clausal resolution, which may lead to concluding inconsistency, but this is prevented from leading to irrelevant formulas being inferred. In contrast, Techne addresses directly the identification of maximally consistent submodels from which inconsistency cannot be concluded.

Techne by its very design avoids asking stakeholders for quantitative estimates of preference, in contrast to, for example, the language from Sotirios Liaskos et al. [97]. Preferences are binary relations, and two preferences cannot be compared in a Techne model itself, but only after the comparison table is constructed. Techne thereby recognizes that there are different approaches to decision making in the presence of multiple criteria and no ideal decision rules, leaving it to the designer who makes a new requirements modeling language from Techne to choose herself the decision rules to apply on the comparison table.

This section inevitably leads to the conclusion that requirements modeling languages come in different shapes and forms. In sum, RMF is a custom formal language with built-in abstraction mechanisms, including aggregation, classification, and generalization. KAOS uses the language of linear temporal logic and categorizes ground formulae as instances of concepts, such as goals, requirements, constraints, while categorizing proof patterns as goal refinement, conflict, or other relations of interest when doing requirements engineering. i-star has a custom visual notation, which comes together with axioms which instruct how to make and read i-star models. LQCL uses the language of classical propositional logic to represent requirements, imposes no classification to requirements, and uses a set of inference rules that are paraconsistent, so that it allows automated reasoning over inconsistent sets of requirements. Techne has its own formal language, where expressions are a subset of propositional Horn clauses, with a mechanism to assign types of requirements to facts and clauses.

Despite the important position that formal languages play in requirements engineering, there are no widely accepted and precise standards that a formal language must satisfy in order to be called requirements modeling language. The evolution of formal languages in requirements engineering is one of testing of and converging on similar ideas, rather than making languages according to strict rules of a requirements modeling language.

4.4 i-Star

This section outlines the requirements modeling language called i-star. A simple example is used to illustrate the language.

This section gives a brief overview of i-star. The aim is not to give a detailed definition, but only give an idea of what the language looks like, the kinds of models that can be made with it, and of what makes its syntax, semantic mapping, and semantic domain. If you are interested in a detailed definition, I suggest looking up Eric Yu's PhD thesis [149].

i-star remains influential since it was proposed in the 1990s. It is the requirements modeling language in the information systems engineering methodology Tropos [23, 50]. There are many extensions of i-star, discussions of its merits and limitations, and 2015 will witness the eight annual i-star research workshop. The state of the art on i-star is discussed in Yu's "Social Modelling for Requirements Engineering" [152].

Unless I indicate otherwise, all citations in this section are from Eric Yu's "Modeling organizations for information systems requirements engineering" [150].

4.4.1 Motivation

The aim of i-star was to be able to represent information about how individuals and systems in an organizational environment interact and depend on one another in their tasks in using resources and achieving individual or joint goals. It is a language focused on "organizational environments—an important class of environments within which many computer-based information systems operate" [150].

The emphasis in i-star is on representing how individuals, software, and other resources coordinate to realize personal and joint goals. Every situation one represents with i-star conveys the organization of agents, and every agent "depends on others for accomplishing some parts of what it wants, and are in turn depended on by others. Agents have wants that are met by others' abilities, run tasks that are performed by others, and deploy resources that are furnished by others. These dependencies form a complex and intricate network of intentional relationships among agents that might be called the intentional structure of the organizational environment."

Using the terms from earlier chapters, i-star is a formal language that can be used to make problem models and solution models. There is usually one i-star model or a set of sentences in the language to represent the problem. There is another to represent the solution. The first is often called the as-is model, and the second the to-be model.

For illustration, consider a system for scheduling meetings. The person scheduling the meeting, the meeting scheduler, should try to select a convenient date and location such that the most potential participants can participate. Each meeting participant should provide acceptable and unacceptable meeting dates based on a personal agenda. The scheduler will suggest a meeting date that falls in as many sets of acceptable dates as possible, and is not in unacceptable date sets. The potential participants agree on a meeting date once an acceptable date is suggested by the scheduler.

A model for such a system can be represented as an instance of the i-star Strategic Rationale model or a Strategic dependency model. The latter kinds of models are made with a subset of i-star and are used when it is not relevant to represent all information that a Strategic Rationale model would include.

An example Strategic Rationale diagram for the scheduler is reprinted in Fig. 4.1 [151]. It shows actors such as *Meeting Scheduler* and *Meeting Participant*, their interdependencies in the achievement of goals, the execution of tasks, and the use of resources, and their internal rationale when participating in the given system. For example, the *Meeting Be Scheduled* goal of the *Meeting Initiator* can be achieved (represented via a so-called means-ends link) by scheduling meetings in a certain way, consisting of (represented via task-decomposition links): obtaining availability dates from participants, finding a suitable date (and time) slot, proposing a meeting date, and obtaining agreement from the participants. Cloud-shaped elements designate so-called softgoals which differ from goals in that there are no clearly defined and agreed criteria for their satisfaction. Softgoals are commonly used to represent nonfunctional requirements in a goal diagram.

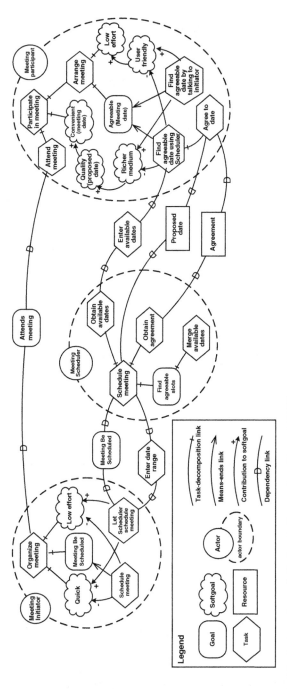

Fig. 4.1 An i-star Strategic Rationale diagram from Yu et al. [151]

4.4.2 Syntax

The legend in Fig. 4.1 gives the symbols that can be used in i-star models. There are shapes labeled "goal" "softgoal," "resource," "task," "actor," and those labeled "task-decomposition link," "means-ends link," "contribution to softgoal," and "dependency link." In any given model, each shape has its own label, and the label is in a natural language, such as English in the figure.

Rules missing from the legend are those of grammar. They are as follows, for the Strategic Rationale diagram:

- Inside the dashed area of "actor boundary" symbol, there can be any number of i-star symbols, as long as they satisfy all i-star grammar rules.
- "Task-decomposition link" symbol has its source side and its target side drawn with a short line across the long line. Its source side must be drawn connected only to one "goal," "task," or "resource" symbol. Its target side must be drawn connected to one "task" symbol.
- "Means-ends link" symbol has a source and a target side, drawn with an arrow. Its source side must be drawn connected to one "goal," "task," or "resource" symbol. Its target side must be drawn connected to one "goal" symbol.
- "Contribution to softgoal" symbol has a source and a target side, drawn with an arrow and a label symbol. The label symbol can be exactly one of "+," "++," "-," or "- -." Its source side must be drawn connected to one "goal," "task," "resource," or "softgoal" symbol. Its target side must be drawn connected to one "softgoal" symbol.
- "Dependency link" symbol has a source and a target side, the former on the left-hand side of the symbol "D" and the other on its right-hand side. Its source side must be drawn connected to one "goal," "task," or "resource" symbol. Its target side must be drawn connected to one "goal," "task," or "resource" symbol.

You can draw i-star Strategic Rationale diagrams by applying the grammar rules above to the allowed symbols. There may be other grammar rules, and there are other ways to define them. You can refer to Eric Yu's original work on i-star [149, 150] for the original grammar of i-star.

4.4.3 Semantic Domain and Mapping

The semantic domains of i-star are propositions about the goals of agents, how agents depend on one another to achieve goals, tasks that agents do to achieve goals, and resources used when executing tasks and achieving goals. Identifying goals, tasks, resources, dependencies, and so on is a task for the modeler. She identifies these through observation of the environment and existing systems, during requirements elicitation, among others. To do so, she relies on definitions of notions of goal, task, resource, dependency, and others, which are given in the definition of the i-star language, which at the same time define its semantic domain. For illustration, here is how dependencies are defined, or explained:

- Goal dependency is a relation in which "one agent, the depender, depends on another, the dependee, for the fulfillment of a goal. The dependee is free to choose how to accomplish the goal. The depender is only interested in the outcome."
- In a task dependency, "a depender agent depends on some dependee agent for the performance of a task. The task specification constrains the choices that the dependee can make regarding how the task is to be carried out."
- Resource dependency is a relation in which "a depender agent presupposes the availability of a resource, which is made available by a dependee agent."

Semantic mapping is a function that takes such a proposition, and produces a combination of symbols and labels on symbols, which are all drawn in a Strategic Rationale diagram.

For example, this sentence is a representation of a proposition in written English: "In order to organize a meeting, the meeting initiator depends on meeting participants to attend the meeting." The semantic mapping function would take the proposition and produce an "actor" symbol with a label "meeting initiator," a "task" symbol with the label "organize meeting," have that "task" symbol inside the "actor boundary" dashed line of "actor" symbol labeled "meeting initiator," there would be a "dependency link" symbol with the "organize meeting" symbol at its source and "attend meeting" goal, and so on. The results are symbols on top of Fig. 4.1. Clearly, it is hard to automate the application of the semantic mapping function. It is the modeler who does the work of matching symbols and their combinations to the propositions based on her understanding of the definition of the semantic domain of i-star.

4.4.4 Comments

I close this section with my own opinion of i-star, and in relation to the topics of this book. I see it as a language that has an innovative design that makes it perhaps more accessible relative to other requirements modeling languages.

Its innovation is not so much in its mathematical aspects, that is, in the axioms that define its concepts and relations via such concepts as "belief" and "intention" taken from knowledge representation and reasoning research in AI. A major innovation is in the idea that an organizational environment, in which a future system should run, can be looked at not in terms of concrete tasks and processes only, but in terms of less precise notions of dependency which do hint at who needs to do what and perhaps who needs to do it before someone else, but highlight how collaboration and delegation generate vulnerabilities of the actors involved.

With as-is i-star models, you can show goals, tasks, and resources that actors collaborate on and use, and how, because of that collaboration, they are vulnerable to each other (if one fails, perhaps others, who depend on her, will fail in their goals and tasks as well). With to-be i-star models, you can show how the future system would change existing patterns of dependencies, that is, current collaboration and vulnerabilities.

The emphasis on visual syntax, that is, on having models be diagrams (rather than, for example, formulas), and the small set of concepts and relations (relative to, say, KAOS), makes i-star accessible to novices. It is not odd that research on i-star is an active domain.

4.5 Techne

This section outlines the requirements modeling language called Techne. The section uses a simple example to illustrate the language.[2]

4.5.1 Motivation

Alexander Borgida, Neil Ernst, John Mylopoulos, and I made Techne [80] in response to a new so-called Core Ontology for Requirements Engineering, or CORE [84]. In general, an ontology is a specification of a conceptualization of a domain, that is, it is a precise definition of the categories of things or ideas in a domain and of relations between these things or ideas.

What I mean by "in response" is that Techne was made so that CORE defines its semantic domain. This was interesting, because John Mylopoulos, Stéphane Faulkner, and I presented CORE as a revision of the ontology that Pamela Zave and Micheal Jackson defined, when they proposed the rules for when requirements engineering is done in a systems engineering project. I cited these rules in Sect. 3.5, and used them to define the default problem.

When you propose a new ontology such as CORE, which is designed to be a core ontology, meaning, a basis for other ontologies in requirements engineering, and if it is different from the existing core ontology used to define the default problem and default solution, you have also to give the problem and solution concepts which use the concepts and relations of that new core ontology. CORE comes with its own definition of the problem which reflects what triggers requirements problem solving and what problem solving needs to produce.

The problem and solution in CORE are called the CORE problem and CORE solution below.

---

[2]This section (excluding the Figures) has been published before in "Techne: Towards a New Generation of Requirements Modeling Languages with Goals, Preferences, and Inconsistency Handling" in "RE 2010, 18th IEEE International Requirements Engineering Conference," see [80]—©IEEE 2010, reprinted with permission.

Definition 4.1 *CORE problem:* there are

1. a set G^p of goal propositions, which are propositions believed to be true of what stakeholders expect and whose truth can be verified without a doubt, and
2. a set Q^p of quality constraint propositions which are propositions believed to be true of the quality stakeholders expect from the system and whose truth can be verified without a doubt,
3. a set U^p of softgoal propositions, which are vague propositions believed to be true of the quality stakeholders expect from the system, but whose truth (because they are vague) cannot be verified without a doubt,
4. a set K^p of environment propositions which are propositions believed to be true about the environment in which the system will be used,
5. a set M^p of mandatory propositions, which are propositions that are required to be true, and can be goals, quality constraints, or softgoals, that is, $M^p \subseteq G^p \cup Q^p \cup U^p$, and
6. a set P^p of preference propositions that are true of stakeholders' preference for some goals, quality constraints, and softgoals over others,

and it is not sufficient for the environment propositions alone to be true, in order for all mandatory goal and quality constraint propositions to be true.

I will clarify later what is meant by goals, quality constraints, softgoals, and preferences. The CORE solution is defined as follows.

Definition 4.2 *CORE solution:* there are

1. a goal model **G**, which stakeholders agreed on, and which may represent propositions from G^p in the CORE problem,
2. a softgoal model **S**, which stakeholders agreed on, and which may represent propositions from U^p in the CORE problem,
3. a quality constraints model **Q** which stakeholders agreed on, which may represent propositions from Q^p in the CORE problem, and which are said to approximate the mandatory propositions in the softgoal model U,
4. an environment model **K**, which stakeholders agreed on, and which may represent propositions from K^p in the CORE problem,
5. a preference model **P**, which stakeholders agreed on, and which may represent propositions from P^p,
6. a task model **T**, which describes propositions true of what system and other agents in the environment will do,

and the task model **T** and the environment model **K** are such that

1. if the propositions represented in **K** are true, that is, the environment is as described and the propositions in **T** are true, that is, tasks are done as described, then all mandatory propositions represented in **G** and **Q** will also be true,
2. because of approximation, all mandatory propositions represented in **S** will also be true,

3. tasks in **T** are feasible, meaning that executing them does not falsify the propositions represented in **K**, and
4. none or some of nonmandatory (optional) propositions represented in **G**, **Q**, or **S** are also true.

The last condition in the CORE solution is due to there being preferences over propositions that can be false. It follows that you could find different solutions, and preferences could tell you which of them is "the best." I will return to preferences and the issue of identifying the best solution in Chap. 14.

CORE and its problem recognized that in addition to goals (which correspond to requirements in the default problem) and tasks (which correspond to the system model there), different stakeholders have different preferences over goals or tasks that they are interested in choosing among alternative solutions to the problem, that potentially many such solutions can be identified, and that requirements are not fixed but change with new information from the stakeholders or the environment. In the absence of preferences, as in RMF, KAOS and i-star to some extent, it is (i) not clear how solution models can be compared, (ii) what criteria (should) serve for comparison, and (iii) how these criteria are represented.

Techne takes CORE as the definition of its semantic domain. This also influences what problems and solutions amount to in Techne, and they are strongly inspired, though not exactly the same as the CORE problem and CORE solution above. The differences come from the fact that Techne wants to give a formal, mathematical definition of the problem and solution, which requires making decisions about how to have mathematics that convey the ideas represented in the various English words and phrases in the definitions above.

As there could be more than one solution, Techne talks of *candidate* solutions that are compared on the basis of which preferred and/or optional goals, quality constraints, and softgoals the corresponding solution models satisfy (make true).

Another distinguishing characteristic of Techne is that it was designed as a language core on which to build new requirements modeling languages. By core language is meant a minimal set of components that are argued as necessary to a requirements modeling language, if it is to model goals, softgoals, quality constraints, domain assumptions, and tasks used to define problem models, to define solution models, to model preferences and optional requirements, and use them as criteria for the comparison of candidate solutions represented in solution models.

The simplest way to make a requirements modeling language from Techne is to add a visual syntax. For example, add a diagrammatic notation and map its syntactic elements to those of Techne's syntax.

4.5.2 Semantic Domain and Mapping

I will follow our original presentation of Techne [80] and explain its semantic domain via categories it uses for the classification of problem-solving information, and relations it is interested in, over pieces of this information.

4.5.2.1 Classification

Elicited information is classified according to the rules in CORE. The overall idea is to distinguish in a statement, which a stakeholder communicates, the psychological mode from the proposition that the statement represents. Then, you establish which CORE concept the statement instantiates and this is based on the psychological mode (belief, desire, and so on) and on some properties of the statement itself. Stakeholders' desires become instances of the goal concept if they refer to conditions, the satisfaction of which is desired, binary, and verifiable (for example, "Deliver music to clients via an online audio player"). If desires constrain desired values of nonbinary measurable properties of the system-to-be, then they are instances of the quality constraint concept ("The bitrate of music delivered via the online audio player should be at least 128 kb/s"). When desired values are vaguely constrained and on not necessarily directly measurable properties, they instantiate the softgoal concept ("Buffering before music starts in the audio player should be short"). Stakeholders' intentions to act in specific ways become instances of tasks to be accomplished either by the system-to-be, or in cooperation with it, or by stakeholders themselves. Beliefs are instances of domain assumption, stating conditions within which the system-to-be will be performing tasks in order to achieve the goals, quality constraints, and satisfy as best as feasible the softgoals. Stakeholder evaluations of requirements—their preferences for some goal (or otherwise) to be satisfied (true) rather than another, or that some must be satisfied, while others are optional—result in relations over requirements subsequently used to compare candidate solutions.

To solve the problem, it is necessary that the categorized statements are recorded, refined, and expanded by iteratively acquiring new ones. To record requirements, Techne maps statements to labels, thereby sorting them. Let p, q, and r (indexed or primed as needed) represent propositions, and $\mathbf{g}()$, $\mathbf{q}()$, $\mathbf{s}()$, $\mathbf{t}()$, and $\mathbf{k}()$ be labels for, respectively, goals, quality constraints, softgoals, tasks, and domain assumptions. A labeling function simply follows the rules of CORE recalled above: if p is an instance of goal, then we write $\mathbf{g}(p)$, if q is an instance of quality constraint, we write $\mathbf{q}(q)$, and so on. Hereafter, *requirement* is a synonym for any labeled representation of a proposition.

4.5.2.2 Relations

There are five relations on requirements in Techne: (i) *inference*, (ii) *conflict*, (iii) *preference*, (iv) *is-mandatory*, and (v) *is-optional* relations. The first two are used to describe and distinguish between candidate solutions and the last three to compare candidate solutions.

Inference

When a requirement (a goal, quality constraint, softgoal, task, or domain assumption) is the immediate consequence of another set of requirements, the former is called the conclusion, the latter the premises, and they stand related through the inference relation.

Say there are two goals, $\mathbf{g}(r_1)$ and $\mathbf{g}(r_2)$, with r_1 for "Music plays in a player integrated in the web page" and r_2 for "Player has all standard functionalities for listening music." If there is also a domain assumption $\mathbf{k}(\gamma_1)$, with γ_1 for "If r_1 and r_3 then music is delivered to clients via an online audio player," then we can conclude the goal $\mathbf{g}(r_3)$, with r_3 for "Deliver music to clients via an online audio player." From two goals and an assumption stating a conditional, the conclusion is another goal.

Reading this backward, from $\mathbf{g}(r_3)$ to the three premises, resemblance to refinement becomes clear: the inference relation can be used to connect the refined requirement to the requirements that refine it. The refinement of a goal by other goals has been a salient feature of KAOS, while other requirements modeling languages had their own proxies (for example, task decomposition in i-star) of the refinement relation. The intuitive meaning of these relations is that if the set of more precise requirements is satisfied, then the less precise requirements are assumed satisfied.

Techne considers that, say, goal refinement and task decomposition ask basically the same question: What more precise requirements should be satisfied in order to assume that the less precise—refined, decomposed—requirement is satisfied as well? Instead of relating less precise to more precise requirements by a refinement or decomposition relation, Techne generalizes these via the inference relation. Note that in both these cases, the form of the rules $\mathbf{k}(\phi)$ is a *definite Horn clause* [112].

Conflict

Contradictory/inconsistent requirements cannot be in the same candidate solution, or equivalently, are in conflict. The conflict relation stands between all members (two or more) of a minimally inconsistent set of requirements. That a candidate solution should be conflict-free means that conflict relations play a crucial role in distinguishing between consistent sets of requirements, and if these sets satisfy some additional properties in distinguishing between candidate solutions. To say that n requirements are in direct conflict, another piece of information is needed, namely an implication which explicitly states that if these requirements together hold, then they imply an inconsistency: for example, to say that $\mathbf{g}(r_1)$ and $\mathbf{k}(r_4)$ are in conflict, where r_4 is for "The user cannot download the audio files," it is necessary to say that the two are contradictory, which is done via an assumption: for example, $\mathbf{k}(\gamma_2)$, with γ_2 for "$\mathbf{g}(r_1)$ and $\mathbf{k}(r_4)$ are contradictory."

Preference

Stakeholders' evaluations of requirements convey that not all requirements are equally desirable. For example, perhaps "The bitrate of music delivered via the online audio player should be at least 256 kb/s" is strictly preferred to "The bitrate of music delivered via the online audio player should be at least 128 kb/s." If a requirement is strictly more desirable than another one, then there is a preference relation between them and by *strictly*, we mean that they cannot be equally desirable.

Is-mandatory

Evaluation is not only comparative, as in the case of preference: individual requirements can be qualified in terms of desirability regardless of other requirements. The is-mandatory relation on a requirement indicates that the requirement *must* be satisfied, or equivalently, that a conflict-free set of requirements which does not include that requirement cannot be a candidate solution. If $k(r_4)$ is mandatory, then every candidate solution will include it, and exclude all requirements contradicting $k(r_4)$ (because a candidate solution cannot include conflicts).

Is-optional

In contrast to the is-mandatory relation, the is-optional relation on a requirement indicates that it would be desirable for a conflict-free set of requirements to include that requirement, but that set can still be a candidate solution if it fails to include the optional requirement; for example, if $k(r_4)$ is optional, then a conflict-free set of requirements which does not contain $k(r_4)$ can still be a candidate solution. Stated otherwise, if there are two candidate solutions which *differ only* in that one has an optional requirement and the other does not, then the former is strictly more desirable than the latter.

4.5.3 Syntax and More Semantic Mapping

Requirements and relations between them are recorded in graphs called *r-nets*. Each requirement and each relation obtains its own node in an r-net, while edges are unlabeled and directed, having contextual informal interpretation: how one reads/calls an edge depends on which requirements and relations it connects (see below). Note already that, as an r-net contains all requirements and all relations for a system-to-be: the r-net thus defines the requirements problem for a given system-to-be, and includes all (if any) candidate solutions to the problem, so that it is by the analysis of the r-net that candidate solutions are sought (see Sect. 4.5.4).

4.5.3.1 Modeling Inference

To show an inference relation, put in the r-net a node (**inf**) for the inference relation, then a line from every premise requirement node to **inf**, and a line from **inf** to the conclusion requirement node.

Example 4.1 Assume the aim is to build a system that would deliver music on-demand: a user visits a website, chooses songs from a database, and can play them in the audio player on the website. Let $\mathbf{g}(p)$, with p for "Generate revenue from the audio player." We can refine it with two goals and a quality constraint: $\mathbf{g}(p_1)$, $\mathbf{g}(p_2)$, and $\mathbf{q}(p_3)$, where p_1 is for "Display text ads in the audio player," p_2 for "Target text ads according to users' profiles," and p_3 for "Maintain the player free to all users." To conclude $\mathbf{g}(p)$ from $\mathbf{g}(p_1)$, $\mathbf{g}(p_2)$, and $\mathbf{q}(p_3)$, we need to assume that $\mathbf{k}(\phi_1)$, with ϕ_1 for "if $\mathbf{g}(p)$ from $\mathbf{g}(p_1)$, $\mathbf{g}(p_2)$ and $\mathbf{q}(p_3)$, then $\mathbf{g}(p)$." Figure 4.2 shows the r-net with this refinement.

Fig. 4.2 Inference as refinement in Example 4.1

Figure 4.2 shows an r-net in a trivial visual syntax, vaguely inspired by the furniture collection "Un piccolo omaggio a Mondrian" by Ettore Sottsass. The mapping to the symbolic syntax of Techne is obvious from this and other figures in this section. My aim was to brighten up the discussion, as it already has its share of dry formulas.

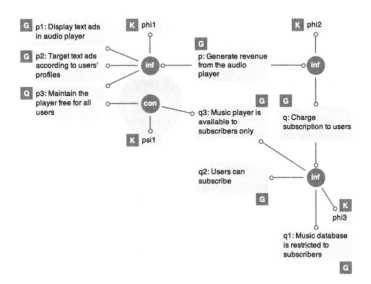

Fig. 4.3 Conflict in Example 4.2

4.5.3.2 Modeling Conflict

To show a conflict between requirements, put a node for each one of the conflicting requirements in the r-net, a conflict node (**con**), and a line from every requirement node in the conflicting set to the conflict node.

Example 4.2 (Contd. Example 4.1) We start with $\mathbf{g}(q)$ with q for "Charge subscription to users," and add $\mathbf{k}(\phi_2)$, with ϕ_2 for "if $\mathbf{g}(q)$ then $\mathbf{g}(p)$." We then refine $\mathbf{g}(q)$ onto $\mathbf{g}(q_1)$, $\mathbf{g}(q_2)$, and $\mathbf{g}(q_3)$, with q_1 for "Music database is restricted to subscribers," q_2 for "Users can subscribe," and q_3 for "Music player is available to subscribers only." This requires the assumption $\mathbf{k}(\phi_3)$, ϕ_3 for "If $\mathbf{g}(q_1)$, $\mathbf{g}(q_2)$, and $\mathbf{g}(q_3)$, then $\mathbf{g}(q)$." It appears that "we cannot both maintain the player free to all users ($\mathbf{q}(p_3)$) and make music available to subscribers only ($\mathbf{g}(q_3)$)" which ψ_1 abbreviates, so we add $\mathbf{k}(\psi_1)$. We thereby have the conflict between $\mathbf{q}(p_3)$ and $\mathbf{g}(q_3)$, highlighted in Fig. 4.3.

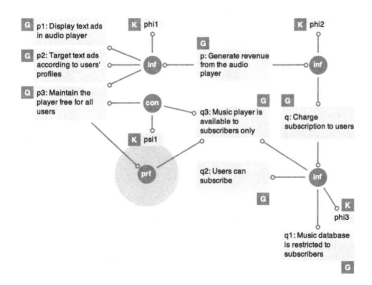

Fig. 4.4 Preference in Example 4.3

4.5.3.3 Modeling Preferences

Preference is a binary relation: if a requirement x is preferred to requirement y, add a preference node (**prf**), and draw a line from the preferred requirement (x) to the preference node (**prf**), and from the preference node (**prf**) to the less-preferred requirement (y).

Example 4.3 (Contd. Example 4.2) The r-net in Fig. 4.3 includes two refinements of $g(p)$. The conflict **con** indicates that these are two *alternative* refinements, as they cannot appear together in a candidate solution. The preference highlighted in Fig. 4.4 says that $g(q_3)$ is strictly preferred to $q(p_3)$. This preference becomes one (of potentially many) criteria for the comparison of candidate solutions: if this were the only criterion, then we would choose the candidate solution which includes $g(q_3)$ instead of another which includes $q(p_3)$.

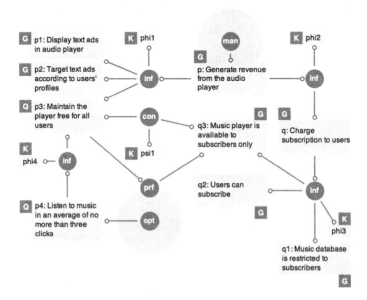

Fig. 4.5 Mandatory and optional in Example 4.4

4.5.3.4 Modeling Mandatory and Optional Relations

Both the is-mandatory and is-optional relations are unary. To say in an r-net that a requirement is mandatory, add a node (**man**) for the is-mandatory relation, and a line from the requirement node to the is-mandatory node. To state instead that a requirement is optional, add a node (**opt**) for the is-optional relation, and a line from the requirement node to the is-optional node.

Example 4.4 (Contd. Example 4.3) If every solution must include $g(p)$, then we add the node **man** to the r-net in Fig. 4.4 and a line from $g(p)$ to **man**, as shown in Fig. 4.5.

To illustrate the use of the is-optional relation, suppose that maintaining the player free to all users ($q(p_3)$) will allow new users to listen to music in an average of no more than three clicks through the audio service (as they do not need to register or provide their billing details); we denote $q(p_4)$ the latter quality constraint. We add

$\mathbf{q}(p_4)$ as a node to the r-net, along with the assumption $\mathbf{k}(\phi_4)$, with ϕ_4 for "if $\mathbf{q}(p_3)$, then $\mathbf{q}(p_4)$," and thus an inference relation. Let $\mathbf{q}(p_4)$ be optional: to make it so in the r-net, we connect it to the node **opt**. If we consider the r-net in Fig. 4.5, it is no longer obvious which of the two refinements is more desirable than the other: if a candidate solution includes $\mathbf{g}(q_3)$, then it will not contain $\mathbf{q}(p_4)$, but will have the preferred $\mathbf{g}(q_3)$; if a candidate solution includes $\mathbf{q}(p_3)$, then it will have $\mathbf{q}(p_4)$, but not the preferred $\mathbf{g}(q_3)$.

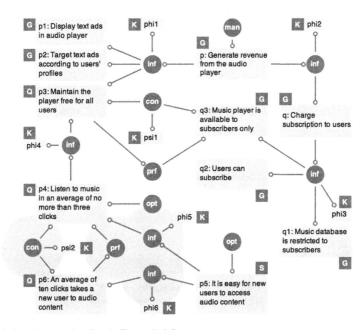

Fig. 4.6 Softgoal approximation in Example 4.5

4.5.3.5 Softgoal Approximation

As softgoals vaguely constrain values of properties that are not necessarily directly measurable, every softgoal ought to be approximated in an r-net. A set of requirements can be an *approximation* of a softgoal if it is assumed that once its members are satisfied, the softgoal will be satisfied to some extent. As different approximations may satisfy the same softgoal to different extents, preference relations can be added between the members of different approximations. These preferences let us compare approximations in terms of how well one satisfies the softgoal relative to others.

Example 4.5 (Contd. Example 4.4) We introduce the optional softgoal $\mathbf{s}(p_5)$, with p_5 for "It is easy for new users to access audio content" into the r-net from Fig. 4.5. There are no universal criteria that tell us what "easy" precisely means in the context of this system-to-be. There are thus different ways to approximate $\mathbf{s}(p_5)$. One of them is to say that the smaller the average number of clicks needed to a new user to access audio content (computed over some number of sessions and for a given focus group), the easier it is to access that content. We can introduce at least two quality constraints, one being $\mathbf{q}(p_4)$ and another $\mathbf{q}(p_6)$, with p_6 for "An average of ten clicks are needed to a new user to get to audio content," with corresponding assumptions $\mathbf{k}(\phi_5)$ and $\mathbf{k}(\phi_6)$, with ϕ_5 for "if $\mathbf{q}(p_4)$, then $\mathbf{s}(p_5)$" and ϕ_6 for "if $\mathbf{q}(p_6)$, then $\mathbf{s}(p_5)$." A preference is added, to indicate that the approximation by $\mathbf{q}(p_4)$ is preferred to the approximation by $\mathbf{q}(q_6)$. Finally, we abbreviate "$\mathbf{q}(p_4)$ cannot be satisfied together with $\mathbf{q}(p_6)$" by ψ_2, and add a conflict between $\mathbf{q}(p_4)$ and $\mathbf{q}(p_6)$, along with the assumption $\mathbf{k}(\psi_2)$.

4.5.3.6 Modeling with Another Visual Syntax

Concrete requirements modeling languages (for example, KAOS, $i*$) have a visual syntax as a diagrammatic notation that aims to simplify the making and reading of requirements models created with these languages. Techne is an *abstract* requirements modeling language as it has no visual syntax. To make a concrete requirements modeling language out of Techne, it would be necessary to add a visual syntax, as I did in the figures in this section.

4.5.4 Analysis

Analysis in Techne should answer two questions: given an r-net (i) what are the candidate solutions to the problem in it? and (ii) what are the preferred and optional requirements that each candidate solution contains? Example 4.6 informally presents how these answers are sought; we then look into the formalization of the r-nets toward the automation of analysis.

Example 4.6 (Contd. Example 4.5) A candidate solution must be conflict-free, so that we are interested in conflict-free subnets of the r-net in Fig. 4.6. There are many conflict-free subnets in Fig. 4.6: for example, $\mathbf{g}(p)$ taken alone is a conflict-free subnet, as is the refinement shown in Fig. 4.2. Since $\mathbf{g}(p)$ is itself a subnet of the said refinement, we are more interested in the entire refinement than in any one of its subnets alone. Stated otherwise, conflict-free (consistent) subnets can be ordered by the subset relation $\subseteq$, and instead of looking for all consistent subnets, those maximal with regards to $\subseteq$ are the most interesting ones. Figures 4.7 and 4.8 highlight two maximal consistent subnets in the r-net from Fig. 4.6. These are, however, *not* also candidate solutions to the requirements problem, as each has goals and quality constraints as source nodes (nodes without incoming lines). Recall that we are interested in finding tasks and domain assumptions which satisfy goals, quality constraints, and softgoals. We can add hypothetical tasks to the r-net in Fig. 4.6 so that no source nodes are goals, quality constraints, or softgoals. Figures 4.9 and 4.10

highlight two maximal consistent subnets of the resulting r-net. Each of these is a candidate solution, because (i) neither has goals, quality constraints, or softgoals as source nodes, and (ii) each includes the only mandatory requirement $\mathbf{g}(p)$.

Once we have found the candidate solutions, the question is how they compare. We can establish that the two candidate solutions, denoted $\mathcal{S}_A$ (the subnet highlighted in Fig. 4.9) and $\mathcal{S}_B$ (the subnet highlighted in Fig. 4.10) have the following mandatory, optional, and preferred nodes:

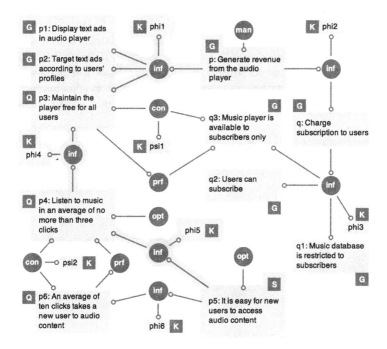

Fig. 4.7 A consistent (sub)net is highlighted

- $\mathcal{S}_A$ (i) has $\mathbf{q}(p_4)$, is both an optional and a preferred requirement; (ii) has $\mathbf{s}(p_5)$ which is an optional requirement, and (iii) has $\mathbf{g}(p)$ which is a mandatory requirement.
- $\mathcal{S}_B$ (i) has $\mathbf{g}(q_3)$ which is a preferred node; (ii) has $\mathbf{s}(p_5)$, an optional requirement, and (iii) has $\mathbf{g}(p)$, a mandatory requirement.

The following comparison table gives the summary:

	$\mathbf{prf} : \mathbf{g}(q_3)$	$\mathbf{prf} : \mathbf{q}(p_4)$	$\mathbf{opt} : \mathbf{q}(p_4)$	$\mathbf{opt} : \mathbf{s}(p_5)$
$\mathcal{S}_A$	no	yes	yes	yes
$\mathcal{S}_B$	yes	no	no	yes

Each column in the comparison table is a criterion for the comparison of candidate solutions. Techne does not suggest how to make a total order over candidates in a comparison table.

4.5.5 Formalization

Automating the search for candidate solutions requires that the elements of Techne introduced so far obtain mathematically formal definitions. To sketch the formalization, recall that a modeling language has four parts: (i) an alphabet of symbols, (ii) rules of grammar to combine symbols into sentences, (iii) a semantic domain with the objects of interest to the purpose of the language, and (iv) mappings from the symbols and sentences to the objects in the semantic domain. As I mentioned earlier, the first and second components are usually called *syntax*, the last two *semantics*.

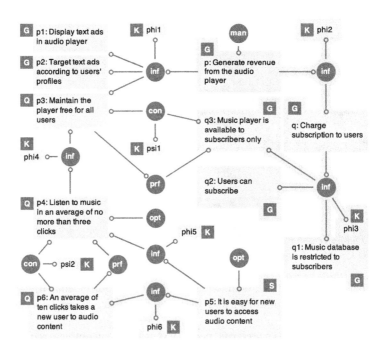

Fig. 4.8 Another consistent (sub)net is highlighted

4.5.5.1 R-Net Alphabet

To draw r-nets, we used symbols for (i) atomic statements (indexed/primed p, q, r), (ii) complex statements (Greek letters), (iii) labels (**k**(), **g**(), **q**(), **s**(), **t**()), (iv) relations (**inf**, **con**, **prf**, **man**, **opt**), and (v) arrow-headed lines.

4.5.5.2 R-Net Grammar

Grammar is dictated by the CORE ontology for the use of labels, and the arity of relations for the use of relation symbols and lines. All allowed sentences are shown in Fig. 4.11, and every r-net is exactly the finite set of elements shown in that figure.

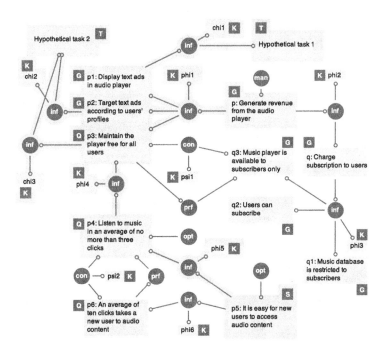

Fig. 4.9 Candidate solution r-net **A** is highlighted

In Fig. 4.11, every p, q is an arbitrary atomic statement, every ϕ an arbitrary complex statement, and every **x** an arbitrary label. For **inf**, ϕ abbreviates "if $\mathbf{x}_1(p_1)$ and ... and $\mathbf{x}_m(p_n)$, then $\mathbf{x}_{m+1}(q)$;" for **con**, ϕ is for "if $\mathbf{x}_1(p_1)$ and ... and $\mathbf{x}_m(p_n)$, then contradiction." As every complex statement refers to an assumption, it must have the label **k**().

4.5.5.3 Semantic Domain and Mapping

The elementary objects in the semantic domain of r-nets are propositions stating the properties of the system-to-be and its operational environment and the inference, conflict, preference, is-mandatory, and is-optional relations between them. Atomic and complex statements in the alphabet refer/map to these pieces of information, relation symbols map to relations, while sentences refer to combinations of the two. Following the statement of the requirements problem and as we want to avoid contradictory solutions, a candidate solution is information which is (i) not contradictory and (ii) from which we can conclude that mandatory goals and quality constraints are satisfied.

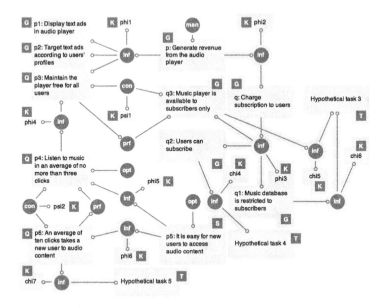

Fig. 4.10 Candidate solution r-net **B** is highlighted

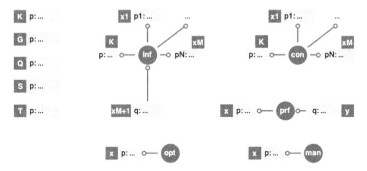

Fig. 4.11 Allowed sentences in an r-net

4.5.5.4 Proof-Theoretic Characterization of Candidate Solutions

To find candidate solutions, we need to find their counterparts in syntax, that is, those parts of r-nets which map exactly to candidate solutions in the semantic domain. As we will be comparing solutions after we find them, we leave out the information for the comparison of candidate solutions (the preference, is-mandatory, and is-optional relations).

In syntax, this means that we focus not on a given r-net but on its *attitude-free* variant: given an r-net $\mathscr{R}$, to make its attitude-free variant $\bar{\mathscr{R}}$, delete all **prf**, **man**, and **opt** nodes and all lines entering and leaving these nodes from $\mathscr{R}$. $\bar{\mathscr{R}}$ contains only the atomic and complex statements, and the inference and conflict relations.

An $\bar{\mathscr{R}}$ can be seen as a set of proofs. To do so, we observe that our complex statements are sentences in the conditional if-then form in which the fragment after the *if* references requirements, while the one after *then* references either a single requirement, or contradiction (see Examples 4.1–4.5). We rewrite every complex statement ϕ in $\mathbf{k}(\phi)$ as a formula with conjunction and implication: every ϕ is such that either

$$\phi \equiv \bigwedge_{i=1}^{n} pl_i \rightarrow pl,$$

or

$$\phi \equiv \bigwedge_{i=1}^{n} pl_i \rightarrow \perp,$$

where every pl is some requirement (for example, $pl \equiv \mathbf{g}(q)$), and $\perp$ refers to logical inconsistency.

Figure 4.12 shows the sentences obtained by applying the said rules on the $\bar{\mathscr{R}}$ in Fig. 4.3.

Fig. 4.12 The $\bar{\mathscr{R}}$ from Fig. 4.3 rewritten as four proofs

$$\frac{\mathbf{g}(\mathsf{p}_1) \quad \mathbf{g}(\mathsf{p}_2) \quad \mathbf{q}(\mathsf{p}_3) \quad \mathbf{g}(\mathsf{p}_1) \wedge \mathbf{g}(\mathsf{p}_2) \wedge \mathbf{q}(\mathsf{p}_3) \rightarrow \mathbf{g}(\mathsf{p})}{\mathbf{g}(\mathsf{p})}$$

$$\frac{\mathbf{g}(\mathsf{q}_1) \quad \mathbf{g}(\mathsf{q}_2) \quad \mathbf{g}(\mathsf{q}_3) \quad \mathbf{g}(\mathsf{q}_1) \wedge \mathbf{g}(\mathsf{q}_2) \wedge \mathbf{g}(\mathsf{q}_3) \rightarrow \mathbf{g}(\mathsf{q})}{\mathbf{g}(\mathsf{q})}$$

$$\frac{\mathbf{g}(\mathsf{q}) \quad \mathbf{g}(\mathsf{q}) \rightarrow \mathbf{g}(\mathsf{p})}{\mathbf{g}(\mathsf{p})} \qquad \frac{\mathbf{q}(\mathsf{p}_3) \quad \mathbf{g}(\mathsf{q}_3) \quad \mathbf{q}(\mathsf{p}_3) \wedge \mathbf{g}(\mathsf{q}_3) \rightarrow \perp}{\perp}$$

Attitude-free r-nets are sets of proofs of the formal system in which the atoms pl of the alphabet are symbols for requirements (for example, $\mathbf{g}(p)$), the only allowed sentences are $\bigwedge_{i=1}^{n} pl_i \rightarrow pl$ and $\bigwedge_{i=1}^{n} pl_i \rightarrow \perp$, and the only rule of inference is modus ponens. Given a set of such requirements and sentences denoted $\bar{S}$ and $x \in \{pl, \perp\}$:

1. $\bar{S} \vdash_? pl$ if $pl \in \bar{S}$, or
2. $\bar{S} \vdash_? x$ if $\forall 1 \leq i \leq n$, $\bar{S} \vdash_? pl_i$ and $\mathbf{k}(\bigwedge_{i=1}^{n} pl_i \rightarrow x) \in \bar{S}$.

The consequence relation $\vdash_?$ is sound w.r.t. standard entailment in propositional logic, but is incomplete in two ways: it only considers deducing positive atoms, and no ordinary proofs based on arguing by contradiction go through, thus being paraconsistent.

The consequence relation leads us to the following conception of the *candidate solution* concept: Given an $\mathscr{R}$ with all of its domain assumptions in the set **K**, tasks in **T**, goals in **G**, quality constraints in **Q**, and softgoals in **S**, *a set of tasks* ***T**** *and a set of domain assumptions* ***K**** *are a* **candidate solution** *to the requirements problem of* $\mathscr{R}$ *if and only if (i)* ***K**** *and* ***T**** *are not inconsistent, (ii)* ***K***, ***T*** $\vdash_? ***G***, ***Q***$, *where* ***G**** $\subseteq$ ***G*** *and* ***Q**** $\subseteq$ ***Q***, *(iii)* ***G**** *and* ***Q**** *include, respectively, all mandatory goals and quality constraints, and (iv) all mandatory softgoals are approximated by the consequences of* ***K**** $\cup$ ***T****, *so that* ***K***, ***T*** $\vdash_? \mathbf{S}^{man}$, *where* $\mathbf{S}^{man}$ *is the set of mandatory softgoals.*

The candidate solution concept leads us in turn to a more precise formulation of the requirements problem: ***Given*** *an r-net* $\mathscr{R}$, ***find*** *its candidate solutions.* Once candidates are found, the comparison table can be constructed in the straightforward way so that they can be compared. It is beyond the scope of this paper to give guidelines on how to rank candidates on the basis of the comparison table. Figure 4.13 highlights the members of these two sets and thus a candidate solution for the r-net from example 4.6. Note that Figs. 4.9 and 4.10 highlight candidate solutions and all of their consequences.

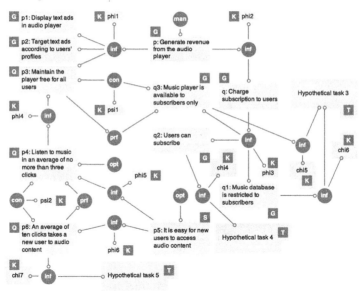

Fig. 4.13 Members of **T*** and **K*** are highlighted

A note on expressiveness: observe that if we treat the *pl*s as atomic propositions, then an r-net is a Horn theory (every formula has at most one positive atom), which is known to be less expressive than full propositional logic, let alone predicate logic. Among others, there is no provision for world knowledge that is disjunctive (for example, composite *pl* like $p \vee q$), but we can express exclusive disjunction (for example, in Fig. 4.3, $\mathbf{g}(p)$ is refined by either $\mathbf{g}(q)$ or by the conjunction of $\mathbf{g}(p_1)$,

$\mathbf{g}(p_2)$, and $\mathbf{g}(p_3)$). There is also no provision for inference nodes that might use lemmas as $\mathbf{k}(\phi)$ which might lead to case-based reasoning. On the other hand, if we consider only attitude-free r-nets, the problem of finding candidate solutions can be reduced to variants of solving nonstandard reasoning problems in logic, such as abduction ("What tasks are needed to ensure the mandatory goals?"). Interestingly, it is known that Horn abduction is one level lower in the polynomial complexity hierarchy than abduction with full propositional logic, so our version of Techne has lower expected computational cost—a typical expressiveness/complexity trade-off. Only extensive practical experience in modeling will show whether more expressive power is needed.

4.5.6 Comments

My involvement in making Techne inevitably colors what I think of it. My own motives for making Techne were to make the language which has the fewest possible concepts and relations, and still achieves two aims. First, that it has concepts which fit the CORE ontology and can produce models which represent CORE problems and CORE solutions. Second, that it can represent common relations in requirements modeling languages which preceded it, such as goal refinement and conflict from KAOS, task decomposition from i-star, and so on. It was also interesting to make a language which does not come with a predefined visual syntax.

In contrast to i-star, which introduced the modeling of dependencies in coordinated work, Techne introduced no new relationships. Concepts in CORE, and thus in Techne, as well as the relationships in Techne can all be seen as a synthesis of various ideas discussed previously in requirements engineering research. For example, quality constraints and softgoals are very much related, and draw on research on nonfunctional requirements [29, 105]. KAOS introduced the concept of "goal" to requirements engineering, and it remains unchanged in Techne. There is novelty in the treatment of conflicts and in having a paraconsistent syntactic consequence relation in Techne which lets it tolerate logical inconsistency when drawing conclusions from models.

Techne 2 [81] was made after trying to apply Techne to the problem of representing problems and solutions in cases when requirements change over time. The challenge is that change of requirements means change of the problem to solve, and thus necessarily the design of, or search for a new solution. This leads to the need for additional tools in a language, such as the ability to represent uncertainty in the degree to which a requirement, say a goal, will be satisfied during some period of time. It also requires being able to show what will happen, in case a goal fails to be satisfied, or some conditions in the environment fail to hold. Overall, it leads to a language which can be used to say more than a Techne model can, but at the cost of having to learn a more complicated language and use more complicated models.

Chapter 5
Requirements Problem-Solving Cases

This chapter presents several genuine problem situations. For some, it outlines the outcomes of only the very first steps of requirements problem solving. One case is used to illustrate the languages defined in this book and the others are given as exercises. In later chapters, there is typically a definition of a requirements modeling language, and models in that language will represent information from a case in this chapter. Confidentiality was important, so names of stakeholders and companies are removed and replaced by generic ones. The name of each case is made the name of a city which was somehow related to the case, and of the domain of expertise of the case. Cases are called Brussels Law, Copenhagen Sports, Dubai Telecom and London Ambulance. London Ambulance is a classical case from requirements engineering research, and it is often used to illustrate requirements modeling languages. The other cases are inspired by my experience in requirements problem solving.

5.1 Brussels Law

This problem occured at a law firm in Brussels. The initial information about it came from a legal professional, shortly after passing the necessary examinations to become a civil law notary in Belgium. Following the country's laws and conventions, and in order to become a practicing notary, this person invested in purchasing the license and the business of a retiring notary in Brussels.

For all practical purposes, you can see the notary business as a small company. It is subject to special regulations (such as limitations on marketing), but they are not relevant for this discussion. At the time, the business had ten employees. These employees assist the notary in performing her principal task, summarily described as follows by the Belgian federation of royal notaries (Fédération Royale du Notariat Belge):

© Springer International Publishing Switzerland 2015
I. Jureta, *The Design of Requirements Modelling Languages*,
DOI 10.1007/978-3-319-18821-8_5

"A civil law notary's task is to advise persons who wish to conclude agreements in areas as diverse as real estate, family, or business matters. A civil law notary informs his or her clients about their rights and duties, and about the consequences—legal, financial, and tax-related—of their commitment. The civil law notary listens to his clients' needs and advises them on all these areas."

The transition from the retiring notary to the new owner was a challenge. The notary observed that employees were making many decisions on their own when interacting with clients. While some degree of autonomy is encouraged, the aim of the notary is to give the best possible advice, and this requires notary's own expertise and involvement.

This overall issue motivated a round of interviews with a sample of the employees, to see if and how they perceive this issue, if they see any related ones, as all this would help understand which problem to solve first and how best to approach its resolution.

The interviews were organized around topics which included explaining the work the individual does at the office, and her impression of problems that may exist in her own work and in work with colleagues. Six employees were interviewed. Each interview lasted approximately 30 min.

The information collected at the interviews was used to produce a summary of the interviews and terminology which defines the terms which have a specific meaning within the notary profession, or within the office itself.

5.1.1 Terminology

The following terms have a specific definition within the Brussels Law problem. They were identified after, and from the information elicited in the interviews.

- *Notary Business:* Notary office led by the notary.
- *Product:* Legal document produced and signed by the notary for a client, in exchange for a fee.
- *Pre-product:* Document prepared by a notary assistant or notary and which has not yet been signed by the notary.
- *Client:* Legal entity purchasing products from the notary business.
- *Notary:* The individual holding the license to perform notary duties who signs legal acts, is legally responsible for the content of the legal acts, owns and leads the notary business, communicates with clients, and prepares legal acts.
- *Prior Notary:* Notary who preceded the current notary. Communicates with clients to ease clients' transition to the new notary.
- *Notary Assistant:* Prepares products for review, validation, and signing by the notary.
- *Secretary:* Manages the expedition of products, handles administration, incoming phone calls, incoming and outgoing mail, finds archived legal acts, etc.
- *Accounting Assistant:* Maintains accounting information through accounting software.

5.1.2 Interviews Summary

Interviews were conducted with the notary business employees, including three notary assistants, two secretaries, and one accounting assistant.

The summary below is organized by the topic that arose during one or more interviews. Topics are neither ordered by priority nor another criterion.

1. Advising clients:

   a. All three notary assistants highlighted that they appreciate giving advice to clients.
   b. By advice, notary assistants seem to mean information related to, but not necessarily included in the product made for the client.
   c. When asked to point to sources of advice, notary assistants indicate their own individual experience.
   d. When asked if they validate the advice with the notary, notary assistants avoid the question, leaving the impression that there is little to no validation of the advice.

2. Methods for delivering advice:

   a. Notary assistants deliver advice to clients in the following ways, from the most frequent to the least frequent: email, phone, live meetings, mail.
   b. All notary assistants indicated that email is the most important form of communication in order to keep a trace of the exchange of information with the client.

3. Supervision of notary assistants in client interaction: When asked when the notary intervenes in the notary assistant's work with a client, the notary assistants indicated that the notary intervenes predominantly at the end of the work with the client, for the transformation of pre-product into product.
4. Client redirection to notary assistants: Client who calls notary business by phone, and asks to speak to a particular notary assistant, is redirected by a secretary to that notary assistant.
5. Affirmation of position:

   a. In all six interviews, every interviewee asserted their relevance and importance for notary business. Every interviewee asserted their importance on their own initiative, as no question was asked which would suggest future changes in positions and responsibilities.
   b. One notary assistant and one secretary suggested that they are the only ones able to discharge the responsibilities they currently hold.

6. Understanding of own position and responsibilities:

   a. One notary assistant stated that for her clients, she is the Notary.
   b. All notary assistants see clients as their own, not as those of the notary business.

    c. The newly hired secretary suggested by herself that—compared to her prior work as secretary of top management—the positions, responsibilities, and hierarchy are not clear at notary business.

7. Transition from past notary. Notary assistant, the spouse of the past notary, highlighted the following:

    a. There is more work compared to the period when prior notary led the office.
    b. Coordination of work is worse now than when prior notary led the office.
    c. Flow of information between employees at notary business is less efficient now than the fully paper-based system was when prior notary led the office.
    d. This notary assistant had the impression that notary is trying to do too much at the same time, and specifically that notary is trying to do both a notary's work and the work of one notary assistant (i.e., the making of Pre-products).

8. Expedition of Products:

    a. There are rules defined in law, for whom to distribute a product (i.e., whom to send a legal act once it is signed by the notary).
    b. One secretary suggested that she is the only person at the moment who knows and applies these rules.
    c. When this secretary was absent, no one could perform her work.

9. Documentation of knowledge: When asked where she is learning the processes and rules of work from, the newly hired secretary suggested that there is no documentation and that she makes her own notes on rules and processes.

5.1.3 Problems

In a summary, interview topics suggest the presence of the following problems:

- Unclear position responsibilities and hierarchy relations;
- Absence of processes and rules to govern the interaction with clients, the making of products, and the expedition of products;
- Absence of processes and rules for documenting knowledge and training of employees;
- No uniqueness and innovation in products and interaction with Clients.

and these problems can have the following interrelated consequences:

- Damage to the notary business brand;
- Inconsistent quality of products;
- Unusual dependence on individual employees and thereby risk of inefficiency in their absence;
- Difficulties in management in absence of means to preserve and transfer knowledge between employees.

Below mentioned are more details on which problem is related to which consequences:

1. No explicit definition of authority relations and position responsibilities. Possible consequences include:

   - Employees do not update the notary of their tasks and deadlines;
   - Employees position themselves as the main point of contact for clients at notary business;
   - Employees give clients advice that has not been validated by the notary.

2. No processes and rules to govern the interaction between clients and notary business. Possible consequences include:

   - Notary assistants interact autonomously with clients, so quality of interaction cannot be monitored, influenced, and standardized;
   - Notary is not informed of communication between client and notary assistant and cannot influence and evaluate the quality of that interaction, when communication takes place via:
     - Email, as notary is not included in CC of emails sent by notary assistants to clients;
     - Phone, as secretaries transfer clients directly to a notary assistant;
     - Meeting outside the notary business office.

3. No processes and rules for monitoring and reporting on delivery of products to clients. Possible consequences include:

   - Task lists of notary assistants are obscure to the notary;
   - Notary assistants fully manage their task lists, and do not report on them.

4. No processes and rules for the preservation of knowledge and no transfer of knowledge between employees. Possible consequences include:

   - Knowledge stays with individuals, who thereby make notary business dependent on them;
   - It seems that rules or procedures in work are not documented, and have not been documented while prior notary was leading the office;
   - There are no rules to govern training between employees. It is up to the employee being trained to document or otherwise formalize and learn the knowledge obtained from another employee.

5. No processes and rules for communicating new and changed rules and processes to employees. Possible consequences include having no clear communication to employees on what rules and processes should be followed.

6. No uniqueness in interaction with clients and no product innovation. Possible consequences include:

   - Notary assistants act autonomously in interaction with clients;
   - Notary is not visible to clients.

5.2 Copenhagen Sports

This case involves a small sports company in Copenhagen. The company sells online coaching software which enables sports coaches to train recreational, amateur, and professional athletes at a distance.

For the coach, the software is a tool to create training plans and training instructions, assign them to individual athletes, and receive their feedback. For the athlete, the software is the place to find training instructions and her training plan, to record training progress, as well as to keep a diary of sports and related activities which can be relevant for the coach, when she designs the training for the athlete (such as the food the athlete ate, if they traveled on a particular day, etc.). For both coaches and athletes, the software provides data visualization tools as well as other means designed to facilitate their communication and interaction.

The majority owner, himself a coach, was interested in how the software could help coaches with two activities that take considerable time, namely invoicing and payments. Up to that point, all invoicing and payment between a coach and an athlete was the responsibility of the coach. In the case where the coach worked for, say, a gym or a sports club, then that legal entity was invoicing and receiving payments from the athletes. Someone at the gym or sports club still had to manage invoicing and payments, and the coaching software offered no help.

This initial idea led to an interview with the owner, in his role as a coach who uses the software with his athletes. The rest of this section gives the terminology required to understand the interview summary, and then the problem description.

5.2.1 Terminology

The following terms have a specific definition within the Copenhagen Sports case. They were identified after, and from the information elicited in the interview with the coach.

- *Coaching Company:* Company that makes and sells the online coaching software.
- *Customer Invoice:* Invoice to an individual who should pay to coaching company.
- *Custom Customer Invoice:* Customer invoice which should be made using a non-standard template defined by the customer, and/or include information which other customer invoices do not include.
- *Company Invoice:* Invoice to a company that should pay the coaching company. It includes specific company information (for example, company registration number) which is not included in customer invoice.

5.2.2 Interview Summary

The aim of the interview was to understand what invoicing and payments tasks a coach usually has to do. Without this information, any proposed solution may entirely ignore constraints which these tasks are currently subject to.

The summary of the interview is given below. It lists first the invoicing tasks, and then the payments tasks that a coach typically performs.

Invoicing tasks include the following:

1. *Subscription invoicing* focuses on having customers pay for their monthly subscriptions to coaching company services. Subscription Invoicing involves the following tasks:

   a. Update spreadsheet with names of all customers who should receive customer invoice for current month; a coach does this;
   b. Make all customer invoices for the current calendar month. Make custom customer invoices for all customers who requested them; coach's accountant does this;
   c. Send all customer invoices and custom customer invoices to all customers at the end of current calendar month; the coach's accountant does this;
   d. Check every Monday if every sent customer invoice has been paid by checking coaching company bank account and matching incoming payments with customer invoice numbers; the coach does this;
   e. For each customer invoice that has not been paid, inform relevant OOB coach to remind the customer to pay; the coach does this;
   f. Send reminders to customers who have not paid, that they have a customer invoice to pay.

2. *Event invoicing* focuses on having companies pay for coaching company services, which are not paid by subscription. Event invoicing typically involves these tasks:

   a. Elicit instructions from client for company invoice;
   b. Make company invoice;
   c. Send company invoice;
   d. Check if company invoice is paid;
   e. If company invoice is not paid, remind client to pay company invoice.

The coach does all the tasks listed above.

Accounting tasks include the following:

1. Keep a record of all invoices sent.
2. Keep a record of all invoices paid.
3. Record every expense of coaching company, and store proofs of expenses.
4. Keep a record of all invoices received and to be paid by coaching company.
5. Pay all invoices received and to be paid by coaching company.
6. Keep a record of all payments of invoices received and paid by coaching company.

7. Provide records of all coaching company expenses and proofs of expenses to danish accountants of coaching company.

The coach does all the accounting tasks above.

5.2.3 Problem

The owner of the coaching company asked for the coaching software to be changed to support coaches with the invoicing and payment tasks described in the interview. In one or several next releases, the software should do at least some of the tasks in place of a coach, or in some other way facilitate these tasks to a coach.

5.3 Dubai Telecom

This case involves a company which specializes in making business-to-consumer software products for telecommunication service providers (TSPs), such as companies offering prepaid and contract mobile telephony and data services. The products are used by TSPs to run their consumer websites, where they promote products and services, to run their online services, such as online technical support, to sell their services and products, and so on.

The company made a new product, called TSPAppDev in this book. The product is software which allows TSP's customers to make apps for mobile devices through an intuitive interface, to minimize the time to make an app and appeal to customers who need to make simple apps quickly. The overall idea is that the TSP buys the software, lets its customers use it through a free trial period, and then charges a monthly subscription for customers who wish to continue to use it.

The chief executive officer of the company wanted to have a clear plan of action, for how to deliver TSPAppDev to a TSP which buys it. This motivated interviews with him, and subsequently with the product director. The rest of the section gives the information elicited after these interviews.

5.3.1 Interviews Summary

5.3.1.1 CEO Interview

The interview with the CEO resulted in the information about the main lifecycle phases of the TSPAppDev product. This information is given below.

TSPAppDev is directed at telecommunications companies, TSPs, interested in introducing new revenue streams and strengthening loyalty of corporate and residential customers.

TSPAppDev is delivered in three phases:

- Phase 1—TSPAppDev Competition: TSPAppDev is delivered to enable a 3 months or longer competition, the goals of which are to

  - Increase brand awareness in local market;
  - Promote local Mobile App development community;
  - Collect market information on business and residential users interest in mobile app development.

- Phase 2—Campaign Evaluation: Analysis of data acquired during competition.

  - If significant market potential is recognized in the competition, the project is transferred into service setup;
  - Alternatively, 3-month competition is repeated or client exits the process;
  - Data collected and analyzed includes: number of registered users, number of created and submitted mobile apps; number of mobile apps ready for distribution in mobile app stores, number of downloaded mobile apps, number of social network fans, number of competition website visitors.

- Phase 3—TSPAppDev Service: TSPAppDev is delivered under a software as a service model to TSP, in order to enable TSP's residential and business customers to make mobile apps.

In addition to making free mobile apps, residential and business customers can create premium mobile apps. Premium mobile apps create new revenue streams for TSP, through per-Mobile App setup and monthly subscription fees paid by residential and business customers.

5.3.1.2 Product Director Interview

The product director highlighted that it is important to understand what the product does for the TSP and its customers. This should suggest what needs to be done, in order to deliver it to the TSP, and set it up so that it can be used by the TSP's customers.

TSPAppDev Competition works as follows:

- Competition is a competition in making mobile apps using TSPAppDev;
- Any user in TSP country can participate;
- To participate, users register to competition website, create, and submit apps;

- Users can create free apps only. Free apps are limited in three ways:
  - Include advertising managed by TSP;
  - Publisher is TSP, not the author of the app;
  - Apps are created using limited set of TSPAppDev features;

- TSP reviews the submitted apps, publishes selected Apps to TSPs and global apps stores;
- Jury and users rate submitted apps and select winners;
- Winners receive awards at an award ceremony.

  TSPAppDev Service works as follows:

- TSP uses TSPAppDev service to enable its residential and business customers to make and distribute free and premium mobile apps;
- For the countries where TSP purchased TSPAppDev service, no other telecommunications company can purchase TSPAppDev service;
- TSPAppDev is distributed under a software as a service model;
- All customers can make free mobile apps;
- Every residential customer pays for each premium mobile app a monthly subscription fee. When purchasing each premium app, the residential customer pays the equivalent of 6 months' subscription, which pays for her first 6 months. After the first 6 months, the residential customer pays the subscription fee per month;
- Every business customer of the TSP pays for each premium mobile app a monthly subscription fee. When purchasing each premium app, the residential customer pays the equivalent of 6 months' subscription, which pays for her first 6 months. After the first 6 months, the residential customer pays the subscription fee per month.

5.3.2 Problem

Given the information from the interviews, the problem is to define how TSPAppDev should be delivered to a TSP which purchased it. Who should do it at the company? How? Are TSP's employees involved? If yes, what expertise do they need to have? When are they involved? What for? All such questions had to be answered.

5.4 London Ambulance

This case draws on the London Ambulance Service's Computer-Aided Dispatch (LASCAD) system [3] which has often been used in requirements engineering to illustrate requirements modeling languages [74, 96, 142, 143]. The information in this case borrows Beynon–Davies' presentation of LASCAD [12].

LASCAD was intended to replace manual dispatching of ambulances to incident locations. A manual dispatching system consists of the following [12]:

"Call taking. Emergency calls are received by ambulance control. Control assistants write down details of incidents on pre-printed forms. The location of each incident is identified and the reference coordinates recorded on the forms. The forms are then placed on a conveyor belt system that transports all the forms to a central collection point.

Resource identification. Other members of ambulance control collect forms, review details on forms, and on the basis of the information provided decide which resource allocator should deal with each incident. The resource allocator examines forms for his/ her sector and compares the details with information recorded for each vehicle and decides which resource should be mobilized. The status information on these forms is updated regularly from information received via the radio operator. The resource is recorded on the original form that is passed on to a dispatcher.

Resource mobilization. The dispatcher either telephones the nearest ambulance station or passes mobilization instructions to the radio operator if an ambulance is already mobile."

The rationale for replacing manual dispatching is that the manual identification of the precise incident location, production of paper-based records, and tracking of ambulance locations were seen as time-consuming and error-prone. Replacing the manual system with a computer-aided one was considered as a way to improve service to patients.

A computer-aided dispatch system would be designed to support the following [12]:

1. *"Call taking: acceptance of calls and verification of incident details including location.*
2. *Resource identification: identifying resources, particularly which ambulance to send to an incident.*
3. *Resource mobilization: communicating details of an incident to the appropriate ambulance.*
4. *Resource management: primarily the positioning of suitably equipped and staffed vehicles to minimize response times.*
5. *Management information: collation of information used to assess performance and help in resource management and planning."*

The problem in the case is to design the computer-aided dispatch system in an environment where dispatching is done manually.

Although there is relatively little information above, it is rich. It mentions various activities that dispatching involves (for example, call taking and resource identification), the normal sequence of these activities (call taking precedes resource identification), the organizational positions involved in these activities (control assistants, resource allocators, dispatchers), the responsibilities of the positions (resource allocator decides which ambulance to mobilize), and so on.

Chapter 6
Checklists, Templates, and Services for Requirements Modeling Language Design

This chapter presents three simple tools called language checklists, templates, and services, and explains why and how they are used in this book. They help make it manageable to define many languages, compare them, and carry their features from one to another. Language checklists give items to include in a definition of a requirements modeling language and its parts. Each checklist suggests a template, so that when it is relevant to define a requirements modeling language or its part according to a checklist, there is a corresponding template to fill out. Services describe specific problem-solving tasks that a language and relevant algorithms automate for a human problem solver. I use services to describe the purpose a language and its parts in problem solving, checklists to avoid missing important parts of definitions, and templates to standardize the presentation of definitions.

6.1 Problem-Solving Services

Let Q denote a question, such as, for example, "Which requirements are satisfied in the given Model?" To answer this question, you need to have elicited requirements, find ways to satisfy them, represent all this in a model, and then analyze the model to see if it answers the question.

But the question itself has nothing to do with how you made the model, that is, the elicitation and any treatment of information that was needed to make the model. The question is not influenced by how the model was made. Moreover, the question is not specific to one particular requirements modeling language. The same question can be asked for various models, made in various languages, as long as these languages have a notion of "requirement" and "satisfaction." The question would otherwise be meaningless, but again, only for those languages which fail to distinguish requirements in a model from other information in the model, and to distinguish when something in the model can be called "satisfied" and when it cannot.

© Springer International Publishing Switzerland 2015
I. Jureta, *The Design of Requirements Modelling Languages*,
DOI 10.1007/978-3-319-18821-8_6

Answering the question Q may be an ill-structured problem, even when you do have a model. This is the case precisely if, for example, the language of the model does *not* give the exact conditions that have to hold, in order to say that, without a doubt some requirement in that model and according to that model, is satisfied. In other words, "being satisfied" is not precisely defined in the language.

In some languages, however, *answering question Q will be a well-structured problem.* In other words, you will know the steps to take and the tools to use in order to answer Q when given *any* model in that language. And *if someone else applies the same steps and tools according to instructions, they will reach the same answer for the same model.*

In some cases, these languages may be such that you or anyone else can apply algorithms to models, and automatically obtain the answer.

The interesting conclusion of the above is that you can describe a language and algorithms for requirements problem solving by the questions they can answer for a human problem solver.

In the rest of the book I will say that a language, and if needed algorithms, that is, Artificial Intelligence for requirements problem solving, have services, and each service is a question that the AI can answer.

Definition 6.1 *Problem-Solving service*: A requirements modeling language has the Problem-Solving service X, or simply the service X, if answering the question X for any reasonably sized model in that language is a well-structured problem.

The definition is loose. Services cannot be used to fully describe *all* that a language can do for a human problem solver. Some people are more inventive than others, and perhaps manage to use a language to answer more questions than others would think of. For example, when does a model have a reasonable size? I do not have a definite answer to this, and if I did, I would have proposed a better definition.

But despite its obvious limitations, services are interesting when used *to guide the design of a requirements modeling language*. This is what I use them for in this book. It is an important role. Services can be used to justify features a language has, the concepts and relations in its ontology, its formalization, etc.

The introduction and use of services is motivated by the assumption mentioned in Sect. 4.2, that a requirements modeling language should influence how one thinks about and solves problems. More specifically, I will assume that a requirements modeling language will effectively do so, if it can *do* something for its user, the human problem solver, that is, *if its user can delegate part of the problem-solving effort to the requirements modeling language*.

You can think of it this way: there is a language user, a person who needs to solve a problem, and suppose that there is software which she uses to make requirements models. To find the solution to the problem, as well as to properly formulate the problem to solve, she invests some effort. Problem solving is the name for what she does.

Part of that effort goes into making and changing the model itself, the *modeling*, and part of it goes into asking questions and finding answers to them by inspecting the model, the *reasoning*. Such questions can be, for example, "Which requirements in the model cannot be satisfied together?" or "Does the model describe how to satisfy some requirement X in it?" and so on. Now, she can probably find answers to many such questions by having natural language as her modeling language, and ordinary text her models; she brings the text up on a screen, or prints it out, then searches through it and reads it to find the answer.

But there are two problems with this, if not more. If another person tries to find the answer to the same question, from the same model, what guarantees that the answer will be the same? Yet it should, unless you want models to cause confusion.[1] And if the model gets big—the text is long—will it not become, at some point, too difficult to find answers, and will there not be questions to which you want answers, yet cannot find them within some reasonable time?

To make problem solving easier, I can add rules on how to make diagrams that represent things, actions, and so on, in the text, and can change the software to enable it to answer questions by doing some processing on the models. The software will then process a model, and return an answer. To abstract from implementation specifics, I will say that *the engineer delegates part of the effort to the requirements modeling language*, and the language has to say what its models are, and how to process them to answer questions.

services are used to describe parts of the problem-solving effort which the engineer can delegate to a requirements modeling language. If a requirements modeling language can answer some specific question, then I can define this as a service, and I will say that that requirements modeling language has that service. Languages can be compared in terms of services that each delivers.

services are not defined as some specific concepts, relations, rules, or algorithms that are part of a language. It follows that two languages may be said to have the same service, even if they have very different components and work in different ways to answer the corresponding question.

How I define and use services will become clearer in and after Chap. 7, when I start defining the first requirements modeling languages specific to this book.

6.2 Checklists and Templates

A checklist lists questions that you need to answer in order to define, for example, a relation or a category that is used in a formal language. For example, to define a relation, it is necessary to say what its domain is, what rules every instance of that relation has to satisfy (such as those due to the relation being transitive, for example), its arity, and so on.

---

[1] Any model probably can be read in different ways by different people, but it is feasible, when making models that have to answer very specific questions, to make sure that they do not give confusing answers *to those questions*. If one writes $x + 5 = 7$, and says to another that these are numbers of apples, the other might debate if they are of the Granny Smith or Golden Spire variety, but both would answer 2 if asked for the value of x.

There are various checklists in this book, and each is related to recurring components of a requirements modeling language. For example, requirements modeling languages typically provide categories for different kinds of elicited information, and there is a checklist that suggests what a definition of a category has to say. Checklists are not exhaustive, but are instead used to ensure that basics are covered.

When there is a checklist that recommends what goes in a definition, the natural next step is to define a corresponding template to use when writing the definition. The template includes slots, which if adequately filled out make sure that the definition answers the questions in the checklist.

There is a template for every checklist in this book. There are two primary uses of the templates, one being to standardize the presentation of languages and their modules in the book, and the other to make it easier to present the information that the corresponding checklist asks for.

6.3 Language and Module Names

Every language defined in this book has two names. One is its so-called module name and the other is its common name.

The *module name* lists the abbreviations of all modules in that language. Section 7.3 explains what a language module is. For now, it is enough to know that a module is a self-contained part of a language, which can appear in more than one language. That is, it can be reused when making different languages.

For example, a module name for one of the languages in Sect. 7.4 is (r.inf.pos, r.inf.neg, f.map.abrel.g). This says that the language is made of three modules, denoted by r.inf.pos, r.inf.neg, and f.brel2g.

Each language module in the book has a unique abbreviation, and those abbreviations are used to form the module names of languages. The point is to know what modules a language includes, simply by looking at its module name.

The *common name* has nothing to do with the module name of a language, in that neither is inspired by the other. The common name is chosen simply to make it easier to refer to a language, when the module name is unnecessary. Common names are the common names of navigational stars in celestial navigation, taken from the Nautical Almanac [75].

Chapter 7
Relations

This chapter is about defining relations over bits and pieces of information used in problem solving. The discussion revolves around how to define individual relations, issues in defining languages that have many relations, and on two requirements engineering concerns, called influence and rationale below, which have usually been addressed via specialized relations in requirements modeling languages. More specifically, the chapter is on:

1. How to represent in requirements models that we start to design with less-detailed information, and incrementally add details to it. (Sect. 7.2)
2. How to define oft-needed relations in such a way that they can be reused when defining new requirements modeling languages. (Sect. 7.3)
3. How to represent that satisfying some requirements influences the satisfaction of others. (Sect. 7.4)
4. How to represent the rationale for design decisions. (Sect. 7.5)
5. If a requirements modeling language includes several relations, then how to avoid errors in using these relations together. (Sect. 7.6)

7.1 Motivation

Problem solving in requirements engineering involves working with information, obtained through interviews, observation, simulation, role-playing, from documentation, through reflection, creativity, and so on. You need to organize this information in order to understand the concrete problem to solve, to design one or alternative solutions, compare them, and do everything else that might be necessary in order to produce a solution.

You can organize this information by making representations of it, splitting representations into pieces, and stating relations over the pieces. The first part of the book focuses on how you can define relations in requirements modeling languages, so that their models can represent instances of these relations over pieces of

© Springer International Publishing Switzerland 2015
I. Jureta, *The Design of Requirements Modelling Languages*,
DOI 10.1007/978-3-319-18821-8_7

information. In turn, relations let you reconstruct, from the pieces, your initial under-standing of the initial whole, and also to identify interactions between these pieces, which was not feasible when they were not split up.

There are two practical reasons to start by focusing on relations *only*, and so have only one category of information. First, I can postpone the discussion of such issues as, when a piece of information should be called a requirement, a goal, a task, a specification, or otherwise, that is, the issue of categorization, to which I return in Chap. 9.

Second, committing already now to some specific categories would bias the dis-cussion to a specific class of problems. This is because problem classes come with their own information categories: in DRP, for example, they are "requirement," "do-main knowledge," and "specification." There is no need to privilege one problem class over the others this early in the book.

Note that, while I am discussing relations before categories, I do not suggest, for example, that in general, relations should be the primitives in requirements modeling languages. I already introduced the notion of fragment as a primitive, and fragments are not relations. Also, when I start introducing more categories later, I do not define categories only in terms of relations. So I am not saying, for example, that pieces of information are in relations *because* they satisfy some monadic properties first and foremost, and that their having these properties influences the relations in a language. For example, this amounts to saying that it is because there are things called requirements and others called specifications that I am interested in relations that indicate how performing according to specifications influences if we satisfy requirements. The opposite approach, where relations are primitives, would be to say that I have to distinguish categories of information that describe what to satisfy (requirements) from those on what to do (specifications), because I am interested in relations that reflect correlation of satisfaction.

7.2 Single Relation Language

As usual, a relation R over some sets $X_1, \ldots, X_n$ of things, be they requirements, laws, (or representations of) people, cars, buildings, or clouds, of the same or of differ-ent kinds, is a subset of the Cartesian product of these sets, that is, $R \subseteq X_1 \times \cdots \times X_n$.

A relation is used to say that the things it relates share the property which the relation stands for. For example, if *in love with* denotes a binary relation over people, and people are identified by first names, then *Pierre in love with Marie* is an instance of the *in love with* relation, and is intended to convey that they share the property that we conventionally understand as Pierre being in love with Marie, and that Marie is the person whom Pierre is in love with.

Suppose you need to define the simplest requirements modeling language which lets you show that information about requirements increases incrementally as system design progresses. By simplest, I mean something that is easy for others to understand. It can help to consider the following questions.

- What is, or are the language services that this language should deliver? Why? Define them.
- How would you represent that information increases? Try with a relation.
- What is the domain of that relation, what is the relation over?
- How should relation instances read informally? What is it that they should be saying to other people who are using models in that language?
- What are the formal properties of that relation? Is it, for example, transitive?

7.2.1 Choose a Language Service

I will start by choosing the language service which I want the new language to deliver. To do this, recall that the default view in requirements engineering is that problems are solved incrementally, moving from incomplete or otherwise deficient information, toward less-deficient information that describes the problem and its solution.

At each iteration, I want to add information to the model. This new information may be adding details to the information already there. The additional detail may come from explaining how to satisfy some requirement, that satisfying a requirement involves satisfying several more specific requirements, making a requirement less ambiguous, and so on. The same applies to any information in the model, be it requirements or otherwise (such as domain knowledge and specifications in the default problem).

It is relevant to have models which show how information was added during design. Discovery and indecision in problem solving are two reasons for this, among others.

- *Discovery* refers to starting with relatively little and progressively increasing knowledge of, for example, the relevant requirements and domain knowledge, their relative importance, their completeness, about ways to satisfy requirements, and so on. At a given time during problem solving for the London Ambulance, you may not know the various possible ways to identify the incident location; as you learn more about them, you would be adding more details to the model.
- *Indecision* refers to the unwillingness, at some time in problem solving, to commit to, for example, resolve some conflict between requirements in one way and reject all alternative ways to do so, to give a particular interpretation to an ambiguous requirement, or to some specific way of satisfying a requirement. For example, you may decide not to describe in the model a process for choosing the ambulance to dispatch until you have interviewed the control assistants who have experience in that task.

As I proceed with discovery and postpone commitments, I add more detailed information to the model. Instead of deleting the less-detailed information when this happens, it is relevant *to keep both in the model*. More specifically, it is useful to indicate in the model which information adds details to which other. Doing so results in a record of *what* I am adding details to and *why* I am adding more detailed information in the first place.

Modeling the increase in information in a model raises a number of design challenges and is related to many language services that various well-known requirements modeling languages deliver. For example, in KAOS, the ability to answer "Which requirements are more detailed than (that is, refine) the given requirement?"; in i-star, to answer "Which tasks are more detailed than (decompose) the given task?" This leads me to the following language service for the new requirements modeling language. Let x and y be parts of a model M in that language.

Language service: AddsDetails

Does x add information to y in M?

The language service does not define exactly what the model or its parts are, and thereby remains independent of a particular language.

7.2.2 Models over Fragments

Natural language text is an accessible and neutral way to represent information about problems and their solutions. There is no need to learn something new to use it. It comes with no rules on how to represent, categorize, or work with that information.

If natural language is a casual means of requirements representation, then does ordinary text as a means of representation deliver s.AddsDetails? Consider the following pieces of information, called *fragments*, about the London Ambulance.

- AddRepEm: Emergency calls are responded to.
- RecEmCal: Receive emergency calls.
- SwtchCal: Switch emergency calls to dispatch center.
- NoDropCal: No calls are dropped because of timeout.
- IdIncLoc: Identify the incident location.
- ChkDblLoc: Check if double location.
- FillIncRep: Fill out the incident report.
- FillSwIncRep: Fill out incident report form via software.

As shown above, fragments are ordinary sentences with an abbreviation for easier referencing. I impose no rules on, for example, how to decompose and combine fragments. Later, I will in some languages. Moreover, while fragments can be representations of *propositions*,[1] not all of them are: questions arise during problem solving, and while they cannot be propositions [52, 136, 140] (What do you answer to "Is that question Q true or false?"), it is relevant to have a record of them, and inevitably, then, have them in models.

But fragments need not only be parts of natural language text. Datasets, diagrams, photographs, videos, can all be representations of requirements, or of other information which is relevant when defining requirements, solving conflicts between them, getting stakeholders to approve requirements, and so on [35, 117].

Consequently, *a fragment is any available representation of information, as long as the model user judges it to be relevant for problem solving in requirements engineering.* This is important to keep in mind, as all languages in the rest of this book create models over fragments. While the present format makes fragments in natural language text the easiest to use, there is nothing in the languages defined here, which restricts fragments to text only.

Example 7.1 The London Ambulance example suggests that addressing each emergency involves (at least) taking the emergency call, identifying the incident location, and so on.

It follows that RecEmCal, SwtchCal, NoDropCal, IdIncLoc, ChkDblLoc, FillIncRep, FillSwIncRep describe one way of satisfying AddRepEm.

AddRepEm thus looks to be *less detailed than* every one of the former statements. Equivalently, AddRepEm is *more abstract than* each of these statements. Also, each of the latter statements is *more concrete, or more detailed than*, and *adds details to* AddRepEm. FillSwIncRep is one of some alternative ways of doing FillIncRep, which makes FillSwIncRep more detailed than, and adding detail to FillIncRep.

The following paragraph summarizes this.

RecEmCal, SwtchCal, NoDropCal, IdIncLoc, ChkDblLoc and FillIncRep describe what to do, in order to satisfy AddRepEm. Each inform to AddRepEm. FillSwIncRep adds details to FillIncRep, because it describes a way of satisfying FillIncRep.

If you replace each abbreviation above with the corresponding fragment, you get an ordinary paragraph of text. •

Taken as a representation of information about ambulance dispatching, the paragraph in Example 7.1 is subject to no particular rules which would influence how you and I represent and communicate about differences in detail. For example, the paragraph can be seen as a single fragment, or multiple fragments, neither of which can be unambiguously established by looking at it alone.

To be able to find the same answer to s.AddsDetails, you and I need to agree on at least two rules, on (i) how to distinguish between fragments and (ii) how to record that one adds details to another. Once we do, the result is that we will no longer be documenting our communication about the adding of details using

---

[1] I take McGrath's view on propositions [101], so that they are "sharable objects of the attitudes and the primary bearers of truth and falsity. This stipulation rules out certain candidates for propositions, including thought- and utterance-tokens, which presumably are not sharable, and concrete events or facts, which presumably cannot be false."

unconstrained text, but text that has to satisfy the new rules. Since these rules are specific to s.AddsDetails, I will call the resulting representations *models*.

7.2.3 Trivial Modeling Language

One way to distinguish fragments is to visually separate them. You can write each in a different paragraph. For referencing, you could have a unique identifier for each paragraph.

To record which fragments add information to others, you and I can agree to write sentences in this format "x informs y", where we replace x and y with relevant fragment identifiers.

"x informs y" reflects the conclusion of comparing two fragments x and y, and concludes that x adds information about y. In other words, saying "x informs y" equates to stating a relation between x and y, and begs the question of what properties this relation has.

It makes no sense to say that "x informs x," so the relation is irreflexive. It is also not the same to say that "x informs y" or that "y informs x"; it is one or the other, so that the relation is antisymmetric. It is also transitive, as the following seems reasonable: if you say that x informs y, and that y informs z, then you are also saying that x informs z. Finally, for every pair of fragments, I will not be saying which fragment informs another. I might do it only for some fragments. In conclusion, the "informs" relation on a given set of fragments is a strict partial order relation.

This gives a language which delivers s.AddsDetails. The language is called L.D1, and is defined only by the rules which you and I agreed on so far:

Every model M in L.D1 is a graph $(X, \text{r.ifm})$, where:

1. every fragment in X is a node,
2. every edge is an instance of r.ifm over X,
3. r.ifm is a strict partial order on members of X, and
4. $(x, y) \in \text{r.ifm}$ reads "fragment x adds details to fragment y".

L.D1 delivers the following language services:

- s.AddsDetails: Yes, iff there is a path from x to y in the transitive closure of M, not otherwise.

Using L.D1 takes me from natural language to a controlled language, and in the process restricts considerably what I can say about why some fragments add detail to others, for example. This is apparent by comparing models in Examples 7.1 and 7.2; the latter was made using L.D1 on fragments in the former example.

Example 7.2 The graph $G = (X, \text{r.ifm})$ is a model in L.D1, where:

- $X = \{$ RecEmCal, SwtchCal, NoDropCal, IdIncLoc, ChkDblLoc, FillIncRep, AddRepEm, FillSwIncRep$\}$ is the set of all fragments,
- The set of edges is this set of r.ifm instances:

r.ifm = {

(RecEmCal, AddRepEm), (SwtchCal, AddRepEm),

(NoDropCal, AddRepEm), (IdIncLoc, AddRepEm),

(ChkDblLoc, AddRepEm), (FillIncRep, AddRepEm),

(FillSwIncRep, FillIncRep) }

Figure 7.1 gives a visualization of this model. The visualization shows a graph, where nodes are fragments, and edges labeled "D" are r.ifm instances. •

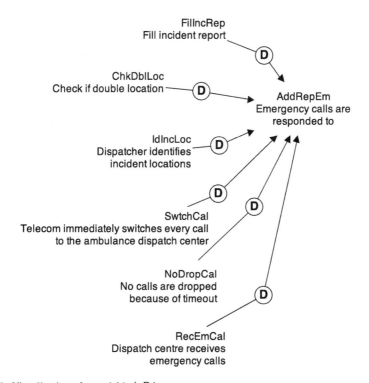

Fig. 7.1 Visualization of a model in L.D1

The example illustrates why language services are interesting. Namely, *if I made the model in Example 7.2 and gave it to you, and you know* L.D1, *then you would not need to ask me for my answer to* s.AddsDetails*since you can get to the same answer as I.* Hence, L.D1 delivers s.AddsDetails.

As an aside, note that L.D1 cannot be used to solve the default problem. Delivering s.AddsDetails is not enough as other language services are needed. If you consider that a language is not a requirements modeling language if it cannot be used to solve the default problem, then L.D1 is not one.[2] L.D1 models cannot be used to answer seemingly simple questions, such as which of the fragments are the most detailed (that is, no other fragments add detail to them). L.D1 does have important limitations, but the book should start from something simple.

7.3 Modular Definitions

I defined a simple language in response to Exercise ex:one-category-one-relation. What if I wanted to define new languages, perhaps many of them, all of which would reuse the relation r.ifm in the same way as L.D1? The challenge is summarized in the following exercise.

Go back to L.D1 and r.ifm, and consider what had to be decided and put into the definition of that relation. I defined r.Inform by answering the following questions:

- What is the name of the relation?
- How should a person read its instances?
- What is its domain?
- What is its dimension (arity)? Is it unary, binary, ternary, n-ary?
- What are its formal properties? More generally, what properties does it have to satisfy?
- Which language services do I want it to deliver?

I will answer the same questions for all relations in this book. Hence the language module template for relations. Slots in it reflect the questions. It is filled out below for r.Inform.

Relation: ifm
Inform
Domain & Dimension
r.ifm $\subseteq$ **F** $\times$ **F**, where **F** is a set of fragments.
Properties
Irreflexive, antisymmetric, and transitive.
Reading

---

[2]i-star, for example, also fails this criterion but is considered a requirements modeling language. There is, to the best of my knowledge, no widely accepted set of criteria for when a modeling language is also a requirements modeling language, despite some suggestions [63, 80, 84, 153].

$(x, y) \in$ r.ifm reads "x adds information to y".

Language services

- s.AddsDetails: Yes, if $(x, y) \in$ r.ifm is in M.

There is a slot for the domain and dimension. Properties are the rules that all relation instances have to satisfy. If some relation r.rel is irreflexive, then you have an error in the model if it includes $(x, x) \in$ r.rel. The properties slot will include all sorts of rules about relation instances, not only common formal properties (as above). Hence the slot's generic name. The "reading" slot says how to read an instance of the relation.

The template includes the abbreviated relation name, r.ifm above. I usually use that abbreviation to refer to the relation, or in general, to language module names in the book.

The template shown with r.ifm focuses on the relation alone. It tries, as much as feasible, to avoid other concerns. For example, it is silent about how sets of relation instances should or could be represented as sets of symbols denoting relation instances, as graphs where edges denote relation instances, or in some other way. The template avoids issues related to the syntax of the language. When I want to use a relation in a language, I will simply use the name of the relation, and leave its definition in its own module, rather than repeat it in the language definition. Given below is the definition of a language which does the same as L.D1.

Language: Alpheratz

Language modules
r.ifm

Domain

Set **F** of fragments and r.ifm $\subseteq$ **F** $\times$ **F**.

Syntax

A model M in the language is a set of symbols $M = \{Z_1, \ldots, Z_n\}$, where every ϕ is generated according to the following BNF rules:

$$A ::= x \mid y \mid z \mid \cdots$$
$$B ::= A \text{ informs } A$$
$$Z ::= A \mid B$$

Mapping

$\mathscr{D}(A) \in F$ and $\mathscr{D}(B) \in$ r.ifm, that is, every A symbol refers to a fragment in **F** and every B symbol to an instance of r.ifm.

Language services

Same as r.ifm.

The template has the common name **L.Alpheratz** and the module name (r.ifm). This follows the conventions set earlier. The module name is in parentheses and says that the language has one module, r.ifm. There is the symbolic syntax defined using BNF notation. You can define it otherwise if you prefer.

I follow Harel and Rumpe [67] on syntax and semantics, and there are consequently slots for syntax, semantic domain and a function that maps elements of the former to those of the latter. The function is denoted $\mathscr{D}$ in all languages in this book, but its definition is always local to a language. The example below gives a model in L.Alpheratz.

Example 7.3 The following is a model in L.Alpheratz:

$$M = \{ \text{ RecEmCal, SwtchCal, NoDropCal, IdIncLoc,}$$
$$\text{ChkDblLoc, FillIncRep, AddRepEm, FillSwIncRep,}$$
$$\text{RecEmCal informs AddRepEm,}$$
$$\text{SwtchCal informs AddRepEm,}$$
$$\text{NoDropCal informs AddRepEm,}$$
$$\text{IdIncLoc informs AddRepEm,}$$
$$\text{ChkDblLoc informs AddRepEm,}$$
$$\text{FillIncRep informs AddRepEm,}$$
$$\text{FillSwIncRep informs FillIncRep}\}$$

M includes individual fragments, which I gave first above, and then instances of r.ifm. •

For every model of **L.Alpheratz**, you can make a corresponding graph. The graph can be a visualization of the model, but more importantly, it can be used to compute answers to new language services such as the following:

- **s.MostDetails**: Which fragments in M are the most detailed?
- **s.LeastDetails**: Which fragments in M are the least detailed?

Suppose $G(M)$ is the graph where every A symbol from M is a node and every B symbol $B = x$ informs y is an edge directed from x to y. Let $Cl(G(M))$ be the transitive closure of that graph. You can then deliver s.MostDetails and s.LeastDetails as follows:

- s.MostDetails: All nodes in $Cl(G(M))$ which have no incoming edges.
- s.LeastDetails: All nodes in $Cl(G(M))$ which have no outgoing edges.

There are well-known algorithms for finding transitive closures of directed acyclic graphs, and for finding paths in them [2, 7]. They can be used to compute answers to the language services above.

In the rest of the book, I define the translations from one syntax to another, or other transformations of models, via Namely. These language modules are functions, taking (parts of) models as input, making changes, and producing new models or otherwise. When I suggested above that you can make a graph from r.ifm and do computations on those graphs, the more general point is that you may want a language to deliver the following language service.

Language service: RelGraph

Given the relation r.R over fragments in **F**, which graph is induced by that relation?

Below is the definition of a function which takes a binary relation and returns a labeled directed graph. It delivers s.RelGraph.

Function: map.abrel.g

Map a binary relation to a graph

Input

Set $X \subseteq \mathbf{F}$ of fragments and a binary antisymmetric relation $\mathsf{r.R} \subseteq X \times X$.

Do

Let $\mathsf{G}(\mathsf{X}, \mathsf{r.R}) = (N, E, l_N, l_E)$ be an empty labeled directed graph:
- For every fragment $f_i \in X$, add a node n_i to N and let the fragment label the node, $l_N(n_i) = f_i$.
- For every relation instance $(f_i, f_j) \in \mathsf{r.R}$, add an edge $(n_i, n_j) \in E$ to the graph, and label the edge r.R.

Output

G(X, r.R).

Language services

- s.RelGraph: G(X, r.R).

A language that would deliver **s.MostDetails** and **s.LeastDetails** would also need additional functions that traverse the graph and return the sink and source nodes.

The more general point is that templates such as the above promote a modular definition of languages. The template for functions is self-explanatory, giving the inputs, the actions to take on these inputs, the result of those actions, and the language services of interest.

You can also have templates for families of languages. You can define analogous languages to **L.Alpheratz** for many other antisymmetric binary relations in this book. The template for all these languages is as follows, where R is the name of the relation. I added the function **f.map.abrel.g**, which enables these languages to deliver more language services than **L.Alpheratz** could. I will not spend much time with such languages as you can define them with the template below.

Language: Alpheratz(R)

Language modules
r.R, f.map.abrel.g

Domain

Set **F** of fragments and r.R $\subseteq$ **F** $\times$ **F**.

Syntax

A model M in the language is a set of symbols $M = \{Z_1, \ldots, Z_n\}$, where every ϕ is generated according to the following BNF rules:

$$A ::= x \mid y \mid z \mid \cdots$$
$$B ::= A \text{ symbol\_for\_R } A$$
$$Z ::= A \mid B$$

Mapping

$\mathscr{D}(A) \in \mathbf{F}$ and $\mathscr{D}(B) \in$ r.R.

Language services

s.AddsDetails, s.RelGraph, s.MostDetails, s.LeastDetails.

I illustrated above how to define a relation as a language module and use this module in a language. Sections 7.4 and 7.5 define several other relations. They are all inspired by well-known ideas such as, say, refinement in programming and correlation in statistics, which are not specific to requirements engineering, as well as relations that are central in well-known requirements modeling languages. The aim is to give more examples of the modular definition of relations, and then combine these sample relations into new languages in Sect. 7.6.

7.4 Some Influence Relations

A recurrent concern in requirements engineering is to represent that *satisfying some x has consequences on satisfying some other y*. (*x* and *y* may be one or more requirements, domain knowledge, specifications, or otherwise; their categorization does not matter at the moment.) Satisfying abbreviates "successfully doing what *x* describes" or if you prefer making clear that these are models of hypothetical actions, conditions, and such (precisely because they are representations), then it abbreviates "as-if what *x* describes is successfully done."

This capability is critical for solving the default problem, for example, because both conditions in that problem are about how the satisfaction of domain knowledge and specifications influences the satisfaction of requirements.

Satisfying some *x* in a requirements model can be independent of the ability to satisfy some other *y* in the same model. If it is not, then the idea is to have an influence relation between *x* and *y*. This relation can indicate positive or negative influence, and various relations have been proposed to do so [119].

You can think of satisfaction as being a value assigned to a fragment. Let *SatVal* denote the satisfaction value of a fragment, and suppose that $\mathscr{V}$ is the set of all allowed satisfaction values, so that $SatVal : X \longrightarrow \mathscr{V}$, where X is a set of fragments. There should be an influence relation from *x* to *y* iff $SatVal(x) = f(\ldots, SatVal(y))$, that is, if the satisfaction value assigned to *x* is function of, among others, the value assigned to *y*.

Due to discovery and indecision in problem solving, I may incrementally be finding out or making decisions about the exact function $SatVal(x) = f(\ldots, SatVal(y))$. To be able to represent partial information about influence, I will define several types of influence relations. Some of them will require that I know very little about how

SatVal(*x*) is sensitive to changes of *SatVal*(*y*), while others may require that I know more, such as the direction and perhaps the strength of that influence.

7.4.1 Presence of Influence

If you want models to show only that influence does or should exist, then you need to deliver the following language service and solve the exercise that follows.

Language service: DoesInfluence

Does the satisfaction of a model part *x* influence the satisfaction of another model part *y* in the model *M*?

The language service can be delivered with a new relation which indicates influence.

Relation: inf

Influence

Domain & Dimension

r.inf $\subseteq$ **F** $\times$ **F**, where **F** is a set of fragments.

Properties

Irreflexive and transitive.

Reading

(*x*, *y*) $\in$ r.inf reads "the satisfaction of *x* influences the satisfaction of *y*", or equivalently, "there is a function according to which the satisfaction value assigned to *y* depends on the satisfaction value assigned to *x*".

Language services

• s.DoesInfluence: Yes, if (*x*, *y*) $\in$ r.inf is in *M*.

Example 7.4 In Example 7.1, the fragments RecEmCal, SwtchCal, NoDropCal, IdIncLoc, ChkDblLoc and FillIncRep described parts of what needs to be done in order to satisfy AddRepEm. This suggests the following r.Influence instances:

(RecEmCal, AddRepEm), (SwtchCal, AddRepEm),

(NoDropCal, AddRepEm), (IdIncLoc, AddRepEm),

(ChkDblLoc, AddRepEm), (FillIncRep, AddRepEm).

Let L.Alpheratz(r.inf) be a language made using the template L.Alpheratz(R) from Sect. 7.3 and r.inf. Let M be a model in that language, which includes all influence relation instances above and all the fragments that these instances relate. The corresponding graph is shown in Fig. 7.2. For brevity, edges are labeled "I", rather than "r.inf". •

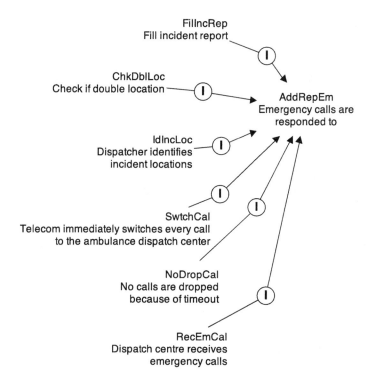

Fig. 7.2 Visualization of a model in L.Alpheratz(r.inf)

The example illustrates that it is only necessary to assume that *there exists* a function f such that $SatVal(y) = f(\ldots, SatVal(x))$. When this is done, it is not necessary to know also how exactly the satisfaction of y depends on that of x. It is also not necessary to define the set $\mathcal{V}$ of allowed satisfaction values. This is useful when that set is still unknown or undecided in problem solving.

7.4.2 Direction of Influence

You may not know exactly how the satisfaction of y depends on that of x, but you may know, or wish to hint that the correlation of their satisfaction values is positive or negative. That is, you want to deliver the following language services:

- **s.PosInfluence**: Does satisfying x influence positively the satisfaction of y in M?
- **s.NegInfluence**: Does satisfying x influence negatively the satisfaction of y in M?

To deliver s.PosInfluence and s.NegInfluence, I define a new relation which can indicate positive or negative influence. I define it as an influence relation that has a parameter. The parameter gives the direction of influence.

Relation: inf.d

Influence.d

Domain & Dimension

r.inf.d $\subseteq$ **F** $\times$ **F**, where **F** is a set of fragments.

Properties

Irreflexive and transitive.

Reading

d is either "pos" for positive or "neg" for negative, and therefore
- $(x, y) \in$ r.inf.pos reads "the satisfaction of x positively influences that of y",
- $(x, y) \in$ r.inf.neg reads "the satisfaction of x negatively influences that of y".

Language services

- s.PosInfluence: Yes, if $(x, y) \in$ r.inf.pos is in M.
- s.NegInfluence: Yes, if $(x, y) \in$ r.inf.neg is in M.

Example 7.5 How would you define a language that can represent both positive and negative influence relations over fragments? How would you define it by making minimal changes to the definition of L.Alpheratz? The language L.Ankaa below does this.

Language: Ankaa

Language modules
r.inf.pos, r.inf.neg, f.map.abrel.g

Domain

Set **F** of fragments. r.inf.pos and r.inf.neg are both over fragments, so that r.inf.pos $\subseteq$ **F** $\times$ **F** and r.inf.neg $\subseteq$ **F** $\times$ **F**.

Syntax

A model M in the language is a set of symbols $M = \{Z_1, \ldots, Z_n\}$, where every ϕ is generated according to the following BNF rules:

$$A ::= x \mid y \mid z \mid \cdots$$
$$B ::= A \text{ influences+ } A$$
$$C ::= A \text{ influences- } A$$
$$Z ::= A \mid B \mid C$$

Mapping

A symbols denote fragments, $\mathscr{D}(A) \in$ **F**, B symbols denote r.inf.pos, and C symbols r.inf.neg instances, $\mathscr{D}(B) \in$ r.inf.pos and $\mathscr{D}C \in$ r.inf.neg.

Language services

s.PosInfluence, s.NegInfluence.

Figure 7.3 shows a graph made by merging the graphs G(**F**, r.inf.pos) and G(**F**, r.inf.neg), both made from the same model M in L.Ankaa. The graph shows positive and negative influence relation instances. Positive influences are labeled with "+" and negative with "−". Note that the merge of G(**F**, r.inf.pos) and G(**F**, r.inf.neg) could be a hypergraph, since L.Ankaa lets me have positive and negative influence relation instances between the same fragments. •

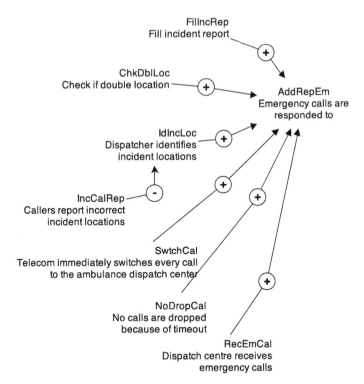

Fig. 7.3 Visualization of a model in L.Ankaa

The difference between $(x, y) \in$ r.inf and $(x, y) \in$ r.inf.d (whichever d is) reflects a difference in the information available about the satisfaction of x and of y. While $(x, y) \in$ r.inf simply says that I believe satisfying x somehow influences satisfying y, $(x, y) \in$ r.inf.d says that I have decided the direction of influence.

7.4.3 Relative Strength of Influence

If you have information about how strongly the satisfaction of a fragment influences that of another fragment, this information cannot be represented in models which can show that there is influence, and/or, the direction of influence.

I will consider the case when the strength of influence of a fragment on some fragment x is relative to the strength of influence of all other fragments which also influence x.

Suppose the satisfaction of y is influenced by the satisfaction of several other fragments $x_1, \ldots, x_n$. How would you indicate that some of them have stronger influence on the satisfaction of y than others? That is, how would you deliver the following language service?

Language service: InfStrength

If the satisfaction of each of $x_1, \ldots, x_n$ influences the satisfaction of y in M, then is the satisfaction of y more sensitive to the satisfaction of x_i than to the satisfaction of x_j, where $x_i, x_j \in \{x_1, \ldots, x_n\}$?

---

s.InfStrength is about the relative strength of influence. To deliver it, it is necessary to compare the strength of influence of satisfying each $x_1, \ldots, x_n$ on the satisfaction of y. If you knew the exact function $SatVal(y) = f(SatVal(x_1), \ldots, SatVal(x_n))$, then this would not be difficult to do. You could compare the covariance of each x_i to y.

I need a new relation to say that x_i has stronger influence on the satisfaction of y than some x_j. The new relation cannot be over fragments, because it does not compare fragments, but the strength of their influence on y. So the new relation, call it r.Stronger_Influence, is over instances of r.inf or those of r.inf.d.

Relation: str.inf

Stronger influence

Domain & Dimension

r.str.inf $\subseteq R \times R$, where R is one of r.inf, r.inf.pos, r.inf.neg.

Properties

Irreflexive, antisymmetric, and transitive.

Reading

$((x_i, y), (x_j, y)) \in$ r.str.inf reads "the satisfaction value assigned to y is more sensitive to the satisfaction value assigned to x_i than to the satisfaction value assigned to x_j".

Language services

- s.InfStrength: Yes, if $((x_i, y), (x_j, y)) \in$ r.str.inf is in M.

Example 7.6 Let L.Schedar be a language made by adding f.str.inf to L.Ankaa. The language is defined as follows.

Language: Schedar

Language modules
r.inf.pos, r.inf.neg, f.map.abrel.g, r.str.inf

Domain

Set **F** of fragments, r.inf.pos $\subseteq$ **F** $\times$ **F**, r.inf.neg $\subseteq$ **F** $\times$ **F**, and

$$\text{r.str.inf} \subseteq (\text{r.inf.pos} \times \text{r.inf.pos}) \cup (\text{r.inf.neg} \times \text{r.inf.neg}).$$

Syntax

A model M in the language is a set of symbols $M = \{Z_1, \ldots, Z_n\}$, where every Z is generated according to the following BNF rules:

$$A ::= x \mid y \mid z \mid \cdots$$
$$B ::= A \text{ influences}+ A$$
$$C ::= A \text{ influences}- A$$
$$D ::= B \text{ infstronger } B \mid C \text{ infstronger } C$$
$$Z ::= A \mid B \mid C \mid D$$

Mapping

$\mathscr{D}(A) \in F$, $\mathscr{D}(B) \in$ r.inf.pos, $\mathscr{D}(C) \in$ r.inf.neg, and $\mathscr{D}(D) \in$ r.str.inf.

Language services

s.PosInfluence, s.NegInfluence, s.InfStrength.

Figure 7.4 is a visualization of a model in L.Schedar. The figure shows that the satisfaction of AddRepEm is more sensitive to the satisfaction of IdIncLoc than it is to all other fragments whose satisfaction influences that of AddRepEm. •

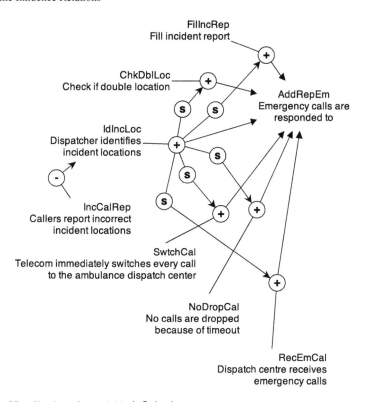

Fig. 7.4   Visualization of a model in L.Schedar

The relation r.str.inf gives no indication about how to evaluate the relative strength of influence. Strength can be a function of covariance, for example. You then need to guess covariance values (in case you have no say about how exactly the satisfaction of x_i influences that of y) or to decide these values (when you can choose exactly how the satisfaction of x_i influences that of y). Both discussions are specific to the concrete problem instance that you are solving. For the former case, multivariate statistics [106, 135] provides general guidelines for estimating covariance. For the latter case, another discipline may provide relevant suggestions, and the discipline in question depends on what the fragments are about. For example, if $x_1, \ldots, x_n$ reflect decisions on the architecture of an information system and y is a requirement about the scalability of that information system, then research on software architecture [122] is relevant.

You can see the absence of precise instructions in r.str.inf as a deficiency. However, this simply reflects the fact that it is in many cases required to call upon experts, among stakeholders or elsewhere, in order to produce relevant models. A language which uses that relation, rough as it is, is only pointing in the direction of relevant areas of expertise, rather than attempting to include some knowledge from them.

7.4.4 Summary on Influence Relations

The purpose of influence relations defined above is to represent that the satisfaction of some fragments depends on the satisfaction of others. I defined several influence relations and a function which illustrated how to assign relative strength of influence to instances of positive and negative influence relations.

None of the influence relations came with predefined levels of satisfaction. I said how to read the satisfied and not satisfied values, when there are only two levels of satisfaction, but I said nothing about cases when there are many levels of satisfaction.

This was acceptable precisely because influence relations are used when we have partial knowledge, due to discovery or indecision about how exactly to compute the satisfaction value $SatVal(y)$ of a fragment y.

The story was that as my knowledge about $SatVal(y)$ increases, I will want to stop using r.inf, and want to use r.inf.pos and r.inf.neg instances. As it further increases, I will want to use f.inf.str to indicate the relative strength of influence. If I knew even more, I could formulate a concrete function $SatVal(y) = f(SatVal(x_1), \ldots, SatVal(x_n))$, which I might revise at later iterations in problem solving.

When you can formulate

$$SatVal(y) = f(SatVal(x_1), \ldots, SatVal(x_n)),$$

you have reached a point in problem solving when influence relations alone represent less than you know about the influence of $x_1, \ldots, x_n$ on the satisfaction of y. At that point, you need a language with more complicated satisfaction scales, and functions assigning those values. I will return to this in Chap. 10.

7.5 Arguments in Models

A recurring concern in requirements engineering is to make justified models. A model is justified if the rationale for its content is acceptable to everyone involved in making and using that model (or at least to those having the authority to complain about the content of a model).

The rationale explains why something is in the model. If the content of a model is contested, and nothing is given to settle the debate, then the model is not justified. If it is not justified, it is unclear whether the problem and solution it may represent are relevant at all.

Checking if a model is justified can be done once it is completed. Another approach is to check every change of the model to make sure that the change itself is justified. In both cases, the idea is that there are some properties that the model should have, and must be satisfied in order to say that the model is justified. These ideas about justification are inspired by a central notion in program refinement.

Program refinement [40, 41, 72, 148] consists of replacing a piece of abstract program with a piece of more concrete program, the benefit being to delay lower level detail to later steps of program development. This is related to the idea of incrementally adding detail discussed earlier, but I want to focus on another important idea in program refinement.

A central notion in program refinement is *proof obligations*. They are properties for which it is necessary to produce a formal proof in order to claim that a particular program refinement is correct. The more concrete program a refines a more abstract program b if and only if all the specific proof obligations for that refinement relation are satisfied. In other words, you can say that there is a program refinement relation from a more concrete program a to a less concrete b if and only if all proof obligations are satisfied.

All relations defined so far in this book come with conditions that must be satisfied by model elements, in order to have a relation instance between them. These appear in the slots of the corresponding language modules. For example, the "Reading" slot for r.ifm says that $(x, y) \in$ r.ifm reads that x adds details to y, and thus, that this relation instance should be in a model if the given informal condition is satisfied, namely that x does add details to y.

The issue is that these conditions are not equally precise and unambiguous for all relations, and from there, not equally convincing to all those making and using models. Proof obligations would ideally remove, or more realistically reduce the need to debate whether a program a refines a program b: if proof obligations are satisfied, then it does, and anyone using the model can check for themselves if they are satisfied.

However, if I write $(x, y) \in$ r.ifm in a model, then my justification for the existence of that relation instance is, just as the definition of r.ifm says, my own judgment that x adds details to y. This might be fine if I am the only person using that model. But you cannot know from that model and its language *why* I concluded that x adds details to y. And this is a practical problem, because if you wanted to know, you would need to ask me, and that would take time and other resources away from more relevant uses.

As should be clear by now, problem solving in requirements engineering involves working with partial information. So it is often simply not feasible to provide conditions as clearly verifiable as proof obligations.[3]

---

[3]There are at least two reasons for this. One is that I may not know a clear enough and complete set of conditions to satisfy for a relation instance to be present. This makes it less relevant to use a formal language, such as a formal logic, to define proof obligations. The issue is not that I cannot formalize something because the formalism is limited in some way, but that I do not know what exactly to formalize. So just as I have partial information about the problem to solve, I also have partial information about the problem-solving method that I am applying. Another reason is that partial information may change quickly. For example, stakeholders may say something at a meeting one day and change their mind at the next. In such cases, formalization may be left for later phases of problem solving and restricted only to problem and solution information which is considered as more stable. For example, it may involve formalizing some aspects of a system design which the stakeholders approved (more on this in Chap. 10).

7.5.1 Support and Defeat

The obligation to have a justified model can perform a similar role to proof obligations when information is partial or otherwise deficient. Justification consists of recording reasons for and against the inclusion of fragments and relations in a model, and checking which of these are "accepted". I will consider "accepted" and "justified" to be synonyms. Reasons may come from model users, other stakeholders, or from anyone else who gives them. Justification comes with rules which define when something is "accepted."

To do justification, I will use a pair of relations called *support* and *defeat*. With them, I will be able to record arguments for and against parts of models. They will be used to deliver the following language services:

- **s.DoesSupport**: Does accepting x support accepting y as well in M?
- **s.DoesDefeat**: Does accepting x support rejecting (not accepting) y in M?

Support and defeat also make it possible to define languages that can deliver such language services as, for example, "Why is it that x adds details to y?", "Why is it that x influences y positively?", "Do stakeholders agree that x influences y positively?", and similar. The relations are defined as follows.

Relation: sup

Support

Domain & Dimension

r.sup $\subseteq X \times X$, where X is either a set of fragments or relation instances.

Properties

Irreflexive, antisymmetric, and transitive.

Reading

$(x, y) \in$ r.sup reads "if x is accepted, then y should be".

Language services

- s.DoesSupport: Yes, if there is $(x, y) \in$ r.sup in M.

In contrast to r.sup, r.def is intransitive. This is an important property and reflects the idea that if x defeats y and y defeats z, then it cannot be that x defeats z. By defeating y, x removes the argument against z, and thereby is not defeating z.

Relation: def

Defeat

Domain & Dimension

r.def $\subseteq X \times X$, where X is either a set of fragments or relation instances.

Properties

Irreflexive, antisymmetric, and intransitive.

Reading

$(x, y) \in$ r.def reads "if x is accepted, then y should not be".

Language services

- s.DoesDefeat: Yes, if there is $(x, y) \in$ r.def in M.

The following example illustrates how to use r.sup and r.def to give reasons for and against instances of the r.ifm in a model.

Example 7.7 How would you define a language which should represent the incremental adding of detail to models, and reasons for and against the additional details that are added?

Let L.Diphda be a new language that can represent r.ifm instances, and fragments as reasons for and against these instances. Moreover, it can be used to say that one fragment is an argument for or against another fragment.

Language: Diphda

Language modules
r.ifm, r.sup, r.def, f.map.abrel.g

Domain

F is a set of fragments. r.ifm is over fragments, so r.ifm $\subseteq$ **F** $\times$ **F**. A fragment can act as a reason, or argument in favor or against a r.ifm instance or another fragment, so that

$$r.sup \subseteq (\mathbf{F} \times r.ifm) \cup (\mathbf{F} \times \mathbf{F}),$$
$$r.def \subseteq (\mathbf{F} \times r.ifm) \cup (\mathbf{F} \times \mathbf{F}).$$

Syntax

A model M in the language is a set of symbols $M = \{Z_1, \ldots, Z_n\}$, where every Z is generated according to the following BNF rules:

$$A ::= x \mid y \mid z \mid \cdots$$
$$B ::= A \text{ informs } A$$
$$C ::= A \text{ supports } A \mid A \text{ supports } B$$
$$D ::= A \text{ defeats } A \mid A \text{ defeats } B$$
$$Z ::= A \mid B \mid C \mid D$$

Mapping

A symbols denote fragments, so $\mathscr{D}(A) \in \mathbf{F}$. B symbols denote r.ifm instances, $\mathscr{D}(B) \in r.ifm$. C symbols and D symbols denote, respectively, instances of r.sup and r.def.

Language services

s.DoesSupport, s.DoesDefeat.

A way to see L.Diphda is that I take a model of L.Alpheratz as a basic model in L.Diphda, and then add arguments in favor or against r.ifm relation instances in the L.Alpheratz model.

In Example 7.1, fragments RecEmCal, SwtchCal, NoDropCal, IdIncLoc, ChkDblLoc and FillIncRep described parts of what needs to be done, in order to satisfy AddRepEm. In Example 7.2, I added instances of r.ifm over these fragments. A reason why I added these relation instances is that each of RecEmCal, SwtchCal, NoDropCal, IdIncLoc, ChkDblLoc and FillIncRep said *how* to satisfy AddRepEm. Moreover, SwtchCal says that the telecom switches the call, so that it says *who* is involved in satisfying AddRepEm. Similarly, RecEmCal and IdIncLoc also identified other positions, respectively, the dispatch center and dispatcher, who have responsibilities in satisfying AddRepEm.

This leads to the following new fragments that justify the said r.ifm instances:

- HowSwtchCal: SwtchCal says how to satisfy AddRepEm.
- WhoSwtchCal: SwtchCal says who is involved in satisfying AddRepEm.
- WhenSwtchCal: SwtchCal says when some events happen when satisfying AddRepEm.
- HowNoDropCal: NoDropCal says how to satisfy AddRepEm.
- HowRecEmCal: RecEmCal says how to satisfy AddRepEm.
- WhoRecEmCal: RecEmCal says who is involved in satisfying AddRepEm.
- HowIdIncLoc: IdIncLoc says how to satisfy AddRepEm.
- WhoIdIncLoc: IdIncLoc says who is involved in satisfying AddRepEm.
- HowChkDblLoc: ChkDblLoc says how to satisfy AddRepEm.
- HowFillIncRep: FillIncRep says how to satisfy AddRepEm.

All of the above give reasons in favor of the various r.ifm instances. The following are these instances of r.sup:

$$(\text{HowSwtchCal}, (\text{SwtchCal}, \text{AddRepEm})),$$
$$(\text{WhoSwtchCal}, (\text{SwtchCal}, \text{AddRepEm})),$$
$$(\text{WhenSwtchCal}, (\text{SwtchCal}, \text{AddRepEm})),$$
$$(\text{HowNoDropCal}, (\text{NoDropCal}, \text{AddRepEm})),$$
$$(\text{HowRecEmCal}, (\text{RecEmCal}, \text{AddRepEm})),$$
$$(\text{WhoRecEmCal}, (\text{RecEmCal}, \text{AddRepEm})),$$
$$(\text{HowIdIncLoc}, (\text{IdIncLoc}, \text{AddRepEm})),$$
$$(\text{WhoIdIncLoc}, (\text{IdIncLoc}, \text{AddRepEm})),$$
$$(\text{HowChkDblLoc}, (\text{ChkDblLoc}, \text{AddRepEm})),$$
$$(\text{HowFillIncRep}, (\text{FillIncRep}, \text{AddRepEm})).$$

Figure 7.5 shows a visualization of the resulting L.Diphda model. r.sup relation instances give arguments in favor of r.ifm relation instances. r.sup instances are shown as white circles labeled "A+", connected to the fragment that is the argument, and to the relation instance which the argument supports. •

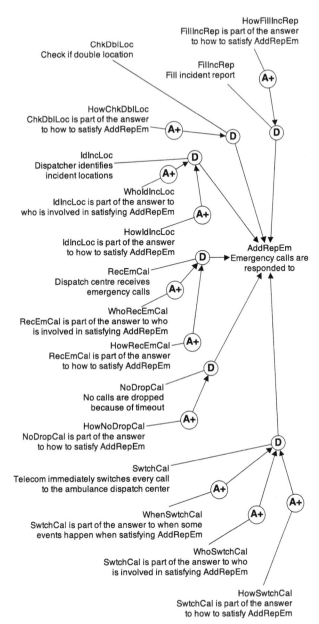

Fig. 7.5 Visualization of a model in L.Diphda

Example 7.7 illustrated how to give one or more arguments in favor of individual r.ifm instances. I did not, for example, give arguments for or against other arguments, yet this can be done. It follows that I can represent that x is an argument in favor of y, and that z is an argument in favor of x, and then, that w is reason against z.

In general terms, it allows me to represent the outcome of *argumentation*, the adding of arguments as chains of r.sup and r.def instances. The following example illustrates this.

Example 7.8 James and Jill are modeling requirements for London Ambulance. James made the model discussed in Example 7.7, visualized in Fig. 7.5. Jill disagrees that FillIncRep adds details to AddRepEm by answering how AddRepEm should be satisfied. The reason why Jill disagrees is that FillIncRep is not in the scope of AddRepEm, and is an administrative matter, to be discussed separately from how to satisfy AddRepEm, that is, of how to respond to emergency calls. This can be recorded in the model by adding the fragment RepFillOutScp.

• RepFillOutScp: To respond to an emergency call, it is not necessary to fill out an incident report.

And then, by adding the r.def instance

(RepFillOutScp, HowFillIncRep)

I would update Fig. 7.5 by adding a fragment node for RepFillOutScp and an r.def instance from it to HowFillIncRep. •

r.sup and r.def are similar in purpose to relations in existing languages in requirements engineering and elsewhere, which are used to represent the design rationale [32, 83, 85, 87, 91, 93, 94, 99, 114, 123, 124], that is, reasons for and against the content of models, or if we look at it from the perspective of the modeling process, then a record of why different model elements were added or removed.

The idea of representing design rationale with arguments for and against model elements is related to two important observations [118]. First, many design and engineering problems are ill-defined, so-called *wicked problems*, lacking a clear scope and formulation, known optimal solutions, or known systematic processes for producing solutions. Second, solving such problems, therefore, cannot involve a known systematic process, but involves finding pieces of the problem and pieces of potential solutions, and collaboratively debating their pros and cons by giving arguments for and against these pieces or their combinations. Such problem solving ends rarely because one finds the best solution, but because of practical time and resource constraints. This makes it interesting to record the design rationale as arguments that led to modeling decisions, whereby the resulting models represent the problem and its solutions, together with explanations of why you were solving that problem instance and not another, and why you produced that or those solutions, and not others.

7.5.2 Accepted or Rejected

Having chains of r.sup and r.def instances raises the issue of *acceptability*. Acceptability is interesting, because something being acceptable is synonymous to being justified. In Example 7.8, there was a chain made from (RepFillOutScp, HowFillIncRep)∈r.def and

(HowFillIncRep, (FillIncRep, AddRepEm))∈r.sup

that is, HowFillIncRep was in favor of saying that FillIncRep adds details to AddRepEm, and then an argument against HowFillIncRep. Asking about acceptability in this case equates to asking this: Should (FillIncRep, AddRepEm) ∈r.ifm be used in problem solving, given the said r.sup and r.def instances, or should it be ignored (do as if it were not in the model at all)? So we need rules to compute acceptability.

I will see acceptability as a value assigned to relata of r.sup and r.def instances.

There is a nuance to how to use that value in problem solving. Instead of saying that acceptable elements should stay in a model, and unacceptable ones be removed, I will remove nothing from a model. (You can have different visualizations of the same model, some showing all, some only parts, so there really is no need to remove model parts.) Instead, I will say that only acceptable elements should be used in problem solving. The reason for this is that new elements and r.sup and r.def instances may change the acceptability of existing elements. This is because argumentation, in the form outlined above with a relation for supporting arguments and another for counterarguments is a form of nonmonotonic reasoning, a point made in philosophy, in relation to, for example, informal logic [10, 71, 144], and in artificial intelligence, in relation to argumentation systems [9, 27, 45] and defeasible logics [111, 113, 126].

While acceptability and satisfaction are values assigned to model elements, they are *different kinds of values, because they are used differently in problem solving.* I said earlier that satisfying x amounted to doing successfully what x describes. If you think in terms of satisfaction, then *the acceptability value of x tells you if you should worry about the satisfaction of x at all.* If x is not acceptable, then it is irrelevant to problem solving, and it does not matter, for example, how it influences other model elements. This makes it unnecessary to evaluate the satisfaction of x. If x is acceptable, then it makes sense to evaluate the consequences of satisfying or not satisfying it.

The following gives a rough idea about how to compute acceptability. Suppose y supports x, and z defeats y, and that nothing else relates via argued relations to any of x, y, and z. What is the acceptability of x, y, and z? A common rule in argumentation systems in artificial intelligence [27] is that z is acceptable since there is no argument against it. So because z is acceptable, and is an argument against y, then y is not acceptable (rejected). Finally, as y was in favor of x, and y is now not acceptable, then the convention is that x is also rejected, as the only argument in its favor is rejected. This is usually a bit more complicated as there can be more than one argument in favor of and against any one element.

Example 7.9 To illustrate the computation of acceptability, I start with the simpler case, when a model has only one so-called "extension." An extension includes all acceptable model parts. Depending on the language in which the model is made, and on the content of the model, it is possible to have models with more than one extension.

Figure 7.6a shows a visualization of a L.Diphda model which takes the fragments AddRepEm, FillIncRep, HowFillIncRep, and RepFillOutScp from earlier examples and adds six new fragments x1–x6. The rationale relations matter for this example, not the specifics of actions or conditions these new fragments describe.

Which fragments in Fig. 7.6a are acceptable? Consider first the leaves, and observe that there are no arguments against AddRepEm, FillIncRep, x2, x3, x5 and x6, so that they are acceptable. x6 supports x5. Since x5 is acceptable and is against x4, x4 is not acceptable. Consequently, it does not matter for the acceptability of x1 that x4 is against x1.

However, x3 is acceptable and attacks x1. I therefore need to choose if arguments against or arguments for are stronger, since this determines whether x1 is acceptable (as x5 is an acceptable argument in its favor). I take the cautious approach, and decide that negative arguments cancel positive ones, and therefore, x1 is not acceptable. It follows that RepFillOutScp is acceptable, and HowFillIncRep is not. So HowFillIncRep is no longer an acceptable argument in favor of the r.ifm relation from FillIncRep to AddRepEm. This leads me to a second decision, which is whether the absence of a positive argument in favor of a model part also means that that model part is not acceptable. I will assume that it is acceptable, as I did the same for, for example, x6 which also lacks positive arguments in its favor.

The resulting acceptability values are shown as additional markers on model elements in Fig. 7.6b. The model there has exactly one extension, and it includes all model parts which are marked with the acceptability value 1.

Figure 7.7a shows what happens when there is an additional r.def instance, which leads to two extensions. For a designer of the language, the possibility for alternative extensions means that the language could suggest which of the extensions to choose. •

I use Dung's definition of acceptability [45]. This is convenient because it is simple and generalizes many others in artificial intelligence. The rough idea is similar (but not the same as explained in Example 7.10) to that explained above with x, y, and z and in Example 7.9. The main difference is that in his graphs, all edges are instances of the so-called "attack" relation. Attack corresponds to my r.def, but there are no relations to capture supporting arguments. This is not a major issue, but will influence how I convert my models into his. I will call his models "argumentation frameworks".

I need a function that delivers the following language service.

Language service: IsAcceptable

Is w acceptable in W, given relations r.sup and r.def over W?

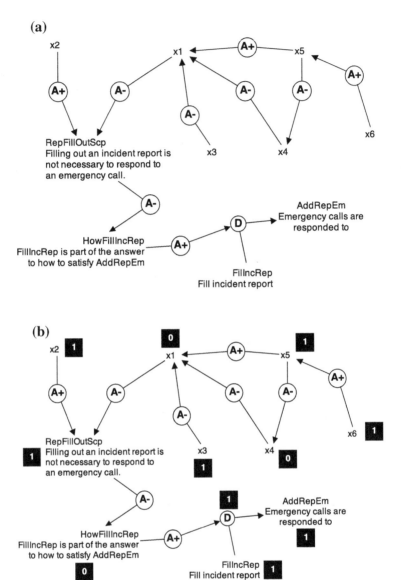

Fig. 7.6 Illustration of acceptability values, part one. (**a**) Visualization of a model discussed in Example 7.9. (**b**) Acceptability values for the model in **a**

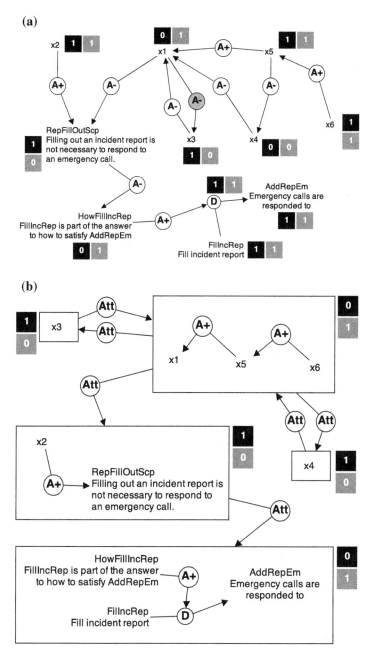

Fig. 7.7 Illustration of acceptability values, part two. (**a**) There are now two extensions. (**b**) Dung argumentation framework from f.accon **a**

The function f.acc below takes instances of r.sup and r.def over some set W, and determines if some $w \in W$ is acceptable or not.

Function: acc

Accepted

Input

A fragment or relation instance w, a set W such that $w \in W$, $A_+ \subseteq$ r.sup, and $A_- \subseteq$ r.def, where r.sup $\subseteq W \times W$ and r.def $\subseteq W \times W$.

Do

1. Let G(W, r.sup) and G(W, r.neg) be graphs made with f.map.abrel.g.
2. Let G(w, W, r.sup) be the subgraph of G(W, r.sup), which includes only the paths of G(W, r.sup) which end in w.
3. Let G(w, W, r.neg) be the subgraph of G(W, r.neg), which includes only the paths of G(W, r.neg) which end in w.
4. Let C include all connected components of G(w, W, r.sup).
5. Let K include every node from G(w, W, r.sup), which is not in a connected component in C.
6. Make an empty set, call it Arg, and let l_{Arg} be a function which will return the label of each element in Arg.
7. For each $c \in C$, add a to Arg and let $l_{Arg}(a) = c$.
8. For each element $k \in K$, add a to Arg and let $l_{Arg}(a) = k$.
9. Make the graph $AF = (Arg, Att)$, with $Att \subseteq Arg \times Arg$ and let Att be empty.
10. For each $(w_i, w_j) \in$ r.def in G(w, W, r.def), add an edge $(a_i, a_j) \in Att$ to AF, so that a_i is such that, either

    - $l_{Arg}(a_i) = w_i$, if $w_i \in K$, or
    - $l_{Arg}(a_i) = c_i$, if $c_i \in C$ if w_i is a node in the connected component c_i,

    and a_j is such that, either

    - $l_{Arg}(a_j) = w_j$, if $w_j \in K$, or
    - $l_{Arg}(a_j) = c_j$, if $c_j \in C$ if w_j is a node in the connected component c_j.

11. The graph $AF = (Arg, Att)$ is a Dung argumentation framework.
12. Use an existing algorithm [102] to compute the acceptability of arguments in AF.
13. If an argument a in AF is acceptable, $l_{Arg}(a) = k$ and $k \in K$, then that element in W is acceptable.

14. If an argument a in AF is acceptable, $l_{Arg}(a) = c$ and $c \in C$, then all elements of W which are in c are acceptable.
15. Let $Acc(W)$ include all acceptable elements of W.

Output

The set $Acc(W)$.

Language services

- s.IsAcceptable: Yes, if w is in the set $Acc(W)$.

Example 7.10 To clarify how f.acc works, recall that a Dung argumentation framework $AF = (Arg, Att)$ is a graph where nodes represent arguments and edges the attack relations. If an argument attacks another, then believing in the former tells us that we should not believe in the latter, or that the former is evidence against the latter. So the attack relation equates in use to r.def. But there is no relation in an argumentation framework which corresponds to r.sup. I therefore have to decide what we do with r.sup when making a Dung argumentation framework. f.acc shows one way to do this.

Applying f.acc to the model in Fig. 7.7a gives the argumentation framework visualized in Fig. 7.7b. The figure also shows the acceptability values in two extensions of the framework. Note the differences between the extensions in the Dung argumentation framework and the extensions in Fig. 7.7a. They are due to the choice in f.acc to equate a Dung argument to a connected component over r.sup instances. •

There are algorithms to find connected components of a graph [73] and to compute extensions of Dung argumentation frameworks [102]. All nodes in a Dung argumentation framework (called arguments there) are considered as acceptable if they are in an extension of the given argumentation framework.[4]

Asking that a relation instance x in a model is acceptable according to f.acc can be seen as an analog to a single proof obligation, in the sense that it is a single condition that the relation instance needs to satisfy in order to be relevant for problem solving.[5] In contrast to proof obligations, which can depend on the properties of x

---

[4] I leave it to the reader to look up the types of extensions, how they differ, and what consequences using one or another type of extension in f.acc would have [45, 125].

[5] It is an analog, because it is a justification and not a deductive proof, as in a formal logic with a monotonic syntactic consequence relation. Namely, if you have a deductive proof of some x in a monotonic logic, then you can still prove x regardless of any new formulas that you are adding, while having a justification for x is sensitive to new formulas, in that new formulas can block proofs which we previously had. As Pollock observes, justification is defeasible reasoning [111]: "[...] inductive reasoning is not deductive, and in perception, when one judges the color of something on the basis of how it looks to him, he is not reasoning deductively. Such reasoning is *defeasible*,

and so be specific to the type of x, acceptability is independent from the properties of x and therefore, it can apply to any x, in any model, in any modeling language. For example, if x is a relation instance, proof obligations may be sensitive to x being reflexive or not, symmetric or not, and so on, while acceptability of x depends solely on those concrete reasons for and against x that we have in a particular model (not a modeling language, and so not *any* model, but exactly *that* model). The benefit is that we can build acceptability into a language when we lack a clear idea for proof obligations. The limitation is precise that it is independent from the properties of x and so involves collecting and confronting anew reasons for and against.

7.6 Combinations of Relations

Suppose you have a language that can represent r.ifm and r.inf instances over fragments, and that it lets you have two relation instances between same fragments. For example, you could have a model with $(x, y) \in$ r.ifm and $(x, y) \in$ r.inf. First of all, would you want the language to allow this in models? And if you do, then, does knowing that x both influences and informs y tell you something more than what these two relation instances tell you each on its own? When it does tell you more, then I will say that the relations interact.

When a language has more than a single relation, the challenge is to decide if these relations interact or not, and if the they do, then how to use their interactions.

If relations interact, then it matters for instances of a relation r.A that there exist instances in the model of another relation r.B. Section 7.6.1 focuses on the simpler case of independence, and Sect. 7.6.2 on interaction.

7.6.1 Independent Relations

L.Diphda included three relations and they were not interacting. It is a permissive language as it imposes no constraints at all on how the presence of some relation between two fragments x and y influences the presence or direction of other relation instances between the same pair of nodes. In other words, the definition of the language is silent on how, if in any way, the relations in it are interacting.

This is unlikely to cause problems if its models are such that there is only one relation instance over any two fragments. When there are two or more edges between two nodes, then it may be unclear how to read this combination of relation instances.

(Footnote 5 continued)

in the sense that the premises taken by themselves may justify us in accepting the conclusion, but when additional information is added, that conclusion may no longer be justified. For example, something's looking red to me may justify me in believing that it is red, but if I subsequently learn that the object is illuminated by red lights and I know that that can make things look red when they are not, then I cease to be justified in believing that the object is red".

If there are two nodes, x and y, such that $(x, y) \in$ r.ifm and $(x, y) \in$ r.def, then what can you conclude about these two nodes? The language itself does not say if this is a modeling error, or is somehow useful in a model.

7.6.2 Interacting Relations

The problem with fitting different relations together in a language, and especially if the relations are only informally defined, is that it may allow models that convey unintended information to their users. There is no guarantee that all unintended information will be benign in problem solving, so we are obliged to worry about how relations interact and to sanction problematic interactions.

I will use L.Achernar below to illustrate this discussion. It has the inform relation and the positive and negative influence relations.

Language: Achernar

Language modules
F, r.ifm, r.inf.pos, r.inf.neg, f.map.abrel.g

Domain

Set **F** of fragments, r.ifm $\subseteq$ **F** × **F**, r.inf.pos $\subseteq$ **F** × **F**, and r.inf.neg $\subseteq$ **F** × **F**.

Syntax

A model M in the language is a set of symbols $M = \{Z_1, \ldots, Z_n\}$, where every ϕ is generated according to the following BNF rules:

$$A ::= x \mid y \mid z \mid \cdots$$
$$B ::= A \text{ informs } A$$
$$C ::= A \text{ influences+ } A$$
$$D ::= A \text{ influences− } A$$
$$Z ::= A \mid B \mid C \mid D$$

Mapping

$\mathscr{D}(A) \in$ **F**, $\mathscr{D}(B) \in$ r.ifm, $\mathscr{D}(C) \in$ r.inf.pos, and $\mathscr{D}(D) \in$ r.inf.neg.

Language services

Same as r.ifm, r.inf.pos, and r.inf.neg.

L.Achernar simply puts together several relations, while making sure that the language delivers all the language services that the relations separately could. But it will be clear below that the modeler has to invest significant effort with this language in order to make unambiguous models. One reason for this is that the language definition does not say how relations interact.

For example, suppose that a L.Achernar model includes, among others, the fragments x and y and the following two relation instances.

$$(x, y) \in \text{r.inf.pos}$$
$$(x, y) \in \text{r.inf.neg}$$

Does, then, x influence positively or negatively y? The answer is not *in* the definitions of L.Achernar and of the influence relations as they say nothing about such cases. It is also irrelevant to look *outside* these definitions, since they are neither equivalent, nor subtypes of others that are defined outside this book. The only remaining option is that the influence relations, and therefore the L.Achernar language, leave it up to the model user to decide for herself if x positively or negatively influences y.

If the language definition does not explain what to do with relation interactions, then the language does not provide support to its users on how to deal with these combinations. The language can include language services focused on interactions, such as the following:

Language service: NegWins

If $(x, y) \in$ r.inf.pos and $(x, y) \in$ r.inf.neg, then does x influence positively or negatively y?

Suppose the answer is: x influences y negatively, and remove $(x, y) \in$ r.inf.pos. This answer can be added to a language as a function, for example, to L.Achernar. The new language would deliver s.NegWins.

The more general point is that once there is more than one relation in a language, it is useful to explain how to use each possible interaction between these relations. This may simply result in explicitly stating in the language definition that it is up to the modelers to decide what to do with interactions.

Consider now all possible interactions of relations in L.Achernar. For each interaction, I give a rule which could be applied.

1. $(x, y) \in$ r.ifm and $(x, y) \in$ r.inf.pos is allowed, and indicates that x informs y, and in such a way that satisfying it positively influences the satisfaction of y.
2. $(y, x) \in$ r.ifm and $(x, y) \in$ r.inf.pos can be handled in different ways, of which two are below:

   - One option is to decide what is not allowed, and one of the two should be removed from the model. This can be motivated as follows: if y is adding details to x, this is because it is clearer how to satisfy y and less clear how to satisfy x, so that I will not be looking to satisfy y by satisfying x. (If the language had the relations for justification, then it would not be necessary to remove one of the two relation instances from the model. It would be enough to make one of the two unacceptable.)
   - Another option is to allow this if y adds such details to x by explaining the consequences which will occur if x is not satisfied, so that if x is satisfied, these consequences will occur, which is captured by the positive influence relation.

3. $(x, y) \in$ r.ifm and $(y, x) \in$ r.inf.pos should be handled in the same way as the case $(y, x) \in$ r.ifm and $(x, y) \in$ r.inf.pos.
4. $(x, y) \in$ r.ifm and $(x, y) \in$ r.inf.neg can be handled via analogous options to those for $(y, x) \in$ r.ifm and $(x, y) \in$ r.inf.pos, except that there is negative influence.
5. $(y, x) \in$ r.ifm and $(x, y) \in$ r.inf.neg should be handled in the same way as the case $(x, y) \in$ r.ifm and $(x, y) \in$ r.inf.neg.
6. $(x, y) \in$ r.inf.pos and $(x, y) \in$ r.inf.neg is not allowed, and one of the two should be removed.
7. $(y, x) \in$ r.inf.pos] and $(x, y) \in$ r.inf.neg can be handled in different ways, and two are given below for illustration:

   - Remove one of the two influence relations.
   - Consider that these two influence relations represent a feedback mechanism, and leave them in the model.

The discussion above leads to three important remarks. The first is about incompleteness in language definition, the second on how completing a language definition suggests new language services, and the third on how to define new relations from combinations of existing ones.

- The discussion of relation interactions shows that the definition of L.Achernar was incomplete. It is necessary to consider each of the possible interactions, check if the language definition says something about them, and *if not, then decide what to do with the interaction, that is, make new language design decisions*. So I decided that when x influences y both positively and negatively, one of these two influence relations should be removed.

- The second important remark is that looking at all possible interactions suggests new language services. For example, adding these new rules for interactions to the language can answer, for example, "Is a model M in L.Achernar correct?" A model in L.Achernar was correct as long as the model did not violate the actual definitions of the individual relations (for example, it could violate them if it had two positive influence relations between same two nodes). If the rules on interactions are added to the language, then model correctness gets a new definition in it.
- A particular case of interaction, or more of them, can be used to define new relations in a language. For example, I can define a new relation called r.Feedback[mixed] as a binary relation that exists between fragments x and y if and only if there are $(x, y) \in$ r.Influence[positive] and $(y, x) \in$ r.Influence[negative]. This new relation is not a primitive of the language, as it is equivalent to a particular pattern of instances of other relations in the language.

7.7 Summary on Relations

The following are the main ideas from the preceding sections on relations:

- When defining a relation, it is useful to say, at least, what it relates, what to do to add its instances to models, and its formal properties (which are necessary if you want to do computations over graphs induced by the relation instances.
- The influence relations illustrated how you can have relations that reflect differences in how much you know when making a model. For example, if you think there is influence of satisfying x on satisfying y, and you do not know if that influence is positive or negative, or how strong it may be relative to others that influence the satisfaction of y, then you can use r.inf. If you then decide or discover that the influence is positive, you can represent this with an instance of r.inf.pos.
- Rules for the use of a relation are central to its definition, as they give the conditions to satisfy in order to add a relation instance to a model. Ideally, use rules should be such that any model user can check if a relation instance is correct with regard to its use rules, that is, if it satisfies the required conditions. When you have use rules that are difficult to verify, you can augment them with a justification process which was illustrated with f.Accepted.
- When a language has two or more relations and when instances of different relations can be between the same model elements, then it is necessary to consider all possible relation interactions, decide how to read and use them and how to capture these instructions in the language definition.

There are many other topics on defining relations in requirements modeling languages, and some of them will be discussed in the next sections. Chapter 8 focuses on how guidelines for modeling can be added to language definitions, but shows also how guidelines can suggest new relations and appear in the definitions of these relations. Chapter 9 introduces categories, and illustrates how relations can be restricted to specific fragment categories, which can reduce the number of relation interactions. Chapter 15 looks at how to produce proofs of satisfaction from models, which is required to solve DRP instances, and shows one way of mapping relation instances to formulae in a formal logic. Chapter 12 uses n-ary relations in order to represent alternatives in models.

Chapter 8
Guidelines

This chapter is on how to define guidelines for problem solving in requirements modeling languages. Guidelines recommend how to do something in problem solving so as to move closer to a solution. The chapter focuses on the following questions.

1. How to find guidelines for problem solving and embed them in requirements modeling languages. (Sect. 8.2)
2. How to combine guidelines into new, more complicated ones. (Sect. 8.3)
3. How to strengthen or weaken guidelines and why. (Sect. 8.4).

8.1 Motivation

Guidelines suggest how to do problem solving in requirements engineering. They may recommend how to elicit requirements, how to make them more precise, how to prioritize them, how to validate them with stakeholders, and so on.

Guidelines have a narrow scope when they focus on a specific task in problem solving. An example is f.acc. Guidelines that have broader scope address complicated problem-solving tasks. Suppose, for example, that you know the following rough recommendation:

> Add details to the model until all stakeholders have agreed that the most detailed elements are detailed enough.

To help you apply this recommendation, a language clearly needs r.ifm (or a relation which delivers the same language services as r.ifm) so that you can represent the adding of detail and identify the most detailed model elements. The language also needs to enable stakeholders to express agreement and disagreement, to represent reasons for agreeing or disagreeing, and to help you identify what the stakeholders agree and disagree on. You can do the first two with r.sup and r.def, and if you say that any acceptable model element is also agreed upon, then the language can use f.acc to find what is agreed and disagreed on.

© Springer International Publishing Switzerland 2015
I. Jureta, *The Design of Requirements Modelling Languages*,
DOI 10.1007/978-3-319-18821-8_8

Requirements modeling languages and guidelines are intertwined, in that it is difficult to design one while ignoring the other. If a language should help us address an issue during problem solving, then it will be designed to fit ideas and experience of how such issues should be addressed. A language service summarizes the issue to address, guidelines tell you what to do to address the issue, and the language should deliver the language service.

For example, the inclusion of a relation in a language reflects decisions about what the language should help its users with, that is, which language services it should deliver. A guideline may suggest that you should first add details to model elements and then look for, for example, how the satisfaction of some influences that of the others. To apply the guideline, you need a language that can represent the increase in details of model elements, and how the satisfaction of some influences that of the others.

Sections 8.2 and 8.3 illustrate how to go from identifying an issue to guidelines for addressing it, and to new language services and language modules which help apply these guidelines and embed them in language definitions. Section 8.4 illustrates the ideas of strengthening and weakening guidelines and why that may be relevant.

8.2 Guidelines from Arguments

L.Alpheratz can be used to represent that some fragments add details to others, but it does not suggest how to find new fragments which inform existing ones. It could not deliver the following language services:

- **s.HowInforms**: Given a fragment x, how to find a new fragment y which adds details to x, that is, such that $(y, x) \in$ r.ifm?
- **s.WhyInforms**: Given two fragments x and y such that $(y, x) \in$ r.ifm, why does y add details to x?

More detailed fragments can be found, for example, through further elicitation, analysis of comparable problem instances, by drawing on experience with comparable systems and in related domains, and so on.

If I want guidelines that are independent from the specific domain or problem class, I can look at various existing models that represent the increase in details of fragments. The aim is to find regularities in the differences between fragments that are related by r.ifm instances.

Take Example 7.7. There are patterns in the arguments given for r.ifm instances. The arguments are similar in HowSwtchCal, HowNoDropCal, HowRecEmCal, HowIdIncLoc, HowChkDblLoc and HowFillIncRep, in that they argue for the presence of r.ifm instances by saying each time that a fragment x adds details to fragment y by indicating *how* actions or conditions that y describes are, respectively, executed and satisfied. There are also similarities in the rationale WhoSwtchCal, WhoRecEmCal, and WhoIdIncLoc, where the additional details always say something about *who* is involved in satisfying the conditions that the informing fragment describes.

While looking for rationale patterns may not lead to universally applicable guidelines that are good for all languages, it can still help deliver additional language services relative to L.Alpheratz.

If I find recurring reasons for adding new fragments, and you and I agree that they are sufficiently relevant and generic to build them into a language, then I can document parts of how you and I use the language into that language. The language embeds more of our conventions on its use. While this may result from our joint work on models, it also means that we will be recommending those ways for use to anyone interested in making models with that language. For example, if you use L.Alpheratz, then you also accept that the inform relation is irreflexive, antisymmetric, and transitive; otherwise, you are using another language, not L.Alpheratz.

Given some fragments about the London Ambulance in Example 7.7, I can ask several questions for any given fragment x, including who does the action or satisfies the condition that x describes, how, when, where, and for whose benefit. If another fragment y answers at least one of these questions for the action or condition in x, then y adds details to x. If you and I agree that asking such questions is relevant, we can define the following language modules.

Function: add.ifm

Add details

Input

$x \in$ **F**.

Do

1. Ask the following questions about x:

   - *Who*: Who does (satisfies) x?
   - *How*: How is x done (satisfied)?
   - *When*: When is x done (satisfied)?
   - *Where*: Where is x done (satisfied)?
   - *WhoFor*: Who needs x to be done (satisfied)?

   Above, "does" is used if x describes actions; "satisfies" if it describes conditions.
2. Define sets $\mathbf{F}_q$ and R_q, for

$$q \in \{Who, How, When, Where, WhoFor\},$$

   such that:

a. each $y \in \mathbf{F}_q$ answers the question q for x,
b. if y answers the question q for x, then there is $(y, x) \in$ r.ifm in R_q.

Output

Sets $\mathbf{F}_q$ and R_q, for $q \in \{Who, How, When, Where, WhoFor\}$.

Language services

- s.HowInforms: Apply f.add.ifm to fragments in a given model M and add the resulting sets back to M.
- s.WhyInforms: If R_q is the output of applying f.AddsDetails, and $(y, x) \in R_q$, then y adds details to x because it answers the question q for x.

The function f.add.ifm suggests finding more detailed fragments via five questions. All new fragments go in the sets $\mathbf{F}_q$. When a fragment $y \in \mathbf{F}_q$ answers a question q for x, then I also add a relation instance $(y, x) \in$ r.ifm and it goes in R_q.

In order to keep the information in models, about which fragment answers which questions, I define five new unary relations on instances of r.ifm. The idea is that, if $(y, x) \in$ r.ifm and y answers the question q for x, then there will be an instance of a unary relation r.q on $(y, x) \in$ r.ifm. The relations are defined with the following template, where $q \in \{Who, How, When, Where, WhoFor\}$.

Relation: q

Answers question q

Domain & Dimension

r.q $\subseteq R$, where R is a set of r.ifm instances.

Properties

None.

Reading

$r \in$ r.q, where $r = (y, x)$, reads "y adds details to x by answering question q for x".

Language services

- s.WhyInforms: If $(y, x) \in$ r.q, then y adds details to x because it answers the question q for x.

Example 8.1 How would you define a language that has r.ifm and all five r.q relations? The language L.Hamal below has these relations.

Language: Hamal

Language modules
r.ifm, r.Who, r.How, r.When, r.Where, r.WhoFor, f.add.ifm

Domain
F is a set of fragments. r.ifm $\subseteq$ **F** $\times$ **F**, r.q $\in$ r.ifm, for every

$$q \in \{Who, How, When, Where, WhoFor\}$$

Syntax

A model M in the language is a set of symbols $M = \{Z_1, \ldots, Z_n\}$, where every Z is generated according to the following BNF rules:

$$A ::= x \mid y \mid z \mid \ldots$$
$$B ::= A \text{ informs } A$$
$$C ::= Who \mid How \mid When \mid Where \mid WhoFor$$
$$D ::= B \text{ answers } C$$
$$Z ::= A \mid B \mid D$$

Mapping

A symbols denote fragments, $\mathscr{D}(A) \in$ **F**. B are for r.ifm instances, that is, $\mathscr{D}(B) \in$ r.ifm. D symbols denote r.q instances,

$$\mathscr{D}(B \text{ answers } Who) \in \text{r.Who}, \ldots,$$
$$\mathscr{D}(B \text{ answers } WhoFor) \in \text{r.WhoFor}.$$

Language services

- s.WhyInforms: If $q.(y, x) \in$ r.q, then y adds details to x because it answers the question q for x.

Figure 8.1 is a visualization of a model in L.Hamal. It shows r.ifm instances and questions associated with each of these instances. The model was made by applying f.add.ifm to the fragments in Example 7.1. •

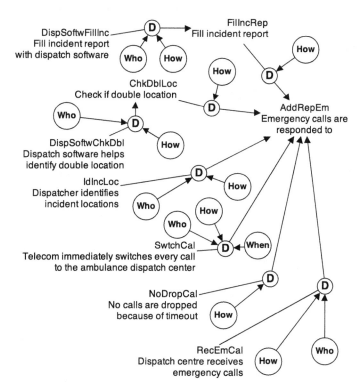

Fig. 8.1 Visualization of a model in L.Hamal

8.3 Composite Guidelines

The function f.add.ifm gave guidelines on how to add instances of one relation, r.ifm, with the side effect that you added new relations, r.q over instances of r.ifm. The aim now is to define guidelines which rely on several relations and functions. As with f.add.ifm, the result will be a function.

Adding details to model elements, and then evaluating how the satisfaction of some influences that of others, are closely related to the issue of operationalization in requirements engineering. The basic guideline in operationalization can be stated as the rule *Op* below, and is inspired by analogous notions in KAOS, Tropos, and Techne.

> *Op*: Add details to model elements until the most detailed ones are judged as detailed enough that it is known how to satisfy them, and satisfying them results in satisfying all the least detailed model elements.

The guideline assumes that I start with fragments that say what needs to be satisfied and/or executed, but that it is not clear how or who will do it. Operationalization is the process by which I need to find and decide who and how to make sure that these initial fragments are satisfied.

To make a function inspired by the operationalization guideline, you need r.ifm and r.inf.pos to represent, respectively, the increase in detail and the influence on satisfaction. You also need f.add.ifm to find new and more detailed fragments. Finally, you want this function to deliver the following language service.

Language service: AreOpr

Are all fragments in W operationalized?

The function is f.opr.all and is defined as follows.

Function: opr.all

Operationalize all fragments in a set

Input

Set W of fragments.

Do

1. Let X be an empty set, add all members of W to X.
2. Apply f.add.ifm to every fragment $w \in X$, and add to X all new fragments which you thereby find. If a fragment $y \in X$ is detailed enough that it is known how to satisfy and/or execute what it describes, and it is known who takes the responsibility to do so, then do not apply f.add.ifm to y.
3. For every $(a, b) \in$ r.ifm, where $a, b \in X$, check if there should be $(a, b) \in$ r.inf.pos or $(a, b) \in$ r.inf.neg and if yes, then add it. Stop when it is known how the satisfaction of each more detailed fragment influences the satisfaction of the fragment to which it adds details.

4. If there is a set $Z \subseteq X$ such that satisfying all fragments in Z positively influences the satisfaction of all fragments in W and there are no fragments in $W \setminus Z$ which inform those in Z, then stop. Otherwise, go back to step 1 above.

Output

Set Z of fragments which are said to operationalize all fragments in W.

Language services

- s.AreOpr: Yes, if there is a set Z made by applying f.opr.all to W.

Example 8.2 f.opr.all can work with models of languages which have r.ifm, r.inf.pos, and r.inf.neg. L.Acamar below has these relations, and so can include f.opr.all.

Language: Acamar

Language modules
r.ifm, r.inf.pos, r.inf.neg, f.add.ifm, f.opr.all

Domain

$\mathbf{F}$ is a set of fragments, r.ifm $\subseteq \mathbf{F} \times \mathbf{F}$, r.inf.pos $\subseteq \mathbf{F} \times \mathbf{F}$, and r.inf.neg $\subseteq \mathbf{F} \times \mathbf{F}$.

Syntax

A model M in the language is a set of symbols $M = \{Z_1, \ldots, Z_n\}$, where every Z is generated according to the following BNF rules:

$$A ::= x \mid y \mid z \mid \ldots$$
$$B ::= A \text{ informs } A$$
$$C ::= A \text{ influences+ } A$$
$$D ::= A \text{ influences– } A$$
$$Z ::= A \mid B \mid C \mid D$$

Mapping

$\mathscr{D}(A) \in$ **F**, $\mathscr{D}(B) \in$ r.ifm, $\mathscr{D}(C) \in$ r.inf.pos, and $\mathscr{D}(D) \in$ r.inf.neg.

Language services

Those of r.ifm, r.inf.pos, and r.inf.neg.

Figure 8.2 is a visualization of a model in L.Acamar, made by applying f.opr.all to the fragment AddRepEm. •

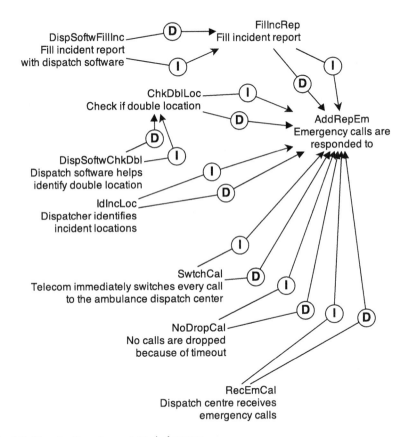

Fig. 8.2 Visualization of a model in L.Acamar.

8.4 Stronger and Weaker Guidelines

f.opr.all uses f.add.ifm, and therefore, also produces graphs $G_{I[q]}$ for various questions q. f.opr.all also says that we should not apply f.add.ifm to those fragments that are detailed enough, and a fragment is, if it is known how to satisfy it and who is responsible for doing so. Notice, then, that f.opr.all did not define "being detailed enough" by the presence or absence of r.q relations for, for example, *How* and *Who* questions. Instead, f.opr.all made no commitment about what exactly needs to be satisfied, in order for a fragment to be "detailed enough."

If you want to define more precisely the conditions that a fragment should satisfy to be detailed enough, this can be done with another function. In that function, call it f.opr.all.b, all is identical to f.opr.all, except that the second step is replaced by the following:

> Apply f.add.ifm to every fragment $w \in X$, and add to X all new fragments which you thereby find. *A fragment a is detailed enough if both Who and How questions are answered for that fragment, and do not apply f.add.ifm to that fragment.*

As given above, the italics mark the part which differs relative to f.opr.all. The difference is that we now use r.q in judging if a fragment is detailed enough.

Verifying if a fragment is detailed enough is simpler in f.opr.all.b than in f.opr.all, as it involves checking for the presence of r.Who and r.How instances, while in f.opr.all, you would have had to read the individual fragments, to say if they are detailed enough.

While f.opr.all.b did make it easier to check if a fragment is detailed enough, it did not necessarily result in a better guideline, since it is easy to find examples of fragments that would be detailed enough for f.opr.all.b and not for f.opr.all. For example, answering a *Who* question does not necessarily identify who is responsible, only who is involved in satisfying what the fragment describes. In short, the guideline documented in f.opr.all.b gives more precise and clearer instructions on what to do than f.opr.all, but neither function gives precise and clear sufficient conditions for a fragment to be detailed enough.

Suppose there are *new* conditions (which are neither in f.opr.all, nor f.opr.all.b) a fragment has to satisfy in order to be considered detailed enough. Let f.opr.all.c be the function made by adding these new conditions to f.opr.all.b. For example, the new conditions are that a fragment is detailed enough if and only if all q questions are answered for it. I will say that f.opr.all.c is *stronger* than f.opr.all.b, and that the former was made by *strengthening* the latter.

Strengthening a guideline involves adding conditions to check when applying the guideline, or to check in order to establish if the guideline is correctly applied. Weakening is the opposite, and consists of removing conditions that need to be checked.

As an additional illustration, recall that I said nothing about negative influences among fragments. It follows that any of the three operationalization functions can produce a set Z that operationalizes its input set X, and we could have had negative influence relations between members of Z. One way to strengthen each of these functions is to add to each of them the condition that there can be no negative influences between members of Z.

8.5 Summary on Guidelines

The following are the main ideas discussed for guidelines:

- Guidelines recommend how to put the language to work when doing problem solving. I can embed guidelines into the definition of the language, and in that way force specific ways of using it.
- You can define narrow guidelines on, for example, how to add a new relation instance to a model. In this book, such guidelines appeared in use rules for relations. You can also combine narrow guidelines into broader ones, which use several relations, functions, or otherwise (other kinds of language modules introduced later in this book), to deliver more complicated language services.
- Guidelines can be strengthened or weakened. I made no suggestions about universal rules on whether to strengthen or weaken a guideline. The stronger a guideline is, the more demanding it is on those involved in modeling, as there are more conditions to satisfy to use the language correctly. There may be situations in which this is not realistic, and consequently makes the language difficult to apply correctly, or makes it inapplicable.
- While experienced users of a language can suggest guidelines, it is also possible to identify guidelines by looking at recurring arguments for modeling decisions.

Chapter 9
Categories

This chapter looks at why and how to organize fragments into categories. "Requirement," "domain knowledge," "specification," "goal," and so on are examples of recurrent categories in requirements engineering. I focus on the following issues, moving from simpler to more complicated topics on categories.

1. Why and how to use independent categories. (Sect. 9.2)
2. What to do when there is a taxonomy of categories. (Sect. 9.3)
3. What is the meta-model and what is the ontology of a language? (Sect. 9.4)
4. Why and how to define derived categories and relations in a language. (Sect. 9.5)
5. How to enforce the intended use of categories in a language. (Sect. 9.6)

9.1 Motivation

A category groups fragments that share the same properties. Categories are used to distinguish between fragments having different properties, and thereby should be used differently during problem solving.

In the absence of categories, it is not possible, for example, to make a language that represents instances of the default problem. This is because the default problem distinguishes three categories, namely "requirement," "domain knowledge," and "specification." As I argue below, categories cut up the information used in problem solving, and thereby reflect the language designer's understanding of the way to cut up the information that is useful in identifying and solving problem instances.

© Springer International Publishing Switzerland 2015
I. Jureta, *The Design of Requirements Modelling Languages*,
DOI 10.1007/978-3-319-18821-8_9

9.2 Independent Categories

Categories are independent if, when adding them to a language, one does not *also* need to add new relations. This also means that, when there is a set of independent categories, you can choose any of its subsets to add to a language.

Categories in the default problem are independent, even though they are used together in the problem and the problem would not be the same if we removed any of these categories from it. They are independent because a fragment belonging to the "requirement" category is independent of the existence of the "domain knowledge" and "specification" categories. This in turn is determined by how these categories are defined [153]:

> The primary distinction necessary for requirements engineering is captured by two gram-
> matical moods. Statements in the "indicative" mood describe the environment as it is in the
> absence of the machine or regardless of the actions of the machine; these statements are often
> called "assumptions" or "domain knowledge". Statements in the "optative" mood describe
> the environment as we would like it to be and as we hope it will be when the machine is
> connected to the environment. Optative statements are commonly called "requirements."
> [...] A specification is also an optative property, but one that must be implementable.

Based on the above definition consider how you would define the minimal set of categories a language would need to make the distinctions suggested in the quote from Zave and Jackson. How many categories are required? What are the properties that decide if a fragment is in one of these categories? Can a fragment be in two or more of these categories? If yes, what conditions does it have to satisfy? If not, then why not?

I define each of the three categories with a language module. The language module has the same slots as for relations, which is unsurprising, since you can also consider categories as unary relations. But it should be clear when I am talking about relations, and when about categories, and hence categories have their own language module. Below is a definition of the requirement category, inspired by the definition of requirement in default problem.

Category: r

Requirement

Domain

c.r $\subseteq$ **F**, where **F** is a set of fragments.

Membership conditions

x is in the optative mood, and describes "the environment as we would like it to be and as we hope it will be when the machine is connected to the environment" [153].

Reading

$x \in$ c.r reads "x is a requirement."

Language services

- **s.IsReq**: Is x a requirement? Yes, if $x \in$ c.r.

The "membership conditions" slot above carries over the informal definition from Zave and Jackson that the requirement must be an optative statement. Following the same approach, there is a category for domain knowledge.

Category: k

Domain knowledge

Domain

c.k $\subseteq$ **F**, where **F** is a set of fragments.

Membership conditions

x is in indicative mood and describes "the environment as it is in the absence of the machine or regardless of the actions of the machine" [153].

Reading

$x \in$ c.k reads "x is domain knowledge."

Language services

- **s.IsDomK**: Is x domain knowledge? Yes, if $x \in$ c.k.

And finally, there is a category for specifications.

Category: s

Specification

Domain

c.s $\subseteq$ **F**, where **F** is a set of fragments.

Membership conditions

x is a statement in optative, which is implementable; that is, it is known who will do what the statement says and how it will be done.

Reading

$x \in$ c.s reads "x is a specification."

Language services

- **s.IsSpec**: Is x a specification? Yes, if $x \in$ c.s.

The three categories above can be used together in a function that categorizes sets of fragments to deliver the following language service.

Language service: WhichKSR

Which fragments in X are requirements, which are domain knowledge, and which are specifications?

---

s.WhichKSR is similar to asking if one specific fragment is in any of the three categories. Such questions are relevant when solving the default problem, because we need to check, for example, if satisfying fragments for domain knowledge and specifications positively influences the satisfaction of requirements fragments. The function below delivers s.WhichKSR.

Function: cat.ksr

Categorize in default problem categories

Input

Set X of fragments.

Do

For each $x \in X$:
- if x is in c.r, then let $cat(x) =$ c.r, else
- if x is in c.k, then let $cat(x) =$ c.k, else
- if x is in c.s, then let $cat(x) =$ c.s.

Output

Function ksr.

Language services

- s.WhichKSR: Function ksr says, for each fragment in X, if it is a requirement, domain knowledge, or specification.

Example 9.1 For illustration, below is the language L.Menkar, which has r.inf.pos, r.inf.neg, r.str.inf, and f.cat.ksr.

Language: Menkar

Language modules
r.inf.pos, r.inf.neg, r.str.inf, f.map.abrel.g, f.cat.ksr

Domain

Fragments are partitioned into requirements, domain knowledge, and specifications, that is, $\mathbf{F} =$ c.r $\cup$ c.k $\cup$ c.s and c.r $\cap$ c.k $\cap$ c.s $= \emptyset$. Influence relations are over fragments, r.inf.pos $\subseteq \mathbf{F} \times \mathbf{F}$, r.inf.neg $\subseteq \mathbf{F} \times \mathbf{F}$. Relative strength of influence is a relation over influence relations of the same type:

$$\text{r.str.inf} \subseteq (\text{r.inf.pos} \times \text{r.inf.pos}) \cup (\text{r.inf.neg} \times \text{r.inf.neg}).$$

Syntax

A model M in the language is a set of symbols $M = \{Z_1, \ldots, Z_n\}$, where every Z is generated according to the following BNF rules:

$$A ::= x \mid y \mid z \mid \ldots$$
$$B ::= r(A) \mid k(A) \mid s(A)$$
$$C ::= B \text{ influences+ } B$$
$$D ::= B \text{ influences- } B$$
$$E ::= C \text{ infstronger } C \mid D \text{ infstronger } D$$
$$Z ::= B \mid C \mid D \mid E$$

Mapping

A symbols denote uncategorized fragments. B symbols denote categorized fragments, so $\mathscr{D}(r(A)) \in$ c.r, $\mathscr{D}(k(A)) \in$ c.k, and $\mathscr{D}(s(A)) \in$ c.s. C symbols denote positive influence relations, $\mathscr{D}(C) \in$ r.inf.pos and D negative influence relations, $\mathscr{D}(D) \in$ r.inf.neg. E symbols denote relative strength of influence, $\mathscr{D}(E) \in$ r.str.inf.

Language services

Those of r.inf.pos, r.inf.neg, r.str.inf, f.map.abrel.g, and f.cat.ksr.

Figure 9.1 is a visualization of a model in L.Menkar. Label "R" marks c.r fragments, "K" those of c.k, and "S" those of c.s. •

9.3 Taxonomy of Categories

A taxonomy of categories is a set of categories related by the is-a relation, also called the specialization relation. If category A is a specialization of category B, then all members of B are also members of A, but not all members of A are necessarily members of B. In technical terms, the extension of category A is a subset of the extension of B.

It is common in requirements engineering to distinguish between two kinds of requirements, often called functional and nonfunctional requirements. I can have two categories for them, both specializations of c.r.

I will consider that a requirement is functional if it can either be satisfied or not. A requirement is nonfunctional if it can be satisfied to some extent, and different stakeholders may judge the requirement to be satisfied to different extents by the

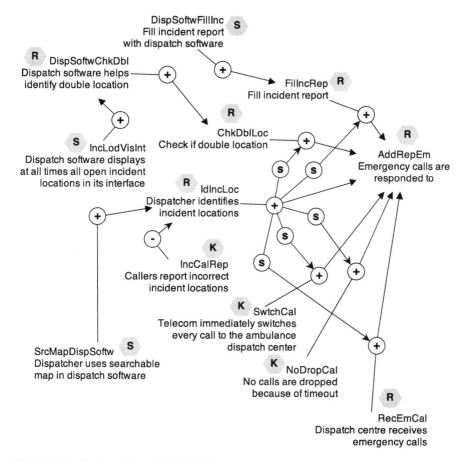

Fig. 9.1 Visualization of a model in L.Menkar

same system. This follows oft-cited research in requirements engineering, such as the NFR framework. According to this view, being able to communicate via radio with an ambulance is a functional requirement, while quickly responding to incidents is a nonfunctional requirement.

Category: r.f

Functional requirement

Domain

c.r.f $\subseteq X$, where $X \subseteq$ c.r.

Membership conditions

x is a member of c.r such that it is either satisfied or not.

Reading

$x \in$ c.r.f reads "x is a functional requirement."

Language services

- **s.IsFunctReq**: Is x a functional requirement? Yes, if $x \in$ c.r.f.

Category: r.nf

Nonfunctional requirement

Domain

c.r.nf $\subseteq X$, where $X \subseteq$ c.r.

Membership conditions

x is a member of c.r such that it can be satisfied to some extent, rather than either satisfied or failed, and different stakeholders may judge it to be satisfied to different extents by the same system.

Reading

$x \in$ c.r.nf reads "x is a nonfunctional requirement."

Language services

- **s.IsNFunctReq**: Is x a nonfunctional requirement? Yes, if $x \in$ c.r.nf.

If you let all fragments be partitioned into requirements, domain knowledge, and specifications, then the latter three categories are specializations of a category for fragments. You can also consider that the fragments category is the most general category, as shown in the taxonomy in Fig. 9.2.

Fig. 9.2 Taxonomy of categories from Sects. 9.2 and 9.3

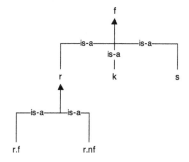

If one category is a specialization of another, then the former inherits the properties of the latter. The modules above captured inheritance by restricting domains wherein functional requirements are some of the requirements. This is clear from the slot "categorizes" in the language modules above.

An important design decision concerns the coverage of the taxonomy. If c.r is specialized into functional and nonfunctional requirements, are these its only subcategories? The taxonomy in Fig. 9.2 shows that these are the only categories while the language modules do not. To add to this constraint, you could add a function to the language that categorizes any requirement either as a functional or a nonfunctional one.

9.4 In Meta-models and Ontologies

A *meta-model* is a conceptual model that represents all the categories and relations of a language. An *ontology* is the specification of a conceptualization in requirements modeling languages; it is the specification of the categories and relations of the domain of the language, the things in the domain that language expressions and formulas are used to represent. The categories and relations are chosen so as to help in the representation and resolution of problems [84]. In *formal ontology*, such a specification is written in a formal logic [61, 129, 131].

The meta-model and the ontology of a language should not be confused [39]. The meta-model usually represents considerations that are purely practical, and concern, for example, the structure of expressions in a language. In the terminology of the languages discussed in this book, a meta-model will, for example, include a category "Graph," which may then be specialized into categories of graphs specific to each relation. However, the fact that graphs are used to represent relation instances is usually simply a practical matter, not something that fundamentally determines the conceptualization of the requirements problems which a language is defined for. In other words, the meta-model of the language may include all categories and relations from the ontology of the language, but will usually also include other categories and relations concerned purely with practical issues of the ways to represent or carry out transformations of the instances of the categories and relations in the ontology of the language.

If a sufficiently expressive ontology specification language is used, the formal ontology of the language could define the language in its entirety. To the best of my knowledge, this has not been done in requirements engineering. At present, the ontology of a language is usually equated to the set of all categories and relations in the language, together with axioms as constraints on how to correctly use the categories and relations. This is the case with i-star, KAOS, Techne, NFR, among others.

One way, then, to think of the ontology of a requirements modeling language is as a definition of the categories and relations needed to define instances of the requirements problem, which the language is made to solve, and the potential solutions to these problems. For example, the definition of L.D1a is a specification of what that language is, and hence is the specification of a conceptualization. The other way is to see the ontology of the language only as all categories and relations of the language. In requirements modeling languages, this has often been equated to a *meta-model* of the language. To represent the language ontology in such a way complements the category and relation definitions with language modules that include information use rules and language services, which the said models do not represent.

Example 9.2 Figure 9.3a shows the categories and relations of two different languages; in Fig. 9.3a and b nodes represent categories and links represent relations.

Figure 9.3a shows the ontology of a language in which r.ifm, r.inf.pos, and r.inf.neg are over the members of any category in the taxonomy in Fig. 9.2.

Figure 9.3b shows an ontology with the same categories as in Fig. 9.3a, but here the influence relations can go only from specification fragments to requirement fragments. •

9.5 Derived Categories and Relations

When new categories and relations are defined only as combinations of other parts of a language, I call them *derived*. Those that are not derived are called *core* language components. The core includes the minimal set of categories and relations needed to define the others in the language. Derived relations will therefore inherit the properties of the core ones.

Derived categories and relations can be used to emphasize specific ideas in a language, or, for example, to simplify modeling. They are syntactic sugar in a requirements modeling language. The following example illustrates this.

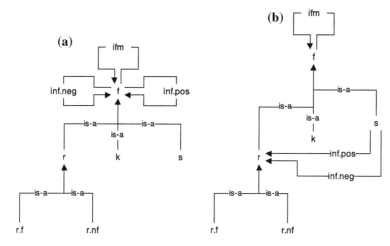

Fig. 9.3 Visualization of two ontologies. **a** Visualization of the ontology of one language. **b** Visualization of the ontology of another language

Example 9.3 Figure 9.3 shows that there can be an influence relation over problem-solving information and, consequently, over any pair of fragments, regardless of either of them being a requirement, domain knowledge, or otherwise. If you want to emphasize that there is a difference between having an influence relation from a specification to a requirement, as opposed to having it between requirements, you can add a derived relation as follows. Call it r.rls.

Relation: rls

Realize

Domain and dimension

r.rls $\subseteq S \times R$, where $S \times R \subseteq$ r.inf, $S \subseteq$ c.s and $R \subseteq$ c.r.

Properties

Irreflexive and transitive.

Reading

$(x, y) \in$ r.rls reads "specification x realizes the requirement y."

Language services

Inherits from r.inf.

r.els is the abbreviation of an influence from a specification to a requirement. You may want to distinguish r.rls from others in a requirements modeling language because there may be guidelines given and so it may be simpler to talk of realization every time the guidelines are applied, rather than of all that it abbreviates. Or, it may be that there is a convention among stakeholders who speak of requirements being realized or not, and you interpret this as being about the presence or absence of influence relations from specifications to these requirements. •

A derived category can not only be defined from categories and relations, but also from combinations of other language components, categories, and functions for example. I look at the former first.

Example 9.4 Suppose I am particularly interested in requirements that are negatively influenced by environmental conditions. If I assume that I cannot change these conditions, then such requirements will likely need to be revised to avoid the system failing them too often at run-time. To highlight them in models, I define a new derived category, c.r.clsh. •

Category: r.clsh

Clashing requirement

Domain

c.r.clsh $\subseteq X$, where $X \subseteq$ c.r.

Membership conditions

x is such that there is $(y, x) \in$ r.inf.neg and $y \in$ c.k.

Reading

$x \in$ c.r.clsh reads "x is a requirement which clashes with environmental conditions."

Language services

• **s.IsClshReq**: Does x clash with environmental conditions? Yes, if $x \in$ c.r.clsh.

Example 9.5 Now suppose I want to categorize a requirement as irrelevant if it is not acceptable. Acceptability works as in Sect. 7.5.2. I use f.Accepted to define the category c.r.irrl. •

Category: r.irrl

Irrelevant requirement

Domain

c.r.irrl $\subseteq X$, where $X \subseteq$ c.r.

Membership conditions

x is not acceptable in a given model M according to f.acc.

Reading

$x \in$ c.r.irrl reads "x is an irrelevant requirement."

Language services

- **s.IsIrrlReq**: Is x an irrelevant requirement? Yes, if $x \in$ c.r.irrl.

9.6 Enforce Category Use

Categories are interesting because they distinguish fragments in terms of how they are used in problem solving. Hence categorizing a fragment is only a part of how categories are used. The other part is to define rules about how to use these categories. This can, for example, be functions that say what to do when there is an instance of some category, or if instances of a category are in some specific relations with instances of other categories.

Another way to view this is that you add new functions to a language in order to make sure that the categories in it are used as intended. In the following example, I use c.r as a completeness check of models.

Example 9.6 Knowing that a fragment is a requirement leads me to ask if this requirement is operationalized in the given model. If it is not, then I might want to conclude that this is negative and say that the model is incomplete. If I want to force this notion of model completeness on language users, I can build it into the language with the following function.

Function: chk.rop

Completeness of requirements operationalization

Input

A set X of fragments, G(X, r.ifm) and G(X, r.inf.pos).

Do

1. Let H be a hypergraph made by merging G(X, r.ifm) and G(X, r.inf.pos).
2. If there is $x \in X$ such that x is in c.r and there is no path in H from $z \in X$ to x, such that z is in c.s, then the model that includes exactly the fragments in X is incomplete with regard to requirements operationalization and $v = 1$.

Output

v.

Language services

- **s.IsROpComp**: Is the model that includes exactly the fragments X incomplete with regard to requirements operationalization? Yes, if $v = 1$, no otherwise.

I can use f.chk.rop as a way to check how close we are to identifying a solution to the problem being solved. If some requirements are not operationalized, then I have to look further for specifications, as I have not solved the problem yet. •

9.7 Summary on Categories

The following are the main ideas discussed on categories:

- To add some category C to a language, it is necessary to define how it is used. At the very least, this involves answering the following questions:

  1. What conditions have to be satisfied for x to belong to (to be in the extension of) the category C?
  2. Can members of the extension of C be members of the extensions of other categories in the given language? If yes, then why and of which categories? This is answered by defining taxonomic (is-a) relations between categories.
  3. How are category instances, if in any way, related to those of other categories? This is answered by the relations over members of extensions, of the categories.

- Using categories for classification is only part of the motivation for having them in languages. After adding a category, such as c.r, you may want to add new relations, functions, and so on in order to use that category in problem solving. For example, having a category for requirements and for specifications begs the question of how the satisfaction of the latter influences that of the former, and to answer it, you need influence relations. Having domain knowledge and requirements categories begs the question of what to do if there is negative influence from the latter to the former, and so requires guidelines for resolving this.
- It is useful to distinguish core categories and relations from derived ones in a language. It is otherwise hard to know what is absolutely necessary in a language, in order to deliver language services as well as to compare languages in terms of their components.

Chapter 10
Valuation

Valuation consists of associating variables to model parts, and functions to relations over the model parts. The aim is to have models where values of some variables depend on the values of others. Given the values of some, you can then compute those of others. Value type, value assignment, and outcome are central notions in valuation. A value type is simply a set of values, such that a variable x has value type T, if and only if any value of that variable must be a member of T. A value assignment is the value that a variable has, among the values of its value type. An outcome is a nonempty set of value assignments. The chapter looks at how to define value types, how to compute value assignments and outcomes, and how to use all of these in a language. This is done by discussing the following:

1. How to define a language with a single binary value type, that is, where model parts take either of two values and why this may be interesting. (Sect. 10.2)
2. How to, and why define a language which has more than one binary value type, so that any model part is assigned a tuple of values instead of a single value. (Sect. 10.3)
3. How to, and why define a language with an unordered set of values as its only value type, (Sect. 10.4)
4. What if the value type for the language is an ordered set, (Sect. 10.5)
5. Why and how to have in a language a value type defined over real numbers (Sect. 10.6).

These discussions will also illustrate how to use value types in new guidelines for a language.

10.1 Motivation

Valuation can enable various interesting language services. It is also related to language services discussed earlier. For example, valuation in a language can say that each fragment is associated with its own variable for satisfaction. The variable might be allowed to take either 1, read "satisfied," or 0 for "not satisfied." A function may then be associated with every positive and negative influence relation, to compute

© Springer International Publishing Switzerland 2015
I. Jureta, *The Design of Requirements Modelling Languages*,
DOI 10.1007/978-3-319-18821-8_10

how the value of the influenced fragment depends on those of fragments influencing it. This section will give many examples unrelated to satisfaction, but satisfaction remains an important motive to think about valuation in a language.

In this book, a language has rules for valuation if, in its models, variables can be associated with model parts, functions to relation instances, and if that language answers the following questions:

1. Which values can be assigned to which variables.
2. Which functions relate the values of the variables.
3. How to compute the values of the variables.

This chapter will illustrate how to answer the questions above for various value types.

10.2 Propagating Binary Values

This section discusses and combines two topics:

- How to have a language in which any fragment and relation instance can be assigned one of the two satisfaction values, namely "satisfied" or "not satisfied"? That is, how to define a language which has only one binary value type? (Sect. 10.2.1)
- Given a model in that language, and knowing the satisfaction value of some fragments and/or relation instances, how to compute the values of others? In other words, how to define functions in a language which return the satisfaction value of a fragment or relation instance and take into account already known satisfaction values of other fragments and relation instances? (Sect. 10.2.2).

I use satisfaction values because I discussed satisfaction already in relation to influence relations. However, the discussion in this section remains relevant for any binary value type. As for how to compute values, I use a simple approach which I refer to as "value propagation." In this approach, a relation instance from y to x is seen, roughly speaking, as a pipe that conducts a value from y to x, whereby the value to conduct depends on the value of y and on the specifics of the relation. Values thus get "pushed" through potentially many such pipes to a fragment, and there is then a rule which aggregates them and outputs a single value for that fragment. There are other ways to compute values on model parts. I will mention some of them and leave others outside the scope of this book.

10.2.1 Binary Value Type

To motivate the use of binary value types recall the first condition in the DRP. It says that there has to be a proof of requirements from domain knowledge and specifications. The more general idea is this: it should be shown that if conditions that domain knowledge and specifications describe are satisfied, then the conditions described with requirements are satisfied as well. This gives the following language service.

Language service: SatReq

Are all requirements satisfied in the model M?

To deliver s.SatReq, it is necessary to have a value type for satisfaction. Given how s.SatReq is phrased, it looks enough to have two values for satisfied and not satisfied. If s.SatReq asked, instead, for how well requirements were satisfied, then a binary value type would not work.

To deliver, then, s.SatReq, I will use v.Satisfaction, a binary value type such that

$$\text{v.Satisfaction} = \{1, 0\},$$

where 1 reads "satisfied" and 0 reads "not satisfied".

s.SatReq mentions requirements, so that the language has to distinguish requirements fragments from others. I will keep using the three categories defined earlier, namely c.r, c.k and c.s.

What, in a model, gets a value of v.Satisfaction? A variable that is associated with every fragment and every relation instance. The language thus also needs a set of variables. There will be as many variables as there are fragments and relation instances. As I am working with a single value type here, all variables will take values from v.Satisfaction.

10.2.2 Value Propagation

The language needs to represent if the satisfaction value of a fragment depends on the satisfaction values of one or more other fragments, and if it does, then how exactly. This is done by having a function which is sensitive to the relations between fragments. Given the motivation discussed earlier for influence relations, the language will include r.inf.pos and r.inf.neg. It will also need another function which is presented later.

Recall that influence relations were not defined specifically with v.Satisfaction in mind, but simply to represent, when it exists, the information that satisfaction of a fragment depends on that of another. The next language design decision to make, then, is to define how exactly the satisfaction value of a fragment influences that of another, when there is an influence relation between them. The following rules come to mind, for $(y, x) \in$ r.inf.pos in a model M:

- if y gets the value 1 from v.Satisfaction, x should get 1 as well, if one ignores all (if any) other influences relation that may be targeting x in M,
- if y gets 0, then x gets 0, too, if one ignores all (if any) other influences relation that may be targeting x in M.

I emphasized in both rules above that they are local: they say which value to assign to x only by considering the value that y has, and that the relation instance is a positive influence (rather than a negative influence). The rules ignore all other positive or negative influences to x, from fragments other than y.

To have these rules in a language, I will add a new function called f.sat.inf.pos. It relies on f.sat to return the satisfaction value of a fragment. f.sat remains undefined for the moment. When I define it later, it will say what the satisfaction value of a fragment is, given potentially many positive and negative influence relation instances to that fragment. This is different from f.sat.inf.pos, which concentrates on the satisfaction value of a single positive influence relation instance.

I will write $\langle x, t, v \rangle$ for a variable of v.t which is associated with the fragment or relation instance x, and whose value is v. This is called a "value assignment".

Function: sat.inf.pos

Positive influence satisfaction

Input

$(y, x) \in$ r.inf.pos and model M.

Do

$v = 1$ if y is satisfied in M, and $v = 0$ otherwise.

Output

$\langle (y, x), $ v.Satisfaction$, v \rangle$.

Language services

- **s.WhPosInfSat**: What is the v.Satisfaction value of $(y, x) \in$ r.inf.pos?: $\langle (y, x), $ v.Satisfaction$, v \rangle$.

The function f.sat.inf.pos is based on the idea of "propagating" values. To see what this amounts to, suppose that there are fragments y and x in a model M, and there is positive influence from y to x. So if y is satisfied, then this positively influences the satisfaction of x. But you cannot simply conclude that x is in fact satisfied, because there may be other influences, positive or negative, which target x, from fragments other than y.

Propagation consists of seeing relation instances as kinds of pipes, each of which propagates a value to its target. There may be many relation instances which propagate different values to the same target, and therefore, it is necessary to have rules which aggregate all these values that a fragment receives, and concludes one satisfaction value for that fragment.

When valuation involves value propagation, the values on relation instances may be somewhat confusing, as in the function below. It propagates satisfaction values of negative influence.

Function: sat.inf.neg

Negative influence satisfaction

Input

$(y, x) \in$ r.inf.neg and model M.

Do

If y is not satisfied in M, then x should be, and $v = 1$. If y is satisfied in M, then x should not, and so $v = 0$.

Output

$\langle (y, x),$ v.Satisfaction$, v \rangle$.

Language services

- **s.WhNegInfSat**: What is the v.Satisfaction value of $(y, x) \in$ r.inf.neg?: $\langle (y, x),$ v.Satisfaction$, v \rangle$.

A satisfied negative influence is thus not an influence which successfully negatively affects its target, but one which fails to do so and therefore propagates 1 to x in f.inf.neg.

The next step is to define f.sat which computes the satisfaction value of a fragment, based on all positive and negative influences on that fragment.

For some fragments, the satisfaction value will be computed; for others, it will be manually assigned. I therefore need rules for how to compute values, as I otherwise cannot answer such questions as "What should be the v.Satisfaction value of a fragment x, when x is the target of two or more positive and/or negative influence relations?" For example, what is the satisfaction value of x, if f.sat.inf.pos$(y, x) = 1$, f.sat.inf.pos$(z, x) = 0$, and f.sat.inf.neg]$(w, x) = 0$?

Let $(p_1, x), \ldots, (p_n, x)$ be instances of r.inf.pos and $(q_1, x), \ldots, (q_m, x)$ be instances of r.inf.neg, all targeting the fragment x. Consider the following rules:

1. if for all $i = 1, \ldots, n$, it is the case that $\mathsf{f.sat.inf.pos}((p_i, x)) = 1$, and for all
   $j = 1, \ldots, m$, $\mathsf{f.sat.inf.neg}((q_j, x)) = 1$, then the satisfaction value of x is 1,
2. in all other cases, the satisfaction value of x is 0.

I can add these rules to a language via the function $\mathsf{f.sat}$, defined as follows:

Function: sat

Satisfaction

Input

Fragment $x \in \mathbf{F}$ and model M.

Do

Let $\{(p_1, x), \ldots, (p_n, x)\} \subseteq \mathsf{r.inf.pos}$ be the set of all positive influence relation instances to x in M, and $\{(q_1, x), \ldots, (q_m, x)\} \subseteq \mathsf{r.inf.neg}$ be the set of all negative influence relation instances to x in M. Then,

$$v = \prod_{i=1}^{n} \mathsf{f.sat.inf.pos}((p_i, x), M) \cdot \prod_{j=1}^{m} \mathsf{f.sat.inf.neg}((q_j, x), M)$$

$\mathsf{f.sat.inf.pos}((p_i, x), M)$ returns the satisfaction value of, or propagated by $(p_i, x) \in \mathsf{r.inf.pos}$ in M. $\mathsf{f.sat.inf.neg}((q_j, x), M)$ returns the satisfaction value of $(q_j, x) \in \mathsf{r.inf.neg}$ in M.

Output

$\langle x, \mathsf{v.Satisfaction}, v \rangle$

Language services

- **s.WhSat**: What is the satisfaction value of x in M? : It is $\langle x, \mathsf{v.Satisfaction}, v. \rangle$

Which rules are relevant for $\mathsf{f.sat}$ depend on what exactly these rules should do for you. The rules above reflect the idea that x will be satisfied only if everything influencing it positively is satisfied as well, and everything influencing it negatively is not satisfied. In some sense, it reflects a demanding and defensive attitude when fragments are satisfied. If any one of these two conditions fails, for example, a fragment is satisfied and negatively influences x, it will not matter that there may be other fragments which are satisfied and positively influence x. The conclusion will be that x is not satisfied.

To give a satisfaction value of some x, f.sat needs all influence relations to x. But what if there are none? f.sat cannot assign a satisfaction value to x, and neither can f.sat.inf.pos and f.sat.inf.neg. You need to choose in another way the values of fragments whose values cannot be computed with these three functions.

In addition to the three functions, another function is needed to assign satisfaction values for every fragment which is target of no influence relation. These are fragments from which you start propagating satisfaction values. If you think in terms of graphs over influence relations, then this amounts to assigning a satisfaction value to every leaf node *only*, and then using the three functions mentioned above, to compute the satisfaction values of other fragments. This leads to f.sat.leaf below, which takes a fragment with no influence relations and assigns a satisfaction value to it.

Function: sat.leaf

Assume a satisfaction value for a non influenced fragment

Input

Fragment x and model M, such that there is no $(y, x) \in$ r.inf, $(y, x) \in$ r.inf.pos, and $(y, x) \in$ r.inf.neg in M with y also in M.

Do

If you assume that x is satisfied, then $v = 1$, else if you assume that x is not satisfied, then $v = 0$, else leave v without value.

Output

$\langle x, v.\text{Satisfaction}, v \rangle$

Language services

- **s.WhAsmSatLf**: Which, if any, is the assumed v.Satisfaction value of x in M?: $\langle x, v.\text{Satisfaction}, v \rangle$ if $v \in \{0, 1\}$, otherwise no v.Satisfaction value is assumed for x.

The four functions, f.sat.inf.pos, f.sat.inf.neg, f.sat and f.sat.leaf are enough to assume and compute satisfaction values on models that relate fragments with positive and negative influence relations. The following language puts these notions together.

Language: Rigel

Language modules
r.inf.pos, r.inf.neg, f.map.abrel.g, f.cat.ksr, f.sat.inf.pos, f.sat.inf.neg, f.sat, f.sat.leaf

---

Domain

There is a set of fragments **F**, a singleton for value types

$$\mathbf{T} = \{\mathsf{v.Satisfaction}\},$$

and a set of value assignments **V**. Fragments have three partitions, namely requirements, domain knowledge and specification fragments, $\mathbf{F} = \mathsf{c.r} \cup \mathsf{c.k} \cup \mathsf{c.s}$ and $\mathsf{c.r} \cap \mathsf{c.k} \cap \mathsf{c.s} = \emptyset$. Influences are over fragments, $\mathsf{r.inf.pos} \subseteq \mathbf{F} \times \mathbf{F}$, $\mathsf{r.inf.neg} \subseteq \mathbf{F} \times \mathbf{F}$. Value assignments are over fragments or relation instances, involve a value type, and a value, so that

$$\mathbf{V} \subseteq (\mathbf{F} \cup \mathsf{r.inf.pos} \cup \mathsf{r.inf.neg}) \times \mathbf{T} \times \mathsf{v.Satisfaction}.$$

Satisfaction is binary, $\mathsf{v.Satisfaction} = \{1, 0\}$.

Syntax

A model M in the language is a set of symbols $M = \{Z_1, \ldots, Z_n\}$, where every ϕ is generated according to the following BNF rules:

$$
\begin{aligned}
A &::= x \mid y \mid z \mid \ldots \\
B &::= r(A) \mid k(A) \mid s(A) \\
C &::= B \text{ influences}+ B \\
D &::= B \text{ influences}- B \\
G &::= \langle A, E, F \rangle \\
Z &::= B \mid C \mid D \mid G
\end{aligned}
$$

Mapping

A symbols denote fragments, $\mathscr{D}(A) \in \mathbf{F}$. B symbols are used to distinguish requirements, domain knowledge, and specification fragments, so that $\mathscr{D}(r(\alpha)) \in \mathsf{c.r}$, $\mathscr{D}(k(\alpha)) \in \mathsf{c.k}$, $\mathscr{D}(s(\alpha)) \in \mathsf{c.s}$. C and D symbols denote, respectively, positive and negative influence relations. E symbols denote value type, $\mathscr{D}(E) \in \mathbf{T}$. F symbols denote a value of a value type, and as there is one value type, $\mathscr{D}(F) \in$ v.Satisfaction. G symbols denote value assignments, $\mathscr{D}(G) \in$ **V**.

Language services

Those of relations and functions in the language, and s.SatReq.

Models in L.Rigel can represent mutually exclusive value assignments on the same fragments and relation instances, and therefore, mutually exclusive outcomes. This is useful because, for example, different people may use f.sat.leaf and they may have different assumptions about the values of leaf fragments. Or the model user wishes to ask what-if kinds of questions, such as "What if all leaf fragments get these satisfaction values, as opposed to these other satisfaction values?" and wishes to compare the outcomes (more on this in Chap. 14). This is illustrated in Example 10.1.

In Example 10.1, Figs. 10.1 and 10.2 do not include outcomes. Figure 10.3 includes one outcome, and Fig. 10.4 includes two. An outcome can be specific to one value type, as in Figs. 10.3 and 10.4, where only v.Satisfaction values can be assigned anyway, due to the specifics of the language used. When I want to say that an outcome has values of only one, or some specific set of value type, I will write so. For example, Figs. 10.3 and 10.4 show v.Satisfaction outcomes.

Example 10.1 This example illustrates how L.Rigel computes value assignments in a model. Figures 10.1, 10.2, 10.3 and 10.4 show four models in L.Rigel.

The first model in Fig. 10.1 shows a model with assignments of satisfaction values to fragments with no incoming positive or negative influence relations. This assignment is a result of applying f.sat.leaf. There can be other assignments, as the values depend entirely on the model user who is assigning them.

The second model, in Fig. 10.2 was made by applying f.sat.inf.pos and f.sat. f.inf.neg on positive and negative influence relation instances which are directly connected to the leaf fragments. You can think of this model as showing one step of propagating the satisfaction values assumed and shown in the first model in Fig. 10.1.

The third model shows the satisfaction values assigned after applying f.sat.inf.pos, f.sat.inf.neg and f.sat to all influence relation instances and fragments in the model.

The model in Fig. 10.4 shows two outcomes, that is, two assignments of satisfaction values to every fragment and relation instance. Values for one outcome are shown on black squares, and on gray squares for the other. •

L.Rigel delivers s.SatReq in the following way. Given a model, you apply f.sat.leaf and assign one satisfaction value to every leaf fragment. You then propagate satisfaction values using f.sat.inf.pos, f.sat.inf.neg and f.sat, until you have one outcome. If that outcome assigns the satisfaction value 1 to every requirement in the model, then the answer to s.SatReq is affirmative, and is "no" otherwise.

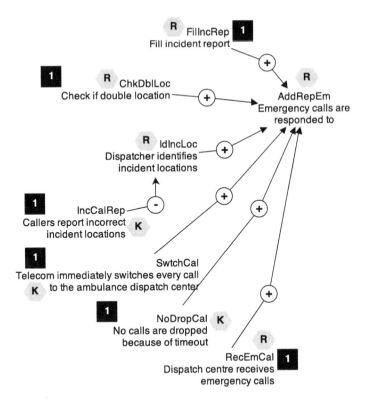

Fig. 10.1 Satisfaction values assigned with f.sat.leaf

10.3 Combining Several Binary Value Types

This section looks at how to have more than one value type in a language. It focuses on a simple case when there are two binary value types. Consider the following language service.

Language services: AppSat

Which requirements in the model M are both approved by all stakeholders, and satisfied?

The language needs two value types, one for satisfaction and the other for approval. They will be called v.Satisfaction and v.Approval. If you allow a stakeholder to either approve or not a requirement, then v.Approval is a binary value type. By analogy to v.Satisfaction, which remains here the same as in Sect. 10.2, there is v.Approval $= \{1, 0\}$, where 1 reads "approved", and 0 "not approved".

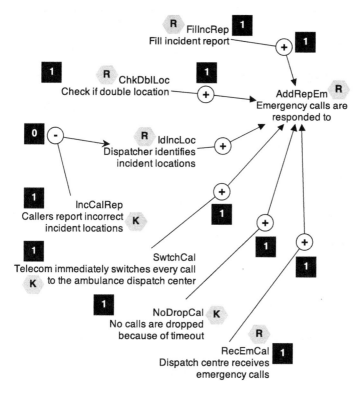

Fig. 10.2 After applying f.sat.inf.pos and f.sat.inf.neg

Then, it is necessary to decide how the approval of a fragment depends on the approval of other fragments, if in any way. One option is to ask stakeholders to assign an approval value to each requirement fragment, and therefore *not* compute the approval value of requirements. Another is to allow influence relations (or some other relations in the language) to be significant for approval, perhaps in the same way that they were significant for satisfaction in Sect. 10.2. That is, if there is $(y, x) \in$ r.inf.pos, and it is known that y is approved, then a rule would say how this should be taken into account to compute the approval value of x.

Section 10.3.1 looks at the case where the approval values are assigned to every fragment manually so that there is no need for rules to compute those values. Section 10.3.2 focuses on the case where missing approval values can be computed from those that exist in a model.

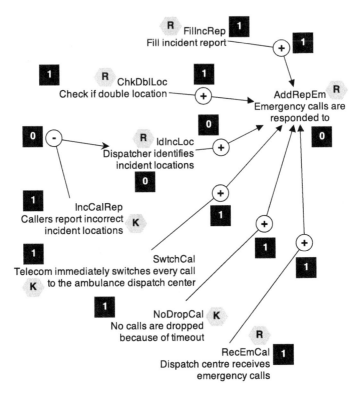

Fig. 10.3 One outcome

10.3.1 Independent Value Assignments

Suppose the approval value of a fragment or relation instance is independent of the approval value of another fragment or of a relation instance. Moreover, suppose the satisfaction values are independent of approval values, and *vice versa*. If I approved fragment x, then this has nothing to do with whether I will approve fragment y, or whether y is satisfied. How would you enable a language to assign approval values in this way and deliver s.AppSat?

You can add v.Approval to L.Rigel, and add a function for asserting approval values which works in the same way as f.sat.leaf. The function is as follows:

Function: app.asg.ind

Assume independent approval value

Input

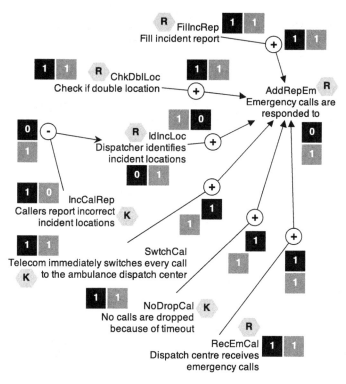

Fig. 10.4 Two outcomes

Fragment $x \in$ **F**.

Do

If a stakeholder approves x, then $v = 1$, else $v = 0$.

Output

$\langle x, \text{v.Approval}, v \rangle$

Language services

- **s.AsmApp**: Is x approved by a stakeholder?: Yes, if $\langle x, \text{v.Approval}, 1 \rangle$, no otherwise.

Assigning approval values in a model M with **f.app.asg.ind** consists of asking a stakeholder to approve each fragment and relation instance.

Two issues arise:

1. There can be many stakeholders, so you should decide if the approval value reflects the approval of a single stakeholder, of some, or of all. The issue is whether to allow the assignment of tuples of approval values to model parts, with one approval value per stakeholder. f.app.asg.ind assigns individual values.
2. How to read and use, if in any way, the combination of a satisfaction and approval value on a fragment? For example, is there some new information to conclude from knowing both that a fragment is satisfied and that it is not approved? Satisfaction and approval values still are independent, but the question is if you should draw some additional conclusion from knowing both the satisfaction and approval value of a fragment or relation instance.

On the first issue, if the models need to show all approval values, from all stakeholders, then the language should allow every model part to carry as many approval values as there are stakeholders. The approval value of a model part would be a tuple, each element being the approval value of one stakeholder.

If it is necessary to decide a single approval value of a model part, when there are many approval values coming from many stakeholders, then the language needs to have rules for aggregating approval values. For example, aggregation rules can be that if all stakeholders approve a model part, then it is approved, or that if the majority approves a model part, then it is approved, and so on. Research in group decision making [33] and social choice [5, 28] is one source of such aggregation rules.

The second issue is if knowing both the satisfaction and approval values *together* gives some additional information for problem solving which is useful for deciding what to do next with the model. For example, if a model part is both satisfied and approved, then it is probably more interesting to look at other model parts in the next steps of problem solving. If model parts are seen as representations of parts of the problem being solved and of its potential solutions, then a satisfied and approved model part can be considered as a solved problem part.

In this same line of thinking, if a model part is not satisfied but is approved, then it will need to be solved, that is, it is necessary to change the model in such a way as to ensure that in the changed model, the model part is both satisfied and approved. There is the case of a satisfied and not approved part, which can be solved by, for example, negotiating its approval with or among stakeholders, or by removing from the model those parts which satisfy it yet are unnecessary for satisfying the approved model parts. The final case is that of a part which is neither satisfied nor approved. It may thereby not even be a part of the problem, even if it is part of the model. Table 10.1 summarizes these ideas.

Table 10.1 Combinations of v.Satisfaction and v.Approval values

	Approved	Not approved
Satisfied	No action needed	Negotiate or remove
Not satisfied	Find a way to satisfy it	Ignore

The more general point for language design is that allowing two or more value types raises the question of how to use the various combinations of these values in problem solving, if they are used at all.

If the value combinations are useful, then this can be captured by a new value type, and functions for assigning and, or computing their values. For illustration, two new value types are defined below, one from combinations of v.Approval only, the other from both v.Approval and v.Satisfaction.

Example 10.2 v.MajApp $= \{1, 0\}$ is such that 1 is given to a model part if half or more of all stakeholders have assigned the v.Approval value 1 to this model part. This gives the following function. •

Function: app.maj

Majority approval

Input

Fragment $x \in$ **F**.

Do

If more than half of all stakeholders approve x, then $v = 1$, else $v = 0$.

Output

$\langle x, \text{v.MajApp}, v \rangle$.

Language services

- **s.IsMajApp**: Is x approved by the majority of stakeholders?: Yes, if $\langle x, \text{v.MajApp}, 1 \rangle$, no otherwise.

Example 10.3 v.SatNext $= \{1, 0\}$ is used to mark model parts which are approved and not satisfied. As they are approved, there is no need to discuss them further with stakeholders, but focus on how to change the model to satisfy them. These values are assigned with the following function. •

Function: sat.nxt

Satisfy next

Input

Fragment $x \in$ **F**.

Do

$v = 1$ if $\langle x, \text{v.Satisfaction}, 0 \rangle$ and $\langle x, \text{v.Approval}, 1 \rangle$, else $v = 0$.

Output

$\langle x, \text{v.SatNext}, v \rangle$.

Language services

- **s.DoSatNext**: Should problem solving focus next on how to satisfy x?: Yes, if $\langle x, \text{v.SatNext}, 1 \rangle$.

Neither v.MajApp, nor v.SatNext is defined over all four possible combinations of v.Satisfaction and v.Approval values. This is because a value type which is defined over all four combinations is not binary, but instead an unordered set of four values. It is discussed in Sect. 10.4.

10.3.2 Dependent Value Assignments

In Sect. 10.3.1, only f.app.maj computed the approval value of a fragment from other approval values on that same fragment. There were no rules about how, for example, to compute the approval value of x from those of other fragments, which x is somehow related to.

If you have a language which cannot assign v.Approval values, how would you change that language so that it can assign these values to fragments and relation instances, along similar lines as f.sat.inf.pos, f.sat.inf.neg, f.sa or f.sat.x, and f.sat.leaf for v.Satisfaction values? Would you need new relations in that language? Which new functions would you add, and why?

To compute approval values in models rather than assigning them manually to all fragments, you need to make analogous decisions tothose made for functions which computed satisfaction values in Sect. 10.2. Therefore, if the language does not represent alternatives, and you want to assign approval values by propagating them, then you need to make the following decisions:

1. What is the relation r whose instance $(y, x) \in r$ should exist, in order for the approval value of the fragment x to depend on the approval value of the fragment y?
2. If there is a relation instance $(y, x) \in r$, and the approval value of y is 1 (or 0), what should be the approval value of x?
3. If there are several relation instances $(y_1, x) \in r_1, \ldots, (y_n, x) \in r_n$, and approval values of $y_1, \ldots, y_n$ are not the same, then what should be the approval value of x?
4. If there are no r relation instances to x, then what should be the approval value of x?

Recall how the questions above were answered for v.Satisfaction. The presence of r.inf.pos or r.inf.neg between two fragments x and y meant that the satisfaction value of one depended on that of the other. If you think in terms of value propagation, positive and negative influence relations were used to propagate satisfaction values that answers the first question. f.sat.inf.pos and f.sat.inf.neg defined how satisfaction value of x depends on that of y, in case when there is, respectively, $(y, x) \in$ r.inf.pos or $(y, x) \in$ r.inf.neg. f.sat answers the third question above. Finally, f.sat.leaf was the answer to the fourth question.

10.4 Sets of Values

Consider now a value type which is a set of values, and there is no order over them. In Sect. 10.3, there were four combinations of binary values from two core binary value type, v.Satisfaction and v.Approval. Table 10.1 gave a reading of these combinations. The four combinations can be used to define the three values of a new value type, called v.ToDo. These values are as follows:

- *Done*, when satisfaction and approval values are both 1,
- *Operationalize*, when satisfaction is 0 and approval 1,
- *Negotiate or remove*, when approval is 0, regardless of satisfaction.

Each value suggests what to do next about the fragment or relation instance it is assigned to, hence the name of the value type. The rules for assigning this value type are straightforward as its values are fully determined by the satisfaction and approval values.

To illustrate a more complicated value type which is also a set of unordered values, recall that I defined five questions, *Who*, *How*, *When*, *Where* and *WhoFor* and the corresponding unary relations. Suppose you want to make a language which delivers the following language service.

Language services: WhichDetail

Which of the questions among *Who, How, When, Where*, and *WhoFor* were not asked for the fragment x?

There are different ways to deliver s.WhichDetail, but I will focus on one which uses a value type, whose values are assigned exclusively to fragments. The assigned value is such that it tells the modeler exactly those questions which were not asked for that fragment. Examples of its values are the set {*When, Where, WhoFor*} when these three questions are not answered for a fragment, or{*Who*} if only that question was not answered for the fragment.

This new value type is v.AskNext and it has 2^5 possible values. The value to assign to a fragment x is computed using simple rules, which look at the presence or absence of r.q instances that target x, where q is any of the five questions. The following function defines these rules.

Function: ask.next

What to ask next

Input

Fragment $x \in$ **F** and model M.

Do

Let V be an empty set. Let $I_x = \{(p_1, x), \ldots, (p_n, x)\} \subseteq$ r.ifm be the set of all instances of r.ifm in M which end in x. For each

$$q \in \{Who, How, When, Where, WhoFor\},$$

if there is $(p_i, x) \in I_x$ such that $(p_i, x) \in$ r.q, then add q to V.

Output

$\langle x, \text{v.AskNext}, V \rangle$.

Language services

- s.WhichDetail: Those missing from V, where V is from $\langle x, \text{v.AskNext}, V \rangle$.

An important idea illustrated with all value types so far, and in particular with v.SatNext, v.ToDo and v.AskNext, is that values on model parts can act as cues for what to do next with the model, and more generally, what next steps to take in problem solving.

10.5 Constraints on Assignments

What if some sequences of assignments of values to the same fragment or relation instance are not allowed? That is, you can assign some value v_1 only to those fragments or relation instances which are already assigned the value v_2, and not some other value. Suppose the aim is to design a language that delivers the following language service:

Language service: WorkProgrRep

What is the progress in the implementation of the specifications in the model M?

This language service can be interesting for teams where the model is used to distinguish specifications that are implemented from those that remain to be implemented. If the model includes requirements, domain knowledge, and specifications, asking about the progress of work may refer to how close the team is to finding a solution such that the requirements are satisfied. Or if a solution was found, if, or what parts of it, are implemented, and thereby get an idea about how much of the system is already in place. These are two different ways to understand "work progress." I will focus on the second one, because the first was discussed earlier, with v.SatNext, v.ToDo and v.AskNext.

Suppose the team is using the following simple steps for each specification fragment x:

1. check if specification x is approved by the system designer, and if yes then
2. check if there is an estimate of time required to implement x, and if yes then
3. check if x is added to product roadmap, and if yes then
4. check if x is ready for testing, and if yes
5. check if x is approved for release, and if yes, then stop.

The process suggests values for a new value type. Call it v.ProgrStatus. Let it have the following values, each corresponding to the respective step above: *DesignApproved*, *EstimateDone*, *InRoadmap*, *TestReady* and *ApprovedForRelease*. Assuming that these values are manually assigned in a model (rather than computed). Given the discussions of valuation so far, it should be clear how to add this value type to any of the languages in the preceding sections.

What I want to emphasize with this value typeis that its values alone do not convey the idea which is informally clear in s.WorkProgrRep and from the steps described above, namely that there is an order, from the approval that x should be done, or implemented, or otherwise completed, to its completion and release.

The order introduces constraints on when a value can be assigned to x, and depends on the value which x already has. Suppose I want to force modelers to assign the values of v.ProgrStatus according to this order. That is, if some x is assigned *DesignApproved*, then it cannot be assigned *InRoadmap*. The modeler can change the value on x from *DesignApproved* to *EstimateDone*, and then only change the value to *InRoadmap*, not go straight from *DesignApproved* to *InRoadmap*. This can be done with a function that checks if the assignment of a value of v.ProgrStatus satisfies the order over the values. The function is as follows:

Function: chk.progrstatus

Check progress status sequence

Input

Fragment $x \in$ **F** and two value assignments $\langle x, \text{v.ProgrStatus}, v_{old} \rangle$ and $\langle x, \text{v.ProgrStatus}, v_{new} \rangle$, where $\langle x, \text{v.ProgrStatus}, v_{new} \rangle$ is the new value that a modeler wishes to add to x, to replace $\langle x, \text{v.ProgrStatus}, v_{old} \rangle$.

Do

Check if (v_{old}, v_{new}) is in the following set

$$\{ \ (none, DesignApproved), (DesignApproved, EstimateDone),$$
$$(EstimateDone, InRoadmap), (InRoadmap, TestReady),$$
$$(TestReady, ApprovedForRelease)\}$$

If yes, then let $v = 1$, else $v = 0$.

Output

v.

---

language services

- **s.ProgrStatusOk**: Can v_{new} replace v_{old} in $\langle x, \text{v.ProgrStatus}, v_{old} \rangle$? : Yes, if $v = 1$, otherwise no.

The function takes the current (old) assignment of a v.ProgrStatus value, and checks if the new value assignment, which replaces the old, satisfies the constraints on the sequence in which the values of this value type can be assigned. Returning to s.WorkProgrRep, notice that it is delivered as soon as it is possible to assign values of v.ProgrStatus to model parts in a language.

10.6 Real Numbers

The hypothetical work process in Sect. 10.5 has a step, when one checks if there exists an estimate of time required to implement what a fragment describes. If these estimates need to be recorded in models, then there can be a new value type, call it v.ImplTime whose allowed values are positive reals.

Depending on the specifics of the language which has this value type, the assignment of implementation time values can be entirely manual or partly automated. In the absence of automation, the language would require that an individual, or more of the them, assign a positive integer value to each fragment.

In the partly automated case, values assigned to some fragments would be used to compute values on others. Let the language have positive and negative influence relations, for example. Suppose there are only two positive influence relations (y, x) and (z, x) to a fragment x. If the assigned implementation time to y is 10 person-hours, and to z is 5 person-hours, the language could include a function which sums these two, and returns 15 person-hours as the implementation time for x. More generally, that function would be summing implementation time over all incoming positive influence relations.

It is up to you to decide if such a function is useful in a language. The point is simply that you can define new functions for such purposes. They can aggregate already assigned values into values of a new value type. Again, I leave it to you as an exercise, to define a language which uses v.ImplTime.

Return now to v.ProgrStatus, where the step called *EstimateDone* was completed for a fragment x if, in the terminology of this section, there is a value of v.ImplTime assigned to x.

Now, suppose the team that uses the language and is designing the system has the rule that if a fragment obtains an v.ImplTime value equal or greater than 20 person-hours, then it has to be approved again by the system designer. Nothing else should change in their work process. Once x is approved, it will immediately enter the product roadmap, because it has the implementation time estimate.

To add this to a language, define a function which is applied for every fragment that has a v.ImplTime value of 20 or more, and which simply removes the value of v.ProgressStatus of that fragment, thereby requiring again the approval of the system designer (the language has to have f.chk.progrstatus). The definition of the function is as follows:

Function: chk.20more

Recheck 20 or more

Input

Model M.

Do

For every fragment x in M, if x is such that its v.ImplTime is 20 person-hours or more, and its v.ProgrStatus is *EstimateDone*, and since it was added to the model, it was only once assigned the value *DesignApproved*, then remove the v.ProgrStatus value from x.

Output

A new model M', where all fragments which were assigned v.ImplTime of 20 person-hours or more, and which were not assigned twice the v.ProgrStatus value *DesignApproved*, now have no v.ProgrStatus value.

Language services

- **s.WhAppAgain**: Which fragments in a model M, among all those that have v.ImplTime of 20 person-hours or more, need to be approved again by the system designer?: All fragments in M, which in M had, and in M' do not have a v.ProgressStatus value.

10.7 Summary on Valuation

Valuation consists of assigning variables to fragments and relation instances, defining functions over these variables, and given an assignment of values to some of the variables, using the functions to compute values of others.

The section gave various illustrations of value types and how to assign values to parts of models. I focused on functions that value binary value types in models. This showed one compelling reason for having value types in the first place, and thinking about valuation in a language.

Many other topics on valuation are important, and I discuss some of them in subsequent sections while others remain outside the scope of the book:

- What if random variables need to be assigned to model parts, to say, for example, that there is a probability for a fragment to get some value? I discuss this in Chap. 11.
- How to say that some value assignments are mutually exclusive, and thereby enable a language to represent alternative problem and solution instances? This is discussed in Chap. 12.
- How to say in models that some values are more or equally desirable than others, on the same fragment or relation instance, or on other fragments and relation instances? This is the topic of Chap. 14.
- How are value types and valuation related to truth values in classical and nonclassical logics? I will revisit this briefly, for classical logic, in Chap. 15.

Chapter 11
Uncertainty

What if you need models to say that a value assignment is uncertain, and to quantify that uncertainty? What if models need to include random variables? This chapter focuses on how to represent that value assignments to model parts are uncertain. This is done by allowing random variables to be associated with model parts, and defining probability spaces for these random variables so that you can give a probability that the random variable takes a specific value, or any value in a range. The section is organized around the following questions:

- How to represent independent random variables in a model. (Sect. 11.2)
- What to do when there are dependent random variables in a model. (Sect. 11.3)

11.1 Motivation

In Sect. 10.6, the implicit assumption was that there is no uncertainty in value assignments of v.ImplTime. This may be unrealistic. There can be changes in requirements, domain knowledge, and/or specifications, errors in the implementation, or other issues. Stakeholders may be unsure about their estimates.

It was not possible to represent uncertainty about estimates with languages discussed so far. I could not deliver the following language service, for example.

Language service: UncImplTime

How uncertain is the assignment of the v.ImplTime value to the fragment x in M?

© Springer International Publishing Switzerland 2015
I. Jureta, *The Design of Requirements Modelling Languages*,
DOI 10.1007/978-3-319-18821-8_11

If a language can deliver s.UncImplTime, then its models can also answer such questions as, for example, "How uncertain is it that the implementation time of x will be v?" where v is the v.ImplTime value assigned to x.

This same assumption was implicit when v.Satisfaction values were assigned. If a model assigns the satisfaction value 1 to a requirement such as, say, AddRepEm, then the model says that *all* emergency calls are responded to. The requirement is idealistic as it is inevitable that among tens of thousands of calls, some will not be responded to or not within some prescribed time. But again there was no way to show more realistic requirements in a model. To avoid this assumption, the language would need to deliver the language service below.

Language service: UncSat

How uncertain is the assignment of the v.Satisfaction value to a fragment x in M?

---

v.Approval value assignments can be uncertain as well. A stakeholder may change her mind and change previously assigned approval values. A model may capture this by describing the uncertainty of an approval value on a fragment, that is, would deliver the following language service.

Language service: UncApp

How uncertain is the assignment of the v.Approval value to a fragment x in M?

If a model can answer the above, then it can also answer questions such as, "How certain is it that the approval value of x will change?" This is relevant if you need to decide whether to ask stakeholders for approving a model again, or if the already assigned approval values are stable enough to avoid another round of approval.

To deliver the language services above, a language needs to have means for qualifying or quantifying uncertainty. Qualifying amounts to having a scale of qualitative values for describing uncertainty, such as, a scale with only the values "low," "medium," and "high." Quantifying usually means assigning and calculating probability values to events. A language can also combine both, by, for example, having rules that map ranges of probability values to values on a qualitative scale (say, if the probability that a stakeholder changes her approval value on x is at most 0.1, then this corresponds to the value "low" on the qualitative scale), but the challenge in having both is being clear on what they are used for.

11.2 Independent Random Variables

To quantify the uncertainty of value assignments, it is necessary to define the probability space of a random variable.

Recall that a *probability space* is a triple $(\mathscr{S}, \mathscr{E}, P)$, where $\mathscr{S}$ is the *sample space* that includes all possible outcomes of a phenomenon, $\mathscr{E}$ is the set of all *events*, where an event can contain zero or more outcomes, and P is a probability measure, a function which given an event, returns a real value in the range [0, 1]. If $e \in \mathscr{E}$, then $P(e)$ is called the *probability of e*. If, for example, the phenomenon of interest is the tossing of a perfect coin, then the sample space is $\mathscr{S} = \{H, T\}$, with two outcomes called H when the "heads" side of the coin is up, and T when the "tails" side is. $\mathscr{E}$ includes all possible combinations of outcomes: that is, it is the power set of $\mathscr{S}$, and the probabilities of events are as follows: $P(\emptyset) = 0$, $P(\{H\}) = 0.5$, $P(\{T\}) = 0.5$, $P(\{H, T\}) = 1$. The probability space would be different if, for example, I was tossing a pair of coins.

An important consequence of allowing random variables in models is that you have to define a probability space for each variable. And there can be many such variables. For example, suppose you have a model in L.Rigel, and all assignments of v.Satisfaction values are uncertain. You know from L.Rigel that because it has f.sat.inf.pos, f.sat.inf.neg, f.sat, and f.sat.leaf, you have to assign all satisfaction values to leaf fragments, and then propagate these values to influence relation instances and fragments. Now to quantify the uncertainty of all these value assignments of satisfaction values, observe that you have as many random variables as there are assignments of satisfaction values. This is because if x is a fragment or relation instance, then there is a random variable x.v.Satisfaction, and you need a probability space for it. So if $\langle x, \text{v.Satisfaction}, 1 \rangle$, or equivalently, x.v.Satisfaction $= 1$, then you need a probability space for x.v.Satisfaction in order to compute the probability of it getting a specific satisfaction value. If that value is 1, you need its probability space if you want a value for $P(x$.v.Satisfaction $= 1)$, which is, given my notational conventions in this book, the same as wanting the value of $P(\langle x, \text{v.Satisfaction}, 1 \rangle)$.

To deliver s.UncImplTime, a language needs to associate a random variable x.v.ImplTime to every fragment x. In addition, each random variable will come with its own probability space, which includes the function that returns the probability of a specific value of x.v.ImplTime.

Recall that v.ImplTime is a positive real. For any fragment x, then, and in the terminology of probability spaces, x.v.ImplTime takes a value from the sample space $[0, \infty)$, and any such value is an outcome. Any event of interest is any one of these outcomes. Furthermore, as it takes a real value, x.v.ImplTime has a continuous probability distribution and has to have a probability density function, which is denoted $pdf(x$.v.ImplTime) below.

For example, perhaps v_x follows a normal (Gaussian) distribution with a mean of 10 man-hours, and a standard deviation of 2 man-hours, so that $pdf(v_x) = (1/2\sqrt{2\pi})e^{-(v_x - 10)^2/8}$. But there can be another fragment y, which has v_y as its random variable, and v_y may have a completely different probability density function (not the one for normal distribution).

Regardless of the specifics of the probability density function, the uncertainty of a value assigned to $x.\mathsf{v.ImplTime}$ is quantified with a probability measure, whereby the probability that implementation time $x.\mathsf{v.ImplTime}$ is in the interval $[a, b]$ is given by

$$P[a \leq v_x \leq b] = \int_a^b pdf(v_x)dv.$$

Similar stories can be told for $\mathsf{v.Satisfaction}$ and $\mathsf{v.Approval}$. If you want to indicate in a model that you are unsure about the satisfaction or approval value on a fragment or relation instance x, then associate the random variable to x and define the probability space for it.

How does the discussion influence the language modules that you define in a language. It is important to see that there are two ways to use random variables.

1. *Probability measurement*: Consists of doing the following. Start by assigning values to fragments and then calculate the probability of these values. For example, if the estimate of implementation time for a fragment x is 13 man-hours, then calculate the probability $P[x.\mathsf{v.ImplTime} \leq 13]$. The probability value thus quantifies the uncertainty of this estimate, with the slight adjustment that it gives the probability that implementation time for x will be at most 13 man-hours and not exactly 13 man-hours. The adjustment is due to $pdf(x.\mathsf{v.ImplTime})$ being a continuous function over reals, so that $P[x.\mathsf{v.ImplTime} = c] = 0$, for any constant c. If $x.\mathsf{v.ImplTime}$ is discrete, and has a probability mass function instead of $pdf(x.\mathsf{v.ImplTime})$, then it makes sense to compute $P(x.\mathsf{v.ImplTime} = 13)$.
2. *Simulation:* Do not assert the value of a random variable $x.\mathsf{v.ImplTime}$, but generate a value for it by simulation. So instead of assigning yourself or asking someone for a value of implementation time, obtain that value through simulation which generates random values that satisfy the specifics of the probability density function or probability mass function of the random variable.

Both approaches add new functions and value types to a language. The measurement approach adds functions which return probability values, while the simulation approach adds functions which return a value of a random variable, produced by simulation. If a model has n random variables, then there have to be n probability spaces, one per random variable. I introduce the convention that each probability space defines a new value type, which is named as follows: if $x.\mathsf{v.ImplTime}$ is the random variable, then there has to be the value type $\mathsf{v.prob}(x.\mathsf{v.ImplTime})$ defined by the probability space for $x.\mathsf{v.ImplTime}$. Illustrations are given below.

For the measurement approach, a language can have a generic function which takes a probability space and returns a probability value. It can be defined as follows.

Function: prob.asg

Assign probability value

Input

- Assignment either of a single value $\langle x, \text{v.T}, w \rangle$ or of a range $\langle x, \text{v.T}, w_1 \leq v \leq w_2 \rangle$ to random variable of value type T on fragment x, and
- Value type v.prob(x.v.T), defined by the probability space $(\mathscr{S}, \mathscr{E}, P)$ for the random variable x.v.T.

Do

If the input is $\langle x, \text{v.T}, w \rangle$, then $p = P(x.\text{v.T} = w)$. If input is $\langle x, \text{v.T}, w_1 \leq v \leq w_2 \rangle$, then $p = P[w_1 \leq v_x \leq w_2]$.

Output

$\langle x, \text{v.prob}(x.\text{v.T}), p \rangle$, that is, the assignment of a probability value, which is the probability that $\langle x, \text{v.T}, w \rangle$ or $\langle x, \text{v.T}, w_1 \leq v \leq w_2 \rangle$, depending on the input to f.prob.asg.

Language services

- **s.WhProbability**: If the probability space for the random variable x.v.T is $(\mathscr{S}, \mathscr{E}, P)$, then what is the probability that $x.\text{v.T} = w$ if w is given, or that $x.\text{v.T} \in [w_1, w_2]$, if $[w_1, w_2]$ is given? $\langle x, \text{v.prob}(x.\text{v.T}), p \rangle$ which f.prob.asg returns.

As it is defined above, f.prob.asg is not specific to particular value types, or to discrete or continuous random variables. The function assumes that a probability space is already defined for a random variable x.v.T, and f.prob.asg returns using the probability function defined for that space, the probability value. f.prob.asg is defined rather loosely, since it says nothing about, for example, how it is ensured that the input value or range for x.v.T matches the properties of the probability space, that is, makes sense for the given probability space (for example, if a single value is input to f.prob.asg, then f.prob.asg will return a zero value if the random variable is not discrete).

If the language does allow the definition of random variables, a major difficulty is to design relevant probability spaces, because the required data may be hard to find and there can be biases [138]. For instance, it may not be clear at all where to look for useful data in order to define the probability space for implementation time of some fragment x.

The simulation approach also involves adding one or more functions to a language. For example, let the aim be to generate values for random variables that follow the normal distribution. A function which takes the mean and standard deviation parameters of the normal distribution that the variable follows is needed. The function may apply, for example, the Box–Muller method [21] to generate and output a value for the random variable.

A model can include random variables, such as some x.v.Tq, whose probability is determined by a joint probability distribution of two or more other random variables, say x_1.v.T1, ..., x_n.v.Tm in the same model.

For illustration, suppose the probability space

$$\text{v.prob}(x.\text{v.Satisfaction})$$

is such that the probability of x.v.Satisfaction is given by the joint probability distribution of the variables

$$x_1.\text{v.Satisfaction}, \ldots, x_n.\text{v.Satisfaction}.$$

If they are all independent variables, then

$$P(x.\text{v.Satisfaction} = b) =$$
$$P(x_1.\text{v.Satisfaction} = a_1) \cdot \ldots \cdot P(x_n.\text{v.Satisfaction} = a_n).$$

If the model says that every fragment $x_1, \ldots x_n$ has to be satisfied, in order for x to be satisfied, then

$$P(x.\text{v.Satisfaction} = 1) =$$
$$P(x_1.\text{v.Satisfaction} = 1) \cdot \ldots \cdot P(x_n.\text{v.Satisfaction} = 1).$$

The above can be shown as a graph, by having an edge from each of the random variables x_i.v.Satisfaction to x.v.Satisfaction. Another approach is to reuse instances of another relation, some r.K, which already generates a graph. This consists of assuming that each r.K instance also indicates that the probability of some value assignment to a fragment is the product of the probabilities of specific value assignments on other fragments. The following example illustrates this.

Example 11.1 Recall that a language can have influence relations to show how a satisfaction value of a fragment or relation instance influences that of another. These relations can be used to define the joint probability distribution to compute the probability of satisfying a fragment. Namely, a language can have a rule which says if to satisfy x it is necessary to satisfy all fragments, say $x_1, \ldots, x_n$ connected via r.inf.pos to x, then the probability of satisfying x is given by the joint probability distribution of the random variables of v.Satisfaction, assigned to $x_1, \ldots, x_n$. The rule can be added to a language with f.prob.prod below.

Function: prob.sat.ind

Compute probability that a fragment is satisfied using probabilities of satisfaction of fragments which influence it positively

---

Input

Fragment $x \in \mathbf{F}$ and model M.

Do

1. Let $\{y_1, \ldots, y_n\} \subseteq$ r.inf.pos be all r.inf.pos to x in M.
2. Let

$$\langle y_1, \text{v.prob}(y_1.\text{v.Satisfaction}), P(y_1.\text{v.Satisfaction} = 1)\rangle,$$

$$\ldots,$$

$$\langle y_n, \text{v.prob}(y_n.\text{v.Satisfaction}), P(y_n.\text{v.Satisfaction} = 1)\rangle$$

   be probability values that each y_1 will take the v.Satisfaction value 1.
3. If y_1.v.Satisfaction, $\ldots$, y_n.v.Satisfaction are independent random variables, and the probability of x.v.Satisfaction is given by the joint probability distribution of

$$y_1.\text{v.Satisfaction}, \ldots, y_n.\text{v.Satisfaction},$$

   then

$$P(x.\text{v.Satisfaction} = 1) \;=\; \prod_{i=1}^{n} P(y_i.\text{v.Satisfaction} = 1).$$

Output

$\langle x, \text{v.prob}(x.\text{v.Satisfaction}), P(x.\text{v.Satisfaction} = 1)\rangle$.

Language services

- **s.WhProbSatInd**: What is the probability of satisfying x, if $y_1, \ldots, y_n$ all positively influence x in M, the probability of satisfying each of y_1 is independent of the probability of satisfying any other y_j, and the probability of satisfying x is given by the joint probability distribution function of satisfying all fragments which influence x?: The answer is

$$\langle x, \mathsf{v.prob}(x.\mathsf{v.Satisfaction}), P(x.\mathsf{v.Satisfaction} = 1)\rangle.$$

The language below allows random variables in models, and has f.prob.asg and f.prob.sat.ind.

Language: Adhara

Language modules
r.inf.pos, r.inf.neg, f.map.abrel.g, f.cat.ksr, f.sat.inf.pos, f.sat.inf.neg, f.sat, f.sat.leaf, f.prob.asg, f.prob.sat.ind

Domain
There is a set of fragments **F**, a singleton for value types

$$\mathbf{T} = \{\mathsf{v.Satisfaction}\},$$

and a set of value assignments **V**. Fragments have three partitions, namely requirements, domain knowledge, and specification fragments, $\mathbf{F} = \mathsf{c.r} \cup \mathsf{c.k} \cup \mathsf{c.s}$ and $\mathsf{c.r} \cap \mathsf{c.k} \cap \mathsf{c.s} = \emptyset$. Influences are over fragments, $\mathsf{r.inf.pos} \subseteq \mathbf{F} \times \mathbf{F}$, $\mathsf{r.inf.neg} \subseteq \mathbf{F} \times \mathbf{F}$. Value assignments are over fragments or relation instances, involve a value type, and a value, so that

$$\mathbf{V} \subseteq W \times \{\mathsf{v.Satisfaction}\} \times \mathsf{v.Satisfaction}$$
$$\cup\, W \times \{\mathsf{v.prob}(x.\mathsf{v.Satisfaction}) \mid x\,W\} \times [0, 1],$$
$$\text{where } W = \mathbf{F} \cup \mathsf{r.inf.pos} \cup \mathsf{r.inf.neg}.$$

The above says that any value assignment is the assignment of a v.Satisfaction to a fragment or influence relation instance, or the assignment of a value from a range $[0, 1]$ of reals, to $x.\mathsf{v.prob}(x.\mathsf{v.Satisfaction})$, where, again, x is a fragment or an influence relation instance. So the first part of **V** is assignment of satisfaction values, and the second part is assignment of the probability of satisfaction value assignments.

The language has many value types,

$$\mathsf{T} = \{\mathsf{v.Satisfaction}\} \cup \{\mathsf{v.prob}(x.\mathsf{v.Satisfaction}) \mid x \in W\},$$
$$\text{where } W = \mathsf{F} \cup \mathsf{r.inf.pos} \cup \mathsf{r.inf.neg}.$$

with v.Satisfaction $= \{1, 0\}$ and v.prob(w.v.Satisfaction) $= [0, 1]$, for every $w \in W$.

Syntax

A model M in the language is a set of symbols $M = \{Z_1, \ldots, Z_n\}$, where every Z is generated according to the following BNF rules:

$$A ::= x \mid y \mid z \mid \ldots$$
$$B ::= r(A) \mid k(A) \mid s(A)$$
$$C ::= B \text{ influences+ } B$$
$$D ::= B \text{ influences− } B$$
$$G ::= \langle A, E, F \rangle$$
$$Z ::= B \mid C \mid D \mid G$$

Mapping

A symbols denote fragments, $\mathscr{D}(A) \in \mathsf{F}$. B symbols are used to distinguish requirements, domain knowledge, and specification fragments, so that $\mathscr{D}(r(\alpha)) \in \mathsf{c.r}$, $\mathscr{D}(k(\alpha)) \in \mathsf{c.k}$, $\mathscr{D}(s(\alpha)) \in \mathsf{c.s}$. C and D symbols denote, respectively, positive and negative influence relations. E symbols denote value types, $\mathscr{D}(E) \in \mathsf{T}$. F symbols denote a value of a value type, and as there is one value type, $\mathscr{D}(F) \in \mathsf{v.Satisfaction}$. G symbols denote value assignments, $\mathscr{D}(G) \in \mathsf{V}$.

Language services

Those of relations and functions in the language, and s.SatReq.

Figure 11.1 shows a model in L.Adhara, when all the random variables of type v.Satisfaction are independent. Each of these variables is denoted $v[m]$, where m is the fragment identifier. Each random variable is of type v.Satisfaction. There is the assignment of a probability value to each fragment. Each indicates the probability that the fragment is satisfied, that the value of the variable is 1. The probability that

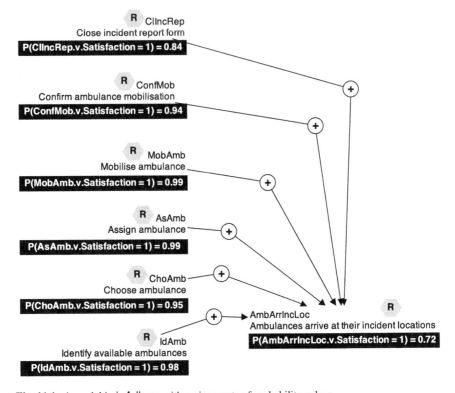

Fig. 11.1 A model in L.Adhara with assignments of probability values

AmbArrIncLoc is satisfied is equal to the joint probability of satisfying all other fragments shown in the figure. •

11.3 Dependent Random Variables

This section drops two assumptions made in Sect. 11.2: (i) that events are independent, so that the occurrence of one does not influence the probability of another to occur and (ii) that random variables are independent, or in other words, that the occurrence of events of one of the variables does not influence the probability of the events of the other random variable.

A language can use Bayesian networks [24, 108] to represent dependency between random variables and to compute probabilities of their events.

A Bayesian network is a directed acyclic graph (V, E), where V is a set of random variables and E of edges. There is an edge from $v_1 \in V$ to $v_2 \in V$, iff $P(v_1) \neq P(v_1 \mid v_2)$, that is, the probability of an event of v_1 is different from the probability of the event, given the occurrence of an event of v_2. If there are two edges to v_1, for example (v_3, v_1) and (v_2, v_1), then this says that $P(v_1) \neq P(v_1 \mid v_2, v_3)$ and that $P(v_1 \mid v_2) \neq P(v_1 \mid v_2, v_3)$. More generally, in a Bayesian network, every random variable is dependent only on its direct parent variables. In an edge (v_2, v_1), v_2 is a direct parent of v_1, while if there another edge (v_3, v_2), then v_3 is an indirect parent of v_1, and so, $P(v_1 \mid v_2) = P(v_1 \mid v_2, v_3)$.

An important property of Bayesian networks is that, to give the joint probability distribution for all random variables in the network (that is, to have the probability value for all events, of all random variables in the network), it is enough to specify only the probability values for all events of all root random variables (those with no parents) and the conditional probability values for all events of all non-root random variables, for all possible combinations of events of their direct parents. While this can require considerable work as well, it is less than the $2^{|V|-1}$ probability values, which would otherwise need to be defined.

There are at least two approaches to enabling a language to represent Bayesian networks in its models, provided this language does allow associating random variables to fragments. The approach in Sect. 11.3.1 ignores relations which may exist in the language. So there is no mapping between a Bayesian network and some graph that a relation gives. This also means that there are no existing graphs in a model in that language, which can be used to produce the corresponding Bayesian network automatically. The approach in Sect. 11.3.2 automatically generates a Bayesian network, based on a graph in a model of the language. I will consider both options below.

11.3.1 Ignoring Existing Relations

The first approach consists of adding a function which takes all random variables assigned to fragments in a model and produces a Bayesian network over these variables (note that the network does not need to be a connected graph). The function is defined as follows.

Function: make.baynet

Make a Bayesian Network

Input

Set $X \subset \mathbf{F}$ of fragments.

Do

Let:

- V_X be the set of all random variables, at most one per fragment in X,
- (V_X, E) be a Bayesian network with no edges,

Then:

1. for every pair x, y in V_X, if $P(x) \neq P(x \mid y)$, then add an edge to E, directed from y to x,
2. for every random variable which is a root node in (V_X, E), define probability values for all its possible events,
3. for every random variable which is not a root node in (V_X, E), define conditional probability values for all events of all non-root random variables, for all possible combinations of events of their direct parents.

Output

Bayesian network (V_X, E).

Language services

- **s.WhProbBN**: What is the probability of an event e of variable v_x to occur, according to the Bayesian network (V_X, E)? : $P(v_x = e)$ obtained by evaluating the Bayesian network (V_X, E).

11.3.2 Using Existing Relations

Given a model in a language, f.make.baynet only uses the random variables assigned to fragments in that model. It ignores all else that may be said in the model, such as the relations that the fragments are in.

When the aim is to reuse more of the information in a model, then it may be relevant to derive (part of) a Bayesian network from some relation in a language.

For illustration, recall that influence relations exist when the satisfaction value of a fragment depends on satisfaction values of others. If I decide that positive influence relations should be interpreted as giving probability dependence between random variables assigned to fragments in these relations, then I can map a graph over influence relation instances to a Bayesian network. The idea is that if there is a positive influence from fragment y to x, and v_y and v_x are the random variables associated with, respectively y and x, then there is an edge in the Bayesian network where v_x and v_y are nodes. The following function does this.

Function: map.inf.pos.baynet

Make a Bayesian Network from r.inf.pos instances

Input

G(X, r.inf.pos), where X is a set of fragments.

Do

Let:
- V_X be the set of all random variables, at most one per fragment in X,
- (V_X, E) be a Bayesian network with no edges.

Then:

1. for every edge (y, x) in G_{I+}, add an edge (v_y, v_x) to E, where v_x and v_y are random variables assigned to, respectively, x and y,
2. for every random variable which is a root node in (V_X, E), define probability values for all its possible events,
3. for every random variable which is not a root node in (V_X, E), define conditional probability values for all events of all non-root random variables, for all possible combinations of events of their direct parents.

Output

Bayesian network (V_X, E).

Language services

s.WhProbBN.

Example 11.2 Figures 11.2 and 11.3 give a simple and hypothetical example of applying f.map.inf.pos.baynet to a graph G(X, r.inf.pos) in Fig. 11.2.

Every fragment in the graph G(X, r.inf.pos) in Fig. 11.2 has an associated random variable of the format $v[\ldots]$ in Fig. 11.3. Figure 11.3 shows a Bayesian network, where edges are marked "B", made by applying f.map.inf.pos.baynet to the graph G(X, r.inf.pos) in Fig. 11.2. Hypothetical probability values to root nodes, and the conditional probability values to the one non-root node were assigned manually. •

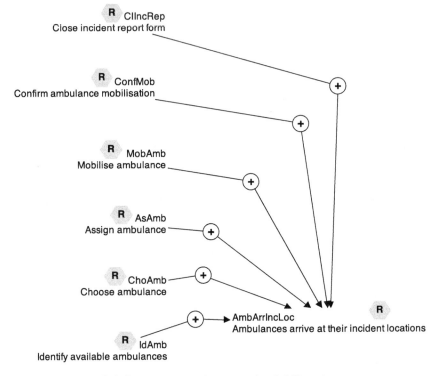

Fig. 11.2 A model in L.Adhara, with no assignments of probability values

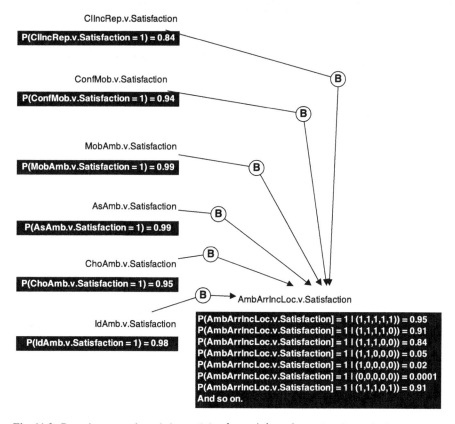

Fig. 11.3 Bayesian network made by applying f.map.inf.pos.baynet to the model in Fig. 11.2

Chapter 12
Alternatives

This chapter focuses on how to represent mutual exclusion in models. If parts A and B in a model are mutually exclusive and the model represents one or more problem and/or solution instances, then none of these problems and solutions includes *both* A and B. In such a model, it may be that some problem (or solution) instances include A, others only B, some perhaps neither, but none include both. I use two notions to discuss how mutual exclusion can work in languages in this book. One, called "alternative," allows me to represent that, say, two value assignments are mutually exclusive. The other is outcome, which was introduced in Chap. 10. Using these notions, I discuss the following questions:

1. How to represent alternatives. (Sect. 12.2)
2. How to find outcomes that include no mutually exclusive value assignment. (Sect. 12.3)
3. How to find outcomes that include no mutually exclusive value assignment when the language has several different value types. (Sect. 12.4)

12.1 Motivation

The exact problem instance to solve is often discovered during problem solving. It is not known up front, but discovered and designed along the way. It is also rarely the case that you discover only one specific problem instance. There may be *different* sets of more concrete requirements, such that each of these sets is an acceptable way to add details to the same less concrete requirement. You are thereby discovering a problem space, that is, a variety of problem instances, one or some of which your solution will solve. The same applies to solutions in that there is a solution space, rather than a single solution. The challenge is then, to understand the problem space and the solution space, and find a pair, made of a problem instance and a solution instance, as the outcome of problem solving.

© Springer International Publishing Switzerland 2015
I. Jureta, *The Design of Requirements Modelling Languages*,
DOI 10.1007/978-3-319-18821-8_12

This chapter focuses on how to represent mutual exclusion in models. If parts A and B in a model are mutually exclusive, and the model represents one or more problem and/or solution instances, then none of these problems and solutions includes *both* A and B. In such a model, it may be that some problem (or solution) instances include A, others only B, some perhaps neither, but none will include both.

In languages in this book, fragments or relation instances are not mutually exclusive themselves, but value assignments on them are. This is because saying that fragments x and y are mutually exclusive is imprecise. Having fragments be mutually exclusive may reflect that they should not be satisfied together, or that they cannot both be approved by stakeholders, or that they should not be included in the same release of the system together, and so on. Yet it could be that they both can be approved by stakeholders, but that they should not both be included in the same release of the system. The point is that when mutual exclusion is about value assignment, then such ambiguities can be avoided.

I use two notions to discuss how mutual exclusion can work in languages in this book. One, called "alternative," allows me to represent that, say, two value assignments are mutually exclusive. The other is outcome, which was introduced in Chap. 10.

There are different ways to fill out an incident report. It can be printed on paper and manually filled out, or there could be a template document of the report for use in word processing software, or by having a dedicated functionality for this in the dispatch software, or in some other way. For each of these, you can probably think of alternative organizational positions whom this responsibility can be assigned, such as dispatcher or administrative assistant.

To represent different ways of doing FillIncRep, and do so with languages defined so far, I would have to make one model each of these mutually exclusive ways. This is impractical. Suppose there are three different ways to fill out a report, and two ways to allocate responsibility for doing so. This gives eight mutually exclusive outcomes, and they cover only some options and only for FillIncRep, not other fragments. Moreover, if the requirements modeling language cannot represent all of them, it will not be able to represent relations between these outcomes. You could thus have many models, but have no information *in these models* about which of them is, for example, more desirable than another one over some criterion, such as cost to implement.

Problem solving involves making decisions, that is, given various possible ways to act, committing to only one. The concept of alternative is a basic notion in decision making. Some x, whatever it may be, can be called an alternative when there are $m \geq 1$ other things, say $y_1, \ldots, y_m$ that can perform the role of x, we have the ability to choose any of $x, y_1, \ldots, y_m$ for that role, and $x, y_1, \ldots, y_m$ are mutually exclusive, that is, neither is compatible with others and neither is part of another.

To use models for decision making, it is necessary to be able to represent alternatives and to represent relations between them. The model becomes a record of alternatives which were encountered during problem solving. This allows you to postpone choosing any one alternative before discovering others and comparing them. You may want to postpone choosing an alternative, because you expect that there may be others that might also be worth considering. Or you may not have the authority to choose alternatives yourself but need to present them to stakeholders who have the authority to decide. Perhaps you also want to first find criteria for the comparison of the alternatives (more on this in Chap. 14), before doing anything else with them.

12.2 Alternatives over Binary Value Types

Suppose you want a language to deliver the following language service.

Language service: SatAlt

Which are all the different ways for satisfying x according to the model M?

This section focuses on the simpler case, where v.Satisfaction is binary.

Recall that L.Rigel can show positive and negative influence relations over fragments, and propagate binary satisfaction values, but it cannot show that some value assignments are mutually exclusive.

How would you represent in models that two or more value assignments are mutually exclusive? Would you do it with a relation, or otherwise? What would you add or remove from L.Rigel to enable it to show in models that some value assignments are mutually exclusive? Would the resulting language deliver s.SatAlt? If yes, then how?

A value assignment becomes an alternative to another value assignment if it participates in a relation. I will call this relation vr.alt.b when it is over value assignments of binary value types. It is a binary relation over value assignments. It should be irreflexive, so that I cannot write that a value assignment is mutually exclusive to itself. It should also be symmetric, because if value assignments v and w are mutually exclusive, then each is mutually exclusive to the other. Finally, it is intransitive, as saying that v is mutually exclusive to w, and w to q does not necessarily mean that v and q are mutually exclusive.

Relation: alt.b

Mutually exclusive value assignments of a binary value type

Domain & Dimension

r.alt.b $\subseteq$ **V** $\times$ **V**, where **V** is a set of value assignments of the same binary value type.

Properties

- Irreflexive, symmetric, and intransitive.
- If $(v, w) \in$ vr.alt.b in a model M, then there is no outcome of M which includes both v and w.

Reading

$(v, w) \in$ vr.alt.b reads "value assignments v and w are alternatives".

Language services

- **s.IsAlt**: Are value assignments v and w alternatives? Yes, if $(v, w) \in$ vr.alt.b.

I define below the language L.Mirfak which can represent positive and negative influences over requirements, domain knowledge, and specifications, just as L.Rigel. L.Rigel, however, cannot represent alternatives. But because of alternatives, L.Mirfak cannot use f.sat from L.Rigel since this function ignores alternatives. I therefore need a new function called f.sat.alt.b. I define it later, as my aim now is simply to illustrate the ability to represent alternatives in models.

Language: Mirfak

Language modules
r.inf.pos, r.inf.neg, f.map.abrel.g, f.cat.ksr, vr.alt.b, f.sat.inf.pos, f.sat.inf.neg, f.sat.alt.b, f.sat.leaf

Domain
There is a set of fragments **F**, a singleton for value types

$$\mathbf{T} = \{\text{v.Satisfaction}\},$$

and a set of value assignments **V**. fragments have three partitions, namely requirements, domain knowledge, and specification fragments, $\mathbf{F} = \text{c.r} \cup \text{c.k} \cup \text{c.s}$ and $\text{c.r} \cap \text{c.k} \cap \text{c.s} = \emptyset$. Influences are over fragments, $\text{r.inf.pos} \subseteq \mathbf{F} \times \mathbf{F}$, $\text{r.inf.neg} \subseteq \mathbf{F} \times \mathbf{F}$. Value assignments are over fragments or relation instances, involve a value type, and a value, so that

$$\mathbf{V} \subseteq (\mathbf{F} \cup \text{r.inf.pos} \cup \text{r.inf.neg}) \times \mathbf{T} \times \text{v.Satisfaction}.$$

Satisfaction is binary, v.Satisfaction = {1, 0}. alternatives are over value assignments, vr.alt.b ⊆ **V** × **V**.

Syntax

A model M in the language is a set of symbols $M = \{Z_1, \ldots, Z_n\}$, where every ϕ is generated according to the following BNF rules:

$$A ::= x \mid y \mid z \mid \ldots$$
$$B ::= r(A) \mid k(A) \mid s(A)$$
$$C ::= B \text{ influences+ } B$$
$$D ::= B \text{ influences− } B$$
$$G ::= \langle A, E, F \rangle$$
$$H ::= G \text{ alternativeTo } G$$
$$Z ::= B \mid C \mid D \mid G \mid H$$

Mapping

A symbols denote fragments, $\mathscr{D}(A) \in$ **F**. B symbols are used to distinguish requirements, domain knowledge, and specification fragments, so that $\mathscr{D}(r(\alpha)) \in$ c.r, $\mathscr{D}(k(\alpha)) \in$ c.k, $\mathscr{D}(s(\alpha)) \in$ c.s. C and D symbols denote, respectively, positive and negative influence relations. E symbols denote value types, $\mathscr{D}(E) \in$ **T**. F symbols denote a value of a value type, and as there is one value type, $\mathscr{D}(F) \in$ v.Satisfaction. G symbols denote value assignments, $\mathscr{D}(G) \in$ **V**. H symbols denote alternatives, $\mathscr{D}(H) \in$ vr.alt.b.

Language services

Those of relations and functions in the language.

How should f.sat.alt.b work? Consider first why this function is needed. Suppose you have the L.Mirfak model in Fig. 12.1. Each node labeled "alt" is an instance of vr.alt.b. There are six such instances in the model.

Each vr.alt.b in the figure represents a constraint on outcomes of the model there. An outcome which has, for example

⟨AutoAmbList influences+ IdAmb, v.Satisfaction, 1⟩,

⟨ManTrckAmb influences+ IdAmb, v.Satisfaction, 1⟩

violates the vr.alt.b instance

$$\langle \text{AutoAmbList influences+ IdAmb, v.Satisfaction, 1} \rangle \text{ alternativeTo}$$
$$\langle \text{ManTrckAmb influences+ IdAmb, v.Satisfaction, 1} \rangle.$$

I will say that such an outcome is incoherent. More generally, if there is a vr.alt.b in a model, and an outcome violates it, then that outcome is incoherent. An outcome may be incoherent for other reasons which will be discussed later.

Figure 12.2 shows value assignments to leaf fragments, made using f.sat.leaf. If you apply f.sat.inf.pos, the resulting value assignments will include

$$\langle \text{AutoAmbList influences+ IdAmb, v.Satisfaction, 1} \rangle,$$
$$\langle \text{UpdAutoAmbList influences+ IdAmb, v.Satisfaction, 1} \rangle,$$
$$\langle \text{ManTrckAmb influences+ IdAmb, v.Satisfaction, 1} \rangle$$

and you can stop propagating v.Satisfaction values, as the resulting outcome will inevitably be incoherent. Figure 12.2 shows circles over the three problematic value assignments, whose propagation gives an incoherent outcome.

I will leave incoherent outcomes aside for now, and consider only value assignments which will give outcomes that are coherent with regard to vr.alt.b. Figure 12.3 shows value assignments to leaf fragments, which will give coherent outcomes. What should be the v.Satisfaction value of IdAmb and ChoAmb in Fig. 12.3?

The value assignment in Fig. 12.3 assures that IdAmb is satisfied. This is because AutoAmbList and UpdAutoAmbList are assumed satisfied via f.sat.leaf, and each positively influences IdAmb. Each of them is also an alternative to ManTrckAmb, which is not satisfied. Any outcome where AutoAmbList and UpdAutoAmbList are satisfied, and ManTrckAmb is not, will satisfy these two vr.alt.b instances. (There can be other outcomes which can satisfy these two vr.alt.b instances. An outcome which makes ManTrckAmb satisfied, but AutoAmbList and UpdAutoAmbList not satisfied, will also be coherent with regard to the two vr.alt.b instances. I will be searching for all such outcomes in Sect. 12.3.)

f.sat will not propagate appropriate v.Satisfaction values when there are vr.alt.b instances as it would assign 0 to IdAmb in Fig. 12.3. f.sat requires all incoming r.inf.pos instances to be satisfied, in order for their target fragment to be satisfied.

f.sat.alt.b should not require all incoming positive influences to be satisfied, in order for the target to be satisfied. It should require a subset of incoming positive influences to be satisfied, as long as none of the members in this subset are themselves alternatives. In other words, there should be no vr.alt.b instance over the members of such a subset. In the case of IdAmb there are two candidate subsets, call them A_1 and A_2,

$$A_1 = \{ \text{AutoAmbList influences+ IdAmb,}$$
$$\text{UpdAutoAmbList influences+ IdAmb} \},$$
$$A_2 = \{ \text{ManTrckAmb influences+ IdAmb} \}.$$

If all members of *either* A_1 *or* A_2 are satisfied, then IdAmb should be satisfied as well. Notice my implicit assumption that *these sets should be the largest subsets* of positive influences. I will make this into a convention, since the idea with f.sat was that *all* positive influences should be satisfied, not some subset thereof. So now, I want to have as many nonalternative positive influences satisfied and not, for example, at least one of them.

The conclusion of the above is that f.sat.alt.b should work as follows when applied to compute the v.Satisfaction value of a fragment x:

1. Find all positive and negative influence relation instances which target x. All these relation instances must have a satisfaction value assigned already. Let V_I be the set that includes v.Satisfaction value assignments to all these positive and negative relation instances.
2. Find all vr.alt.b instances over the value assignments in V_I. Let A_I be the set which includes all these vr.alt.b instances.
3. Find all the largest subsets of V_i such that if o_i is such a subset, then there is no vr.alt.b instance over any pair of its members.
4. For each $o_i \in O$, compute the product of v.Satisfaction values in it.
5. If there is at least one $o_j \in O$, whose satisfaction value is 1, then $\langle x,$ v.Satisfaction$\rangle$, 1, otherwise $\langle x,$ v.Satisfaction, 0$\rangle$.

When applied to the model in Fig. 12.3 and IdAmb, the first step gives

$$V_I = \{ \langle \text{AutoAmbList influences+ IdAmb, v.Satisfaction, 1} \rangle,$$
$$\langle \text{UpdAutoAmbList influences+ IdAmb, v.Satisfaction, 1} \rangle,$$
$$\langle \text{ManTrckAmb influences+ IdAmb, v.Satisfaction, 0} \rangle \}.$$

Note that I had to propagate satisfaction values over the three influence relation instances first, in order to get the members of V_I. The second step gives

$$A_I = \{ \langle \text{AutoAmbList influences+ IdAmb, v.Satisfaction, 1} \rangle$$
$$\text{alternativeTo}$$
$$\langle \text{ManTrckAmb influences+ IdAmb, v.Satisfaction, 1} \rangle,$$
$$\langle \text{UpdAutoAmbList influences+ IdAmb, v.Satisfaction, 1} \rangle$$
$$\text{alternativeTo}$$
$$\langle \text{ManTrckAmb influences+ IdAmb, v.Satisfaction, 1} \rangle \}.$$

The third step results in

$$O = \{ o_1, o_2 \},$$
$$o_1 = \{ \langle \text{AutoAmbList influences+ IdAmb, v.Satisfaction, 1} \rangle,$$
$$\langle \text{UpdAutoAmbList influences+ IdAmb, v.Satisfaction, 1} \rangle \},$$
$$o_2 = \{ \langle \text{ManTrckAmb influences+ IdAmb, v.Satisfaction, 1} \rangle \}.$$

The fourth step calculates the product of satisfaction values in each outcome, in O. The result is 1 for o_1 and 1 for o_2. Finally, the fifth step concludes with

$$\langle \mathsf{IdAmb}, \mathsf{v.Satisfaction}, 1 \rangle.$$

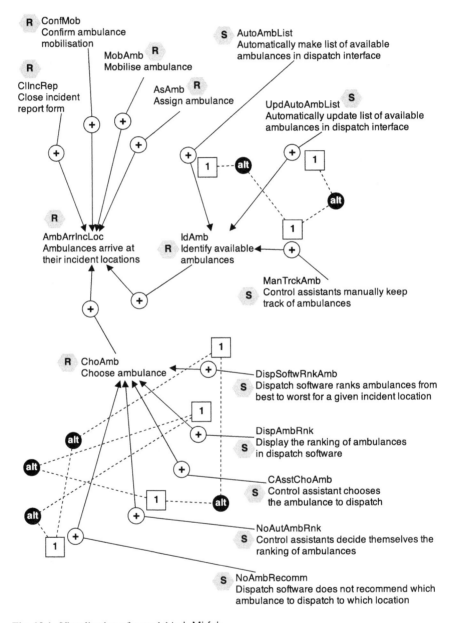

Fig. 12.1 Visualization of a model in L.Mirfak

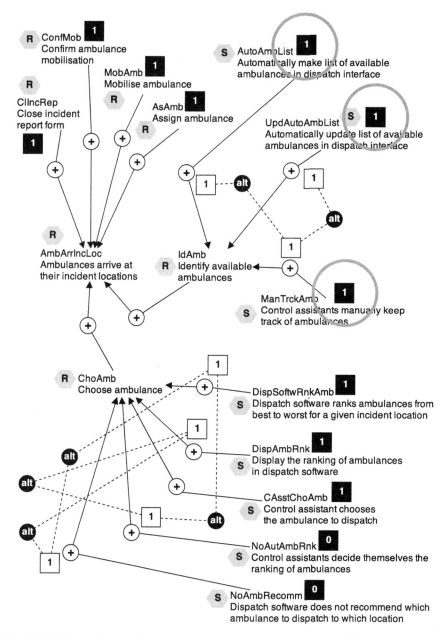

Fig. 12.2 Value assignments for an incoherent outcome

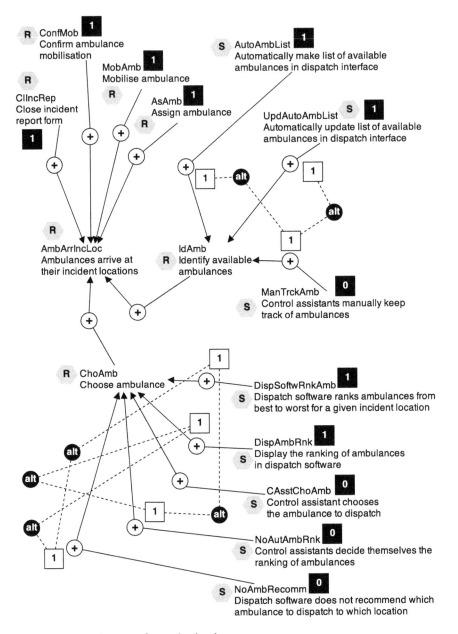

Fig. 12.3 Value assignments for another incoherent outcome

The following is a definition of f.sat.alt.b, which works according to the rules above.

Function: sat.alt.b

Binary satisfaction in presence of alternatives

Input

Fragment or relation instance x, and model M.

Do

1. Find all positive and negative influence relation instances which target x. All these relation instances must have a v.Satisfaction value assigned already. Let V_I be the set which includes v.Satisfaction value assignments to all these positive and negative relation instances. That is, do the following:

   a. Find the set $\{(p_1, x), \ldots, (p_n, x)\} \subseteq$ r.inf.pos of all positive influence relation instances to x in M. Call this set $I_+(x)$.
   b. Find the set $\{(p_{n+1}, x), \ldots, (p_m, x)\} \subseteq$ r.inf.neg of all negative influence relation instances to x in M. Call this set $I_-(x)$.
   c. For each $(p_i, x) \in I_+(x) \cup I_-(x)$, compute its satisfaction value assignment

   $$\langle (p_i, x), \text{v.Satisfaction}, 1 \rangle = \text{f.sat.alt.b}((p_i, x), M),$$

   and add this value assignment to V_I.

2. Find all vr.alt.b instances over the value assignments in V_I. Let A_I be the set which includes all these vr.alt.b instances. Thus, A_I includes all vr.alt.b instances with either this format

   $$\langle p_i \text{ influences+ } x, \text{v.Satisfaction}, 1 \rangle \text{ alternativeTo}$$
   $$\langle p_j \text{ influences+ } x, \text{v.Satisfaction}, 1 \rangle$$

   or this format

   $$\langle p_i \text{ influences- } x, \text{v.Satisfaction}, 1 \rangle \text{ alternativeTo}$$
   $$\langle p_j \text{ influences- } x, \text{v.Satisfaction}, 1 \rangle$$

   where both (p_i, x) and (p_j, x) are members of $I_+(x) \cup I_-(x)$.
3. Find all the largest subsets of V_i, such that if o_i is such a subset, then there is no vr.alt.b instance over any pair of its members.

4. For each $o_i \in O$, compute the product of v.Satisfaction values in it. Let $v(o_i)$ be that value.
5. If there is at least one $o_j \in O$, whose satisfaction value is 1, then let $s = 1$, otherwise let $s = 0$.

Output

$\langle x, \text{v.Satisfaction}, s \rangle$.

Language services

- s.WhSat: $\langle x, \text{v.Satisfaction}, s \rangle$.

Figure 12.4 shows a visualization of a model in L.Mirfak. The value assignments there show one coherent outcome, made by applying f.sat.leaf, f.sat.inf.pos, f.sat.if.neg, and f.sat.alt.b.

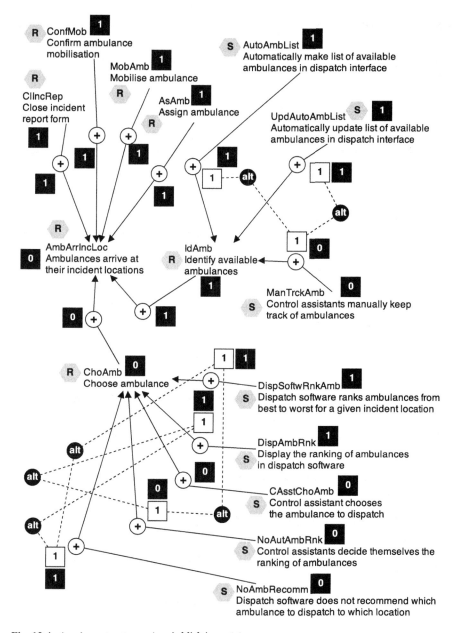

Fig. 12.4 A coherent outcome in a L.Mirfak model

12.3 Picks and Their Use

A pick, denoted P, is an outcome which satisfies the following conditions:

1. It is a coherent outcome,
2. It includes only value assignments which are for some reason desirable to you.

The idea is that you first define a pick for a model, and then search for outcomes which include that pick. It may be that a model can have outcomes which include the pick, but it can also be that there are no such outcomes. If, for example, the pick includes all requirements in a model, and the model itself shows various ways of satisfying these requirements, then looking for outcomes which include this pick amounts to looking for outcomes which ensure that the requirements are satisfied.

There are no constraints on what goes in P. It can, for example, include value assignments over different value types. There are therefore different picks depending on the content of P.

To illustrate how to use picks and what for, consider how the following language service can be delivered.

Language service: MandSat

Given a model in which every fragment can be assigned a binary satisfaction value, and a binary importance value, which are all the complete and coherent outcomes of that model, in which all mandatory fragments are satisfied?

A complete outcome has a value assignment to every variable in a model. Recall that there is one variable per pair of fragment and value type.

s.MandSat can work with a language with two value types. One is a binary satisfaction value, and v.Satisfaction will do. The other is binary importance value, which I will call v.Importance. Importance value is either 1, if satisfying the fragment or relation instance is mandatory, or 0 otherwise. It follows that s.MandSat consists of finding all outcomes of a model, which are a superset of the following pick:

$$P = \{ \langle x, \text{v.Satisfaction}, 1 \rangle \mid \forall x \in M \text{ s.t.}$$
$$x \in \mathbf{F} \text{ and } \langle x, \text{v.Importance}, 1 \rangle \}.$$

Having defined the pick, I need a language whose outcomes can have it as a subset. Let L.Pollux be the language made by adding v.Importance via f.imp.asm to L.Mirfak. For simplicity, there is no propagation of importance values. They are assigned manually to individual fragments only, not to relation instances using f.imp.asm. The new function is defined as follows.

Function: imp.asm

Assume an importance value for a fragment

Input

fragment x and model M.

Do

If you assume that x must be satisfied, then $v = 1$, else $v = 0$.

Output

$\langle x, \text{v.Importance}, v \rangle$

Language services

- **s.WhImpAsm**: Which, if any, is the assumed v.Importance value of x in M? : $\langle x, \text{v.Importance}, v \rangle$.

The language is made by adding f.imp.asm to L.Mirfak. Syntax and mapping remain the same; the domain changes, as it now has v.Importance.

Language: Pollux

Language modules
r.inf.pos, r.inf.neg, f.map.abrel.g, f.cat.ksr, vr.alt.b, f.sat.inf.pos, f.sat.inf.neg, f.sat.alt.b, f.sat.leaf, f.imp.asm

---

Domain

There is a set of fragments **F** and value types

$$\mathbf{T} = \{\text{v.Satisfaction}, \text{v.Importance}\},$$

and a set of value assignments **V**. Fragments have three partitions, namely requirements, domain knowledge, and specification fragments, $\mathbf{F} = \text{c.r} \cup \text{c.k} \cup \text{c.s}$

and c.r $\cap$ c.k $\cap$ c.s $= \emptyset$. Influences are over fragments, r.inf.pos $\subseteq$ **F** $\times$ **F**, r.inf.neg $\subseteq$ **F** $\times$ **F**. Satisfaction value assignments are over fragments or relation instances, involve a value type, and a value, so that

$$\textbf{V} \subseteq (\textbf{F} \cup \text{r.inf.pos} \cup \text{r.inf.neg}) \times \{\text{v.Satisfaction}\} \times \text{v.Satisfaction}.$$

Importance value assignments are over fragments only, so that

$$\textbf{V} \subseteq \textbf{F} \times \{\text{v.Importance}\} \times \text{v.Importance}.$$

Both the satisfaction and importance value types are binary; v.Satisfaction $=$ v.Importance $= \{1, 0\}$. alternatives are over value assignments of the same value type.

Syntax

A model M in the language is a set of symbols $M = \{Z_1, \ldots, Z_n\}$, where every ϕ is generated according to the following BNF rules:

$$A ::= x \mid y \mid z \mid \ldots$$
$$B ::= r(A) \mid k(A) \mid s(A)$$
$$C ::= B \text{ influences+ } B$$
$$D ::= B \text{ influences} - B$$

$$G ::= \langle A, E, F \rangle$$
$$H ::= G \text{ alternativeTo } G$$
$$Z ::= B \mid C \mid D \mid G \mid H$$

Mapping

A symbols denote fragments, $\mathscr{D}(A) \in$ **F**. B symbols are used to distinguish requirements, domain knowledge, and specification fragments, so that $\mathscr{D}(r(\alpha)) \in$ c.r, $\mathscr{D}(k(\alpha)) \in$ c.k, $\mathscr{D}(s(\alpha)) \in$ c.s. C and D symbols denote, respectively, positive and negative influence relations. E symbols denote value types, $\mathscr{D}(E) \in$ **T**. F symbols denote a value of a value type, and as there is one value type, $\mathscr{D}(F) \in$ v.Satisfaction. G symbols denote value assignments, $\mathscr{D}(G) \in$ **V**. H symbols denote alternatives, $\mathscr{D}(H) \in$ vr.alt.b.

Language services

Those of relations and functions in the language.

Figure 12.5 shows a visualization of a model in L.Pollux. As there are two value types, labels are different than in the visualization of L.Mirfak models. Now, label "s1" is for the assignment of the satisfaction value 1, and "s0" if the satisfaction value is 0. "i1" is the assignment of the importance value 1, and "i0" of value 0. According to the model in the figure, ChoAmb is the only fragment which must be satisfied. Therefore, the pick is

$$P = \{ \langle AmbArrIncLoc, v.Satisfaction, 1 \rangle,$$
$$\langle AmbArrIncLoc, v.Importance, 1 \rangle \}$$

that is, the outcomes to find should assign the satisfaction value 1 and importance value 1 to AmbArrIncLoc.

How, then, to find all outcomes of the model in Fig. 12.5 which include the pick P above? In other words, define a function which takes a model in L.Pollux and a pick, and returns all outcomes supersets of that pick, if they exist, or an empty set if there are none.

This function will have to assign values in a different way propagation. It should also not produce outcomes which contradict those that would have been produced on a model, if satisfaction values were propagated from the leaves using f.sat.inf.pos, f.sat.inf.neg, f.sat.leaf, and f.sat, since these functions are part of L.Pollux.

In the model in Fig. 12.5, AmbArrIncLoc must be satisfied and therefore must have the satisfaction value 1. It will have that value only if all positive influences to it, and all negative influences to it have the satisfaction value 1. Otherwise, I would be violating the rules of f.sat.inf.pos, f.sat.inf.neg, and f.sat. It follows that any outcome which includes P must also include the following value assignments:

$$\{\langle ClIncRep \text{ influences+ } AmbArrIncLoc, v.Satisfaction, 1 \rangle,$$
$$\langle ConfMob \text{ influences+ } AmbArrIncLoc, v.Satisfaction, 1 \rangle,$$
$$\langle MobAmb \text{ influences+ } AmbArrIncLoc, v.Satisfaction, 1 \rangle,$$
$$\langle AsAmb \text{ influences+ } AmbArrIncLoc, v.Satisfaction, 1 \rangle,$$
$$\langle IdAmb \text{ influences+ } AmbArrIncLoc, v.Satisfaction, 1 \rangle,$$
$$\langle ChoAmb \text{ influences+ } AmbArrIncLoc, v.Satisfaction, 1 \rangle \}.$$

According to f.sat.inf.pos, an instance of a positive influence relation will have the satisfaction value 1 only if its origin fragment also has the satisfaction value 1. It follows that all outcomes which include P must also include these value assignments:

$$\{\langle ClIncRep, v.Satisfaction, 1 \rangle,$$
$$\langle ConfMob, v.Satisfaction, 1 \rangle,$$
$$\langle MobAmb, v.Satisfaction, 1 \rangle,$$
$$\langle AsAmb, v.Satisfaction, 1 \rangle,$$
$$\langle IdAmb, v.Satisfaction, 1 \rangle,$$

⟨ChoAmb, v.Satisfaction, 1⟩ }.

The resulting outcome is shown in Fig. 12.6. It is an incomplete outcome.

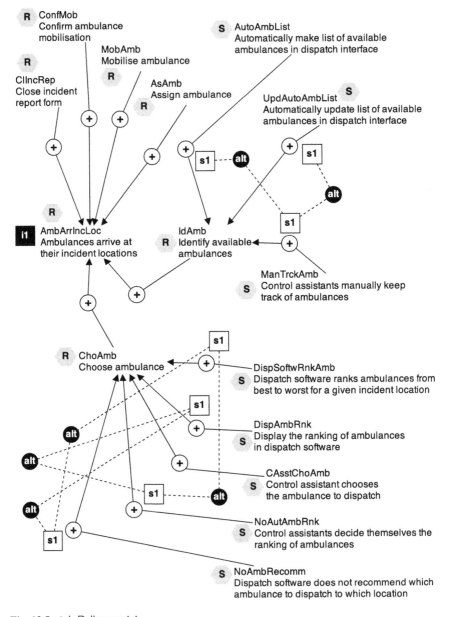

Fig. 12.5 A L.Pollux model

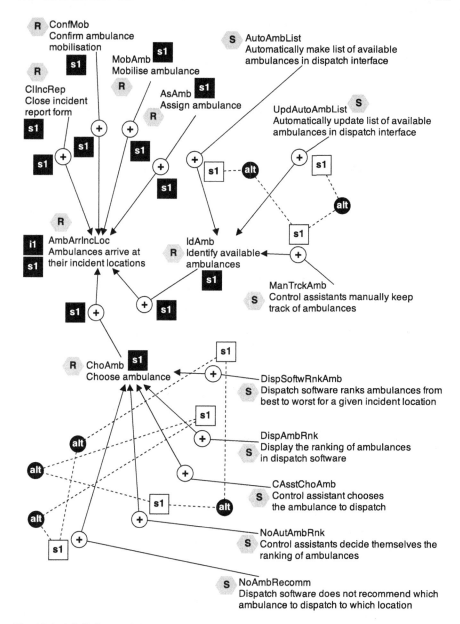

Fig. 12.6 A L.Pollux model with a pick and an incomplete outcome

There are alternatives for satisfying IdAmb in Fig. 12.6. You can find them by solving a system of equations over variables defined by the positive influence relations to IdAmb, and the fragments in which these relation instances originate. To simplify notation and write w_1 for the variable

AutoAmbList.v.Satisfaction,

use the following equivalences:

$w_1 \equiv$ AutoAmbList.v.Satisfaction,

$w_{1.4} \equiv$ (AutoAmbList influences+ IdAmb).v.Satisfaction,

$w_2 \equiv$ UpdAutoAmbList.v.Satisfaction,

$w_{2.4} \equiv$ (UpdAutoAmbList influences+ IdAmb).v.Satisfaction,

$w_3 \equiv$ ManTrckAmb.v.Satisfaction,

$w_{3.4} \equiv$ (ManTrckAmb influences+ IdAmb).v.Satisfaction,

$w_7 \equiv$ IdAmb.v.Satisfaction.

The system of equations is then as follows:

$$0 = w_1 - w_{1.4},$$
$$0 = w_2 - w_{2.4},$$
$$0 = w_3 - w_{3.4},$$
$$1 = |w_{1.4} - w_{3.4}|,$$
$$1 = |w_{2.4} - w_{3.4}|,$$
$$w_4 = |w_{1.4} * w_{2.4} - w_{3.4}|.$$

The first three equations above reflect the rules in f.sat.inf.pos. If $w_1 = 1$, that is, if AutoAmbList is satisfied, then the positive influence from it, to IdAmb, must be satisfied as well, that is, $w_{1.4} = 1$. If $w_1 = 0$, then $w_{1.4} = 0$, and *vice versa*. The fourth and fifth equations are due to r.alt.b instances. If $w_1 = w_{1.4} = 1$, then $w_3 * w_{3.4}$ has to be 0 according to the fourth equation. The sixth equation is due to the rule in f.sat.alt.b, which requires that the largest subset of nonalternative influence relation instances be satisfied, in order for their target to be satisfied.

If you set $w_7 = 1$, there are two solutions to the system of equations above. They are

$$w_1 = 1, w_{1.4} = 1, w_2 = 1, w_{2.4} = 1, w_3 = 0, w_{3.4} = 0, \text{ and}$$
$$w_1 = 0, w_{1.4} = 0, w_2 = 0, w_{2.4} = 0, w_3 = 1, w_{3.4} = 1.$$

The system of equations above is specific to the paths which end in IdAmb in Fig. 12.6. There is another system of equations for alternatives to ChoAmb. Again, for simplicity, start with these equivalences:

$u_1 \equiv$ DispSoftwRnkAmb.v.Satisfaction,

$u_2 \equiv$ DispAmbRnk.v.Satisfaction,

$u_3 \equiv$ CAsstChoAmb.v.Satisfaction,

$u_4 \equiv$ NoAutAmbRnk.v.Satisfaction,

$u_5 \equiv$ NoAmbRecomm.v.Satisfaction,

$u_6 \equiv$ ChoAmb.v.Satisfaction,

$u_{1.6} \equiv$ (DispSoftwRnkAmb influences+ ChoAmb).v.Satisfaction,

$u_{2.6} \equiv$ (DispAmbRnk influences+ ChoAmb).v.Satisfaction,

$u_{3.6} \equiv$ (CAsstChoAmb influences+ ChoAmb).v.Satisfaction,

$u_{4.6} \equiv$ (NoAutAmbRnk influences+ ChoAmb).v.Satisfaction,

$u_{5.6} \equiv$ (NoAmbRecomm influences+ ChoAmb).v.Satisfaction.

ChoAmb has to be satisfied, that is $u_6 = 1$, in order for AmbArrIncLoc to be satisfied. You can consequently find all outcomes which include the fragments and positive influences above by solving the following system of equations:

$$0 = u_1 - u_{1.6},$$
$$0 = u_2 - u_{2.6},$$
$$0 = u_3 - u_{3.6},$$
$$0 = u_4 - u_{4.6},$$
$$0 = u_5 - u_{5.6},$$
$$1 = |u_{1.6} - u_{5.6}|,$$
$$1 = |u_{1.6} - u_{4.6}|,$$
$$1 = |u_{2.6} - u_{5.6}|,$$
$$1 = |u_{2.6} - u_{4.6}|,$$
$$u_6 = u_{3.6} * |(u_{1.6} * u_{2.6} - u_{4.6} * u_{5.6})|.$$

There are two solutions. One is

$$u_1 = u_{1.6} = u_2 = u_{2.6} = u_3 = u_{3.6} = 1,$$
$$u_4 = u_{4.6} = u_5 = u_{5.6} = 0,$$

and the other is

$$u_1 = u_{1.6} = u_2 = u_{2.6} = 0,$$
$$u_3 = u_{3.6} = u_4 = u_{4.6} = u_5 = u_{5.6} = 1.$$

As there are two solutions for each system of equations, and there are two such systems in the model in Fig. 12.5, it follows that there are four complete outcomes of that model, each of which is coherent with regard to f.sat.inf.pos, f.sat.inf.neg, f.sat.leaf, and f.sat.alt.b, and is a superset of P. The four are shown in Figs. 12.7, 12.8, 12.9, and 12.10. In each figure, the circles highlight the fragments and relation instances which are not satisfied.

The following pages show the figures mentioned above. After the figures, I discuss a function that can produce these systems of equations for L.Pollux models.

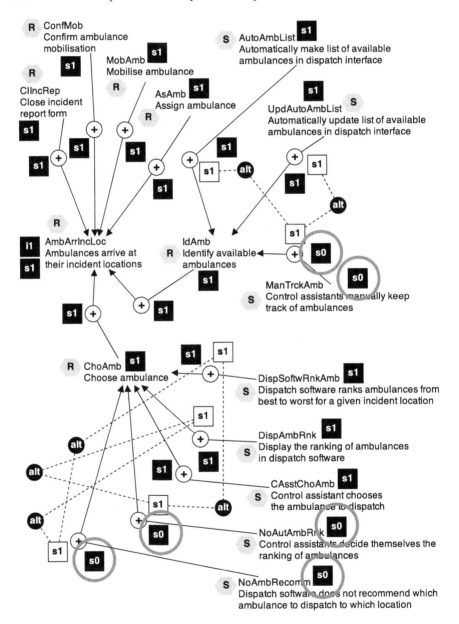

Fig. 12.7 One complete outcome

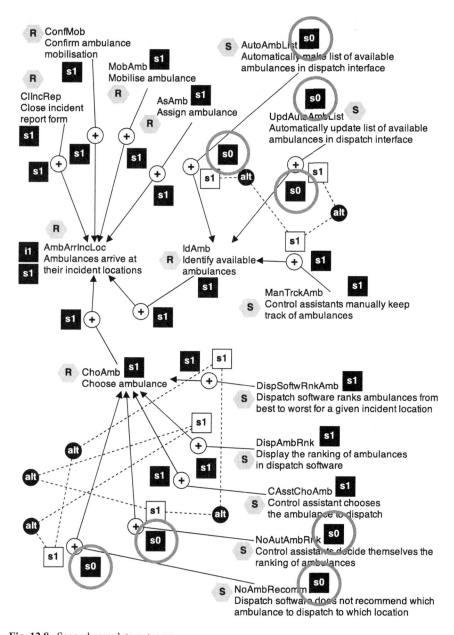

Fig. 12.8 Second complete outcome

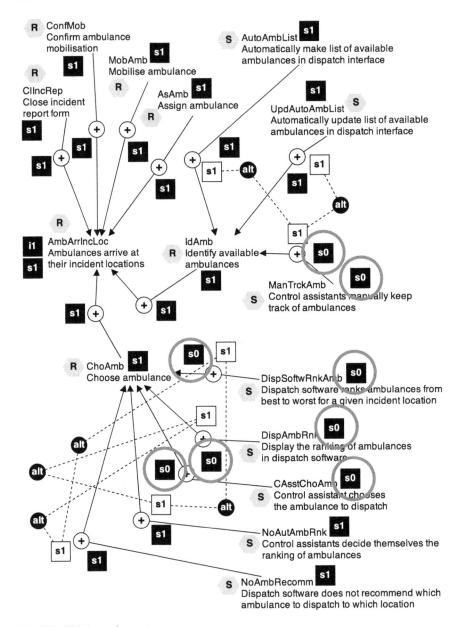

Fig. 12.9 Third complete outcome

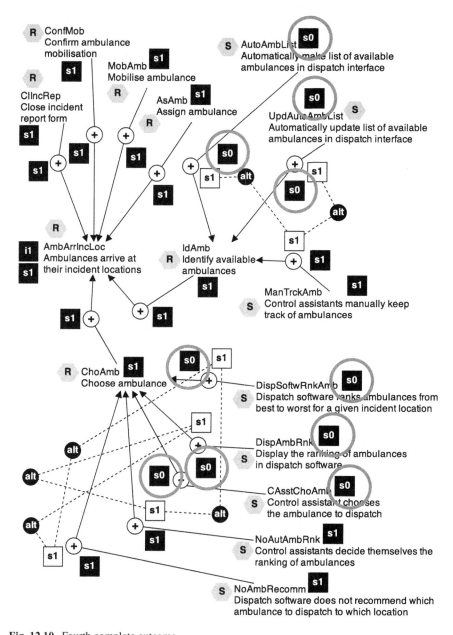

Fig. 12.10 Fourth complete outcome

To find all outcomes which include a particular pick, and do this for models of L.Pollux, I need a function that produces the systems of equations, in the same way I did for the model in Fig. 12.5, then solves them, and finally returns the outcomes. Here is a sketch of how the function could work, based on what I did for the model in Fig. 12.5:

1. Take an L.Pollux model M, and make a directed hypergraph $H(M)$ from it, such that in $H(M)$ there is one node for every fragment in M, and a directed edge for every positive and every negative influence relation instance, in the direction of influence.

Example 12.1 Figure 12.5 shows the graph for a model in L.Pollux. It has at most one edge between any two nodes, and is therefore not a hypergraph. •

2. Check if $H(M)$ includes cycles:

   • If yes, then stop, because the model M is incoherent with regard to r.inf.pos and/or r.inf.neg. These two relations are irreflexive and transitive and therefore, cycles are not allowed in the hypergraph which these relations induce over fragments.
   • If there are no cycles, then go to next step.

Example 12.2 (Example 12.1 continued) The graph in Fig. 12.5 has no cycles. Note that it is a tree, as it is acyclic and has one root. •

3. For each fragment x in M, define a variable w_x

$$w_x \equiv x.\text{v.Satisfaction}$$

which takes a satisfaction value, and add that variable to the set of all variables from M, denoted W_M.

Example 12.3 (Example 12.2 continued) W_M includes one variable per fragment in Fig. 12.5:

$$\begin{aligned}
W_M = \{\ &w_{\text{AmbArrIncLoc}},\ w_{\text{ClIncRep}},\ w_{\text{ConfMob}} \\
&w_{\text{MobAmb}},\ w_{\text{AsAmb}},\ w_{\text{IdAmb}}, \\
&w_{\text{AutoAmbList}},\ w_{\text{UpdAutoAmbList}},\ w_{\text{ManTrckAmb}}, \\
&w_{\text{ChoAmb}},\ w_{\text{DispSoftwRnkmb}},\ w_{\text{DispAmbRnk}}, \\
&w_{\text{AsstChoAmb}},\ w_{\text{NoAutAmbRnk}},\ w_{\text{NoAmbRecomm}}\ \}.\ \ •
\end{aligned}$$

4. For each r.inf.pos instance x influences+ y, from fragment x to fragment y,

   a. define a variable $w_{x.p.y}$

$$w_{x.p.y} \equiv (x \text{ influences+ } y).\text{v.Satisfaction},$$

   and add this variable to W_M,

b. define an equation

$$w_x - w_{x.p.y} = 0$$

that requires that w_x and $w_{x.p.y}$ have the same v.Satisfaction value, following the rules in f.sat.inf.pos, and add this equation to the set of equations E_M.

Example 12.4 (Example 12.3 *continued)* To simplify notation, I introduce the following equivalences:

$w_1 \equiv w_{\text{AmbArrIncLoc}}$,	$w_2 \equiv w_{\text{ClIncRep}}$,
$w_3 \equiv w_{\text{ConfMob}}$,	$w_4 \equiv w_{\text{MobAmb}}$,
$w_5 \equiv w_{\text{AsAmb}}$,	$w_6 \equiv w_{\text{IdAmb}}$,
$w_7 \equiv w_{\text{AutoAmbList}}$,	$w_8 \equiv w_{\text{UpdAutoAmbList}}$,
$w_9 \equiv w_{\text{ManTrckAmb}}$,	$w_{10} \equiv w_{\text{ChoAmb}}$,
$w_{11} \equiv w_{\text{DispSoftwRnkmb}}$,	$w_{12} \equiv w_{\text{DispAmbRnk}}$,
$w_{13} \equiv w_{\text{AsstChoAmb}}$,	$w_{14} \equiv w_{\text{NoAutAmbRnk}}$,
$w_{15} \equiv w_{\text{NoAmbRecomm}}$.	

Using these equivalences, this first part of this fourth step gives the following new variables for W_M, one per positive influence relation instance in Fig. 12.5

$$w_{2.p.1}, w_{3.p.1}, w_{4.p.1}, w_{5.p.1}, w_{6.p.1}, w_{10.p.1},$$
$$w_{7.p.6}, w_{8.p.6}, w_{9.p.6},$$
$$w_{11.p.10}, w_{12.p.10}, w_{13.p.10}, w_{14.p.10}, w_{15.p.10}.$$

The second part of this fourth step gives the following equations for E_M

$0 = w_2 - w_{2.p.1}$,	$0 = w_3 - w_{3.p.1}$,
$0 = w_4 - w_{4.p.1}$,	$0 = w_5 - w_{5.p.1}$,
$0 = w_6 - w_{6.p.1}$,	$0 = w_{10} - w_{10.p.1}$,
$0 = w_7 - w_{7.p.6}$,	$0 = w_8 - w_{8.p.6}$,
$0 = w_9 - w_{9.p.6}$,	
$0 = w_{11} - w_{11.p.10}$,	$0 = w_{12} - w_{12.p.10}$,
$0 = w_{13} - w_{13.p.10}$,	$0 = w_{14} - w_{14.p.10}$,
$0 = w_{15} - w_{15.p.10}$.	

At this point, all fragments and positive influence relation instances have corresponding variables which take a satisfaction value. •

5. For each r.inf.neg instance x influences$-$ y, from fragment x to fragment y,

a. define a variable $w_{x.n.y}$

$$w_{x.n.y} \equiv (x \text{ influences}- y).\text{v.Satisfaction},$$

and add this variable to W_M,
b. define an equation

$$|w_x - w_{x.n.y}| = 1$$

which follows the rules f.inf.neg, and requires that if $w_x = 1$ then $w_{x.n.y} = 0$, and *vice versa*. Add this equation to the set of equations E_M.

At this point, you have the set W_M which includes a variable for every fragment and every positive and negative influence relation instance in M, and the set E_M of equations, one per positive and negative influence relation instance. You still need equations which correspond to r.alt.b instances.

Example 12.5 (Example 12.4 *continued)* There are no negative influence relation instances in Fig. 12.5. This step therefore does not change W_M and E_M updated in the fifth step. •

6. For each r.alt.b instance over values of two variables $w_i \in W_M$ and $w_j \in W_M$,

   • if the instance is

   $$(w_i = 1) \text{ alternativeTo } (w_j = 1),$$

   then add an equation

   $$|w_i - w_j| = 1$$

   to the set E_M,
   • if the instance is

   $$(w_i = 1) \text{ alternativeTo } (w_j = 0),$$

   then add an equation

   $$w_i - w_j \leq 0$$

   to the set E_M,
   • if the instance is

   $$(w_i = 0) \text{ alternativeTo } (w_j = 1),$$

   then add an equation

   $$w_i - w_j \geq 0$$

   to the set E_M,
   • if the instance is

   $$(w_i = 0) \text{ alternativeTo } (w_j = 0),$$

then add an equation

$$|w_i - w_j| \geq 0$$

to the set E_M.

Example 12.6 (Example 12.5 continued) All r.alt.b instances are between the assignments of satisfaction value 1, so that only $|w_i - w_j| = 1$ equations need to be added to E_M. These equations are

$$1 = |w_{7.p.6} - w_{9.p.6}|, \qquad 1 = |w_{8.p.6} - w_{9.p.6}|,$$
$$1 = |w_{11.p.10} - w_{14.p.10}|, \qquad 1 = |w_{11.p.10} - w_{15.p.10}|,$$
$$1 = |w_{12.p.10} - w_{14.p.10}|, \qquad 1 = |w_{12.p.10} - w_{15.p.10}|. \quad \bullet$$

7. For each fragment x in M, do the following:

   a. Make the set W_M^x, so that it only includes all variables of the format $w_{y.p.x}$ and $w_{y.n.x}$, where y is any fragment in M, so that W_M^x includes all variables for positive and negative influence relation instances which end in x.

Example 12.7 (Example 12.6 continued) Of all fragments in Fig. 12.5, only three are targets of influence relation instances, so there are only three sets W_M^x, as follows:

$$W_M^{\text{AmbArrIncLoc}} = \{ w_{2.p.1}, w_{3.p.1}, w_{4.p.1}, w_{5.p.1},$$
$$w_{6.p.1}, w_{10.p.1} \},$$
$$W_M^{\text{IdAmb}} = \{ w_{7.p.6}, w_{8.p.6}, w_{9.p.6} \},$$
$$W_M^{\text{ChoAmb}} = \{ w_{11.p.10}, w_{12.p.10}, w_{13.p.10},$$
$$w_{14.p.10}, w_{15.p.10} \}. \quad \bullet$$

   b. Make the set O_M^x, which includes all the largest subsets of W_M^x which include no alternatives, that is every member o_i^x of O_M^x is the largest subset of W_M^x in which there are no two variables which represent mutually exclusive influence relation instances.

Example 12.8 (Example 12.7 continued) The sets are

$$O_M^{\text{AmbArrIncLoc}} = \{ o_1^{\text{AmbArrIncLoc}} \},$$
$$o_1^{\text{AmbArrIncLoc}} = W_M^{\text{AmbArrIncLoc}},$$
$$O_M^{\text{IdAmb}} = \{ o_1^{\text{IdAmb}}, o_2^{\text{IdAmb}} \},$$
$$o_1^{\text{IdAmb}} = \{ w_{7.p.6}, w_{8.p.6} \},$$
$$o_2^{\text{IdAmb}} = \{ w_{9.p.6} \},$$
$$O_M^{\text{ChoAmb}} = \{ o_1^{\text{ChoAmb}}, o_2^{\text{ChoAmb}} \},$$

$$o_1^{\text{ChoAmb}} = \{\ w_{11.p.10}, w_{12.p.10}, w_{13.p.10}\ \},$$
$$o_2^{\text{ChoAmb}} = \{\ w_{13.p.10}, w_{14.p.10}, w_{15.p.10}\ \}. \quad \bullet$$

c. Add a formula

$$\sum_{o_i^x \in O_M^x} \left(\prod_{w_{y.p.x} \in o_i^x} w_{y.p.x} \cdot \prod_{w_{y.n.x} \in o_i^x} w_{y.n.x} \right) = w_x$$

to E_M, which is used to indicate that only one of all the largest nonalternative sets of influence relation instances to x should be satisfied in one outcome.

Example 12.9 (Example 12.8 *continued)* The three equations to add to E_M are

$$w_{2.p.1} \cdot w_{3.p.1} \cdot w_{4.p.1} \cdot w_{5.p.1} \cdot w_{6.p.1} \cdot w_{10.p.1} = w_1,$$
$$w_{7.p.6} \cdot w_{8.p.6} + w_{9.p.6} = w_6,$$
$$w_{11.p.10} \cdot w_{12.p.10} \cdot w_{13.p.10}$$
$$+w_{13.p.10} \cdot w_{14.p.10} \cdot w_{15.p.10} = w_{10}. \quad \bullet$$

8. Take the pick you want to find outcomes for and add each value assignment $w_i = v$ in the pick to the set of equations E_M.

Example 12.10 (Example 12.9 *continued)* Suppose that the pick is

$$P = \{\ \langle \text{AmbArrIncLoc}, \text{v.Satisfaction}, 1 \rangle\ \},$$

and consequently, add $w_1 = 1$ to E_M. $\bullet$

9. Find all solutions to the system of equations defined by E_M. Each solution is a complete outcome of M.

The above remains a sketch of a function. Its aim is to illustrate how you could generate systems of equations to solve, to find all outcomes which include a pick of interest. I do not provide a proof that it works correctly with any **L.Pollux** model, and I do not discuss how hard it is to actually solve systems of equations it gives, for models of any size. That is, I do not discuss reasoning complexity. These issues are important when defining a new language. I leave them outside this book, as they require deeper expertise in mathematics and formal logic than I can offer.

12.4 Several Arbitrary Value Types

This section focuses on how alternatives and picks can be used when there are several arbitrary value types in a language. Consider this language service:

Language service: AccTime

According to the model M, what is the estimated time required to make a system that satisfies those mandatory requirements for which the specifications are in the product roadmap?

---

s.AccTime can be relevant for a team which needs to

- document requirements, domain knowledge, and specifications,
- distinguish mandatory requirements from others,
- keep track of the progress in implementing specifications, and
- have an estimate of time to implement specifications which are mature enough to be in the road map, and are necessary to satisfy the mandatory requirements.

The language for this team needs to have f.WhichKSR, so as to distinguish requirements, domain knowledge, and specifications in models. v.ProgrStatus from Sect. 10.5 can be used to keep track of progress in implementing specifications. Statuses can be assigned in the sequence prescribed in f.chk.progrstatus. The language also needs a value type for satisfaction, in order to identify the satisfied mandatory requirements. v.Satisfaction will do. It needs a value type to distinguish mandatory from other requirements, and it can use v.Importance. Finally, it should be possible to assign time estimates to specifications, and v.ImplTime can be used.

The resulting language has several arbitrary value types, in the sense that v.Satisfaction and v.Importance are binary, v.ProgrStatus has values on a nominal scale and comes with constraints defined f.chk.progrstatus, and v.ImplTime takes a positive real value. The language is called L.Avior and is defined below.

Language: Avior

Language modules
r.inf.pos, r.inf.neg, f.map.abrel.g, f.cat.ksr, vr.alt.b, f.sat.inf.pos, f.sat.inf.neg, f.sat.alt.b, f.sat.leaf, f.imp.asm, f.chk.progrstatus

---

Domain

- The domain is made of a set of fragments **F**, relation instances **R**, value types **T**, and value assignments **V**.
- Fragments have three partitions, namely requirements, domain knowledge, and specification fragments, $\mathbf{F} = \text{c.r} \cup \text{c.k} \cup \text{c.s}$ and $\text{c.r} \cap \text{c.k} \cap \text{c.s} = \emptyset$.
- Relation instances are binary and either over fragments or value assignments, $\mathbf{R} = (\mathbf{F} \times \mathbf{F}) \cup (\mathbf{V} \times \mathbf{V})$, and are partitioned as follows:

$$R = \text{r.inf.pos} \cup \text{r.inf.neg} \cup \text{vr.alt.b},$$
$$\emptyset = \text{r.inf.pos} \cap \text{r.inf.neg} \cap \text{vr.alt.b},$$

where influences are over fragments, $\text{r.inf.pos} \subseteq \mathbf{F} \times \mathbf{F}$, $\text{r.inf.neg} \subseteq \mathbf{F} \times \mathbf{F}$, and $\text{vr.alt.b} \subseteq \mathbf{V} \times \mathbf{V}$.

• value types are

$$\mathbf{T} = \{\text{v.Satisfaction, v.Importance,}$$
$$\text{v.ProgrStatus, v.ImplTime}\}.$$

$\text{v.Satisfaction} = \{1, 0\}$ and 1 reads "satisfied," 0 "not satisfied." $\text{v.Importance} = \{1, 0\}$ and 1 reads "mandatory", 0 "not mandatory". v.ProgrStatus is called "progress status," and its values are

$$\text{v.ProgrStatus} = \{\textit{none, DesignApproved,}$$
$$\textit{EstimateDone, InRoadmap,}$$
$$\textit{TestReady, ApprovedForRelease}\}.$$

v.ImplTime takes a real positive value, $\text{v.ImplTime} \in \mathbb{R}^+$.

• Value assignments are ternary relations over fragments or relation instances, value types, and values of value types:

$$\mathbf{V} \subseteq (\mathbf{F} \cup \mathbf{R}) \times \mathbf{T} \times \bigcup_{\text{v.t}\in\mathbf{T}} \text{v.t.}$$

and are partitioned as follows:

$$\mathbf{V} = (\mathbf{F} \cup \mathbf{R}) \times \{\text{v.Satisfaction}\} \times \{1, 0\}$$
$$\cup \mathbf{F} \times \{\text{v.Importance}\} \times \{1, 0\}$$
$$\cup \mathbf{F} \times \{\text{v.ProgrStatus}\} \times \text{v.ProgrStatus}$$
$$\cup \mathbf{F} \times \{\text{v.ImplTime}\} \times \text{v.ImplTime},$$

whereby the intersection of the sets above is empty. Note from the above that satisfaction values can be assigned to fragments and relation instances, while values of all other value types can be assigned only to fragments.

Syntax

A model M in the language is a set of symbols $M = \{Z_1, \ldots, Z_n\}$, where every ϕ is generated according to the following BNF rules:

$$A ::= x \mid y \mid z \mid \ldots$$
$$B ::= r(A) \mid k(A) \mid s(A)$$

$$C ::= B \text{ influences+ } B$$
$$D ::= B \text{ influences- } B$$
$$G ::= \langle A, E, F \rangle$$
$$H ::= G \text{ alternativeTo } G$$
$$Z ::= B \mid C \mid D \mid G \mid H$$

Mapping

Symbols map to domain elements as follows:

- A symbols denote fragments, $\mathscr{D}(A) \in$ **F**.
- B symbols are used to distinguish requirements, domain knowledge, and specification fragments, so that $\mathscr{D}(r(\alpha)) \in$ c.r, $\mathscr{D}(k(\alpha)) \in$ c.k, $\mathscr{D}(s(\alpha)) \in$ c.s.
- C and D symbols denote, respectively, positive and negative influence relations.
- E symbols denote value types, $\mathscr{D}(E) \in$ **T**.
- F symbols denote a value of a value type, and as there is one value type, $\mathscr{D}(F) \in$ v.Satisfaction.
- G symbols denote value assignments, $\mathscr{D}(G) \in$ **V**.
- H symbols denote alternatives, $\mathscr{D}(H) \in$ vr.alt.b.

Language services

Those of relations and functions in the language.

Figure 12.11 shows a model in **L.Avior**. Not all fragments have value assignment for all value types. For example, **AutoAmbList** has no satisfaction value, has no importance value, is in the roadmap, and the estimated implementation time is 25 man-days.

To deliver **s.AccTime**, you can define a function which would work as follows on an **L.Avior** model M:

1. Find all complete **v.Satisfaction** outcomes of M, which include a pick which you are interested in. Let O be the set of all these outcomes, and $o_i \in O$ a member of that set. An outcome is complete for **v.Satisfaction** if a satisfaction value is assigned to every fragment and relation instance, which it can be assigned to in a model, according to the language being used.

Example 12.11 Let the pick be

$$P = \{\langle \text{AmbArrIncLoc}, \text{v.Satisfaction}, 1 \rangle,$$
$$\langle \text{AmbArrIncLoc}, \text{v.Importance}, 1 \rangle\}.$$

The pick is shown in Fig. 12.11. Figures 12.7, 12.8, 12.9, and 12.10 show all four complete v.Satisfaction outcomes for the pick above. Although these are models in L.Pollux, they are also models in L.Avior, since the latter was made by adding new value types to the former, and without changing functions or syntax in the former. •

2. For each $o_i \in O$, if a fragment x is such that

   a. $\langle x, \text{v.Satisfaction}, 1 \rangle \in o_i$,
   b. x is a specification fragment, $x \in \text{c.s}$,
   c. x is a leaf fragment, that is, there are no positive and negative influence relation instances which target x in M,
   d. there is $\langle x, \text{v.ProgrStatus}, InRoadmap \rangle$, and
   e. there is $\langle x, \text{v.ImplTime}, v \rangle$, such that $v > 0$.

   then add x to the set T_{o_i}.

Example 12.12 (Example 12.11 continued) Let o_1 be the outcome in Fig. 12.12, so that

$$T_{o_1} = \{\text{AutoAmbList, UpdAutoAmbList,}$$
$$\text{DispSoftwRnkAmb, DispAmbRnk}\}. \quad \bullet$$

3. The answer to s.AccTime in M is given for each complete v.Satisfaction outcome o_i, by summing the v.ImplTime values assigned to every member of T_{o_i}.

Example 12.13 (Example 12.12 continued) For o_1, the total estimated implementation time is

$$25MD + 4MD + 30MD + 5MD = 64MD.$$

•

12.5 Summary on Alternatives

A language that aims to support design may need to represent alternative design options in models via alternatives and outcomes. This section illustrated that discovery and indecision in problem solving make this a relevant capability for a language.

   Enabling a language to represent alternatives raises many challenges and this section focused on the basic ones, namely, how to represent mutually exclusive pairs of value assignments and how to find outcomes which include no mutually exclusive pair of value assignments.

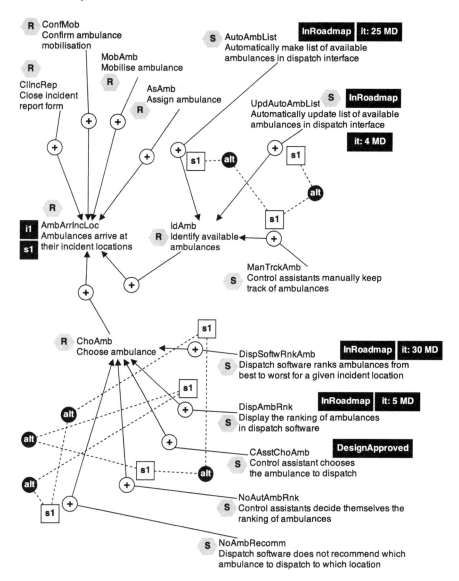

Fig. 12.11 A model in L.Avior

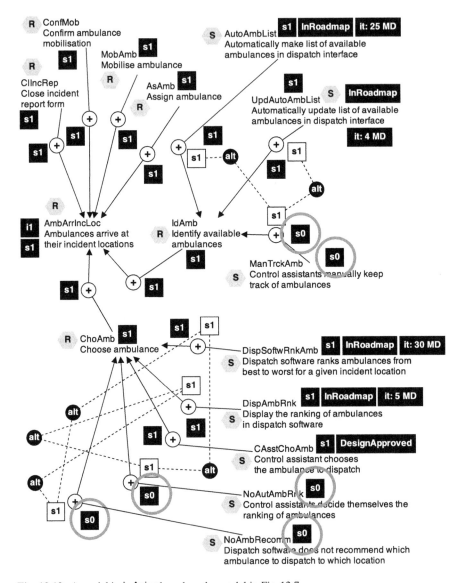

Fig. 12.12 A model in L.Avior based on the model in Fig. 12.7

Mutual exclusion was discussed in a limited way in this section. It remains unclear, for example, how to show that ranges of values that can be assigned to a fragment are mutually exclusive to ranges of values that can be assigned to another fragment. I will show in the next chapter that mutual exclusion, as discussed here, is one kind of constraint over value assignments, and that there are others that can be relevant to show in models.

Chapter 13
Constraints

This chapter focuses on how to have models with constraints over value assignments, which are richer than mutual exclusion from Chap. 12. Here are some constraints other than mutual exclusion:

- If x and z are both satisfied, then the implementation cost of y should double.
- If x is not acceptable, then estimated revenue from y will decrease by 30%.
- If the decision about the acceptability of x arrives after a given date, then implementation cost of x will increase by 50%.
- If the implementation time of x is above a, then implementation time of y cannot be over b.

What is common to the above is that there is an interdependence between value assignments, and that interdependence cannot be reduced, or when it can, it is inefficient to reduce it to mutual exclusion between pairs of value assignments. Given such constraints, the aim is to find one or all outcomes which satisfy them. The overall idea is that you need to define a system of equations which takes into account all constraints in a model, and find all outcomes that are its solutions. The rest of this chapter looks at the following questions:

- How to represent various kinds of constraints (Sect. 13.1)
- How to find outcomes when the model has constraints in a model (Sect. 13.2).

13.1 Representing Constraints

Constraints define n-ary relations over value assignments. The domain of the language needs to reflect the properties of the constraints which are allowed in the language, and the syntax should specify the format in which these constraints are written.

While it was straightforward to represent in graphs that two value assignments are mutually exclusive, there is no corresponding simple representation of many other kinds of constraints.

© Springer International Publishing Switzerland 2015
I. Jureta, *The Design of Requirements Modelling Languages*,
DOI 10.1007/978-3-319-18821-8_13

Consider a language in which a model M is a set of Z symbols, where each Z symbol is generated according to the following BNF rules:

$$A ::= x \mid y \mid z \mid \ldots$$
$$B ::= r(A) \mid k(A) \mid s(A)$$
$$C ::= B \text{ influences+ } B$$
$$D ::= B \text{ influences} - B$$
$$G ::= \langle A, E, F \rangle$$
$$H ::= G \text{ alternativeTo } G$$
$$I ::= A.E$$
$$J ::= G \mid I \mid N$$
$$K ::= J \mid K + K \mid K - K \mid K * K \mid K/K$$
$$L ::= K = K \mid K > K \mid K < K \mid K \geq K \mid K \leq K$$
$$Z ::= B \mid C \mid D \mid G \mid H \mid L$$

As given above, I symbols are variables without an assigned value, as opposed to G symbols where the F symbol stands for the assigned value. N symbol is a real number. K symbols reflect the arithmetic operations and L symbols are used to write equality and inequality. L symbols are symbols for constraints.

Suppose this language is such that it can represent all that L.Avior could, so that the following constraint can be associated with the L.Avior model in Fig. 12.11.

$$\text{ChoAmb.v.ImplTime} \leq 100$$

and if it included in a pick, then you are looking for outcomes which include a value assignment which assigns at most 100 v.ImplTime value to ChoAmb. You may be assuming or computing the v.ImplTime value of ChoAmb, but in any case, you will not be interested in outcomes where the assigned value is greater than 100.

When reading constraints such as above, recall the notational convention that the pair ChoAmb and v.ImplTime defines a variable, which can be written as

$$\text{ChoAmb.v.ImplTime}$$

and if it is assigned a value, say 50, then there are two equivalent ways of writing that value assignment, namely

$$\text{ChoAmb.v.ImplTime} = 50 \equiv \langle \text{ChoAmb, v.ImplTime, 50} \rangle.$$

To illustrate both points above, I define a new language which allows you to write constraints using arithmetic operations over value assignments in L.Avior models.

There can be more complicated constraints, such as

$$\mathsf{AutoAmbList.v.ImplTime} * \mathsf{AutoAmbList.v.Satisfaction} < 20$$

which says that I am interested in outcomes where, if AutoAmbList is satisfied, then its implementation time has to be below 20. Note that this constraint will be satisfied by outcomes where AutoAmbList is not satisfied, since v.Satisfaction is binary. But it will not be satisfied by outcomes where it is satisfied, and implementation time is equal to or above 20.

I could add the following constraint to a pick, to say that I am interested in outcomes in which implementing AutoAmbList takes at most twice the time to implement UpdAutoAmbList if both are satisfied:

$$\mathsf{AutoAmbList.v.Satisfaction} * \mathsf{AutoAmbList.v.ImplTime}$$
$$\leq 2 * \mathsf{UpdAutoAmbList.v.Satisfaction} * \mathsf{UpdAutoAmbList.v.ImpltTime}.$$

Constraints have to be sensitive to the value type, as arithmetic operations do not need to make sense for any value type. For example, multiplying two values of v.ProgrStatus makes no sense if multiplication is used as in arithmetic. You could define new operators for combining such values, but they would not be those of arithmetic.

Note that r.alt.b, when defined over value assignments of value types for which arithmetic operations make sense, can be rewritten as a constraint. I already did this when I rewrote r.alt.b instances in Figs. 12.7, 12.8, 12.9, and 12.10 in a system of equations in Sect. 12.3.

Below is a definition of the language L.Alphard which has the syntax given earlier. Its domain is loosely defined, as it includes no detailed definition of arithmetic operations.

L.Alphard is made by extending L.Avior. Aside from differences in syntax, the domains are also different. In L.Alphard, the domain includes constraints and real numbers $\mathbb{R}$. A constraint in the domain is a set of relation instances over value assignments. Each of these relation instances is such that when the variables in the constraint obtain values given in the value assignments in the relation instance, the arithmetic expression of the constraint is correct. To clarify this, consider the following constraint:

$$\mathsf{ChoAmb.v.ImplTime} \leq 100.$$

Recall that v.ImplTime is the set of positive real numbers. It follows that any positive real which is at most 100, that is, any real in [0, 100], makes the arithmetic expression above correct. This constraint is thus a set of instances of a unary relation and that set is

$$\{ \langle \mathsf{ChoAmb}, \mathsf{v.ImplTime}, v \rangle \mid v \in [0, 100] \text{ and } v \in \mathbb{R} \}.$$

Consider this constraint for another illustration

AutoAmbList.v.Satisfaction $*$ AutoAmbList.v.ImpltTime

$\leq 2 *$ UpdAutoAmbList.v.Satisfaction $*$ UpdAutoAmbList.v.ImpltTime.

In this case, the constraint defines a set of instances of a four-place relation, over assignments of values to these four variables

AutoAmbListv.Satisfaction, AutoAmbListv.ImplTime,

UpdAutoAmbListv.Satisfaction, UpdAutoAmbList.v.ImpltTime.

The set of instances are all assignments of values to all four variables above, such that the arithmetic expression in the constraint is correct. The following is an instance in that set

($\langle$AutoAmbList, v.Satisfaction, 0$\rangle$, $\langle$AutoAmbList, v.ImplTime, 50$\rangle$,

$\langle$UpdAutoAmbList, v.Satisfaction, 1$\rangle$,

$\langle$UpdAutoAmbList, v.ImplTime, 10$\rangle$).

Language: Alphard

Language modules
r.inf.pos, r.inf.neg, f.map.abrel.g, f.cat.ksr, vr.alt.b, f.sat.inf.pos, f.sat.inf.neg, f.sat.alt.b, f.sat.leaf, f.imp.asm, f.chk.progrstatus

---

Domain

- The domain is made of a set of fragments F, relation instances R, value types T, value assignments V, constraints Q, and real numbers $\mathbb{R}$.
- Fragments have three partitions, namely requirements, domain knowledge, and specification fragments, $F = c.r \cup c.k \cup c.s$ and $c.r \cap c.k \cap c.s = \emptyset$.
- Relation instances are over fragments or value assignments, $R = (F \times F) \cup V^n$, and are partitioned as follows:

$$R = r.inf.pos \cup r.inf.neg \cup vr.alt.b \cup \bigcup Q,$$

$$\emptyset = r.inf.pos \cap r.inf.neg \cap vr.alt.b \cap \bigcap Q,$$

where influences are over fragments, $r.inf.pos \subseteq F \times F$, $r.inf.neg \subseteq F \times F$, and $vr.alt.b \subseteq V \times V$. Each constraint is an n-ary relation over value assignments so that $Q \subseteq \wp(V^n)$.

- Value types are

$$\mathsf{T} = \{\mathsf{v.Satisfaction, v.Importance,}$$
$$\mathsf{v.ProgrStatus, v.ImplTime}\}.$$

v.Satisfaction $=$ $\{1, 0\}$ and 1 reads "satisfied," 0 "not satisfied."
v.Importance $=$ $\{1, 0\}$ and 1 reads "mandatory," 0 "not mandatory."
v.ProgrStatus is called "progress status," and its values are

$$\mathsf{v.ProgrStatus} = \{none, DesignApproved,$$
$$EstimateDone, InRoadmap,$$
$$TestReady, ApprovedForRelease\}.$$

v.ImplTime takes a real positive value, v.ImplTime $\in \mathbb{R}^+$.
- Value assignments are ternary relations over fragments or relation instances, T and values of T:

$$\mathsf{V} \subseteq (\mathsf{F} \cup \mathsf{R}) \times \mathsf{T} \times \bigcup_{\mathsf{v.t} \in \mathsf{T}} \mathsf{v.t.}$$

and is partitioned as follows:

$$\mathsf{V} = (\mathsf{F} \cup \mathsf{R}) \times \{\mathsf{v.Satisfaction}\} \times \{1, 0\}$$
$$\cup \mathsf{F} \times \{\mathsf{v.Importance}\} \times \{1, 0\}$$
$$\cup \mathsf{F} \times \{\mathsf{v.ProgrStatus}\} \times \mathsf{v.ProgrStatus}$$
$$\cup \mathsf{F} \times \{\mathsf{v.ImplTime}\} \times \mathsf{v.ImplTime},$$

whereby the intersection of the sets above is empty. Note from the above that satisfaction values can be assigned to fragments and relation instances, while values of all other T can be assigned only to fragments.

Syntax

A model M in the language is a set of symbols $M = \{Z_1, \ldots, Z_n\}$, where every ϕ is generated according to the following BNF rules:

$$A ::= x \mid y \mid z \mid \ldots$$
$$B ::= r(A) \mid k(A) \mid s(A)$$
$$C ::= B \text{ influences+ } B$$
$$D ::= B \text{ influences- } B$$
$$G ::= \langle A, E, F \rangle$$
$$H ::= G \text{ alternativeTo } G$$

$$I ::= A.E$$
$$J ::= G \mid I \mid N$$
$$K ::= J \mid K + K \mid K - K \mid K * K \mid K/K$$
$$L ::= K = K \mid K > K \mid K < K \mid K \geq K \mid K \leq K$$
$$Z ::= B \mid C \mid D \mid G \mid H \mid L$$

Mapping

Symbols map to domain elements as follows:

- A symbols denote fragments, $\mathscr{D}(A) \in \mathsf{F}$.
- B symbols are used to distinguish requirements, domain knowledge, and specification fragments, so that $\mathscr{D}(r(\alpha)) \in \mathsf{c.r}$, $\mathscr{D}(k(\alpha)) \in \mathsf{c.k}$, $\mathscr{D}(s(\alpha)) \in \mathsf{c.s}$.
- C and D symbols denote, respectively, positive and negative influence relations.
- E symbols denote T, $\mathscr{D}(E) \in \mathsf{T}$.
- F symbols denote a value of a value type, and as there is one value type, $\mathscr{D}(F) \in \mathsf{v.Satisfaction}$.
- G symbols denote value assignments, $\mathscr{D}(G) \in \mathsf{V}$.
- H symbols denote alternatives, $\mathscr{D}(H) \in \mathsf{vr.alt.b}$.
- I symbols denote variables, that is, pairs of fragment or relation instance, and a value type, $\mathscr{D}(I) \in (\mathsf{F} \cup \mathsf{R}) \times \mathsf{T}$.
- N symbols denote a real number, $\mathscr{D}(N) \in \mathbb{R}$.
- $K + K$ denotes the sum of K and K,

$$\mathscr{D}(K + K) = \mathscr{D}(K) + \mathscr{D}(K),$$

- $K - K$ denotes the subtraction of K on the right side of "−" from the K on the left side of "−",

$$\mathscr{D}(K - K) = \mathscr{D}(K) - \mathscr{D}(K),$$

- $K * K$ denotes the result of multiplying K and K,

$$\mathscr{D}(K * K) = \mathscr{D}(K) * \mathscr{D}(K),$$

- K/K denotes the result of dividing the K on the left side of "/" with the K on the right side of "/",

$$\mathscr{D}(K/K) = \mathscr{D}(K)/\mathscr{D}(K),$$

- $K = K$ denotes that the two K are equal,
- $K > K$ denotes that the K on the left side of ">" is greater than the K on the right side of ">",
- $K < K$ denotes that the K on the left side of "<" is smaller than the K on the right side of "<",
- $K \geq K$ denotes that the K on the left side of "≥" is equal or greater than the K on the right side of "≥", and
- $K \leq K$ denotes that the K on the left side of "≤" is equal to or smaller than the K on the right side of "≤".

Language services

Those of relations and functions in the language.

Observe how the mapping works in L.Alphard. The arithmetic operations map to standard arithmetic operations, so when I write

$$\mathscr{D}(K + K) = \mathscr{D}(K) + \mathscr{D}(K),$$

the aim of the formula is to show that the "+" symbol should work the same way that addition works in arithmetic, and this is shown by simply taking it out of $\mathscr{D}$. The mapping works in this same way for the rest of the arithmetic operators, equality, and inequality symbols.

13.2 Constraints in Outcome Search

The aim now is to show a way to find outcomes in a model with constraints. The idea is the same as in Sect. 12.3: define a pick, convert the model in a system of equations such that any solution of that system is an outcome which includes the pick. As I will illustrate below, the only change relative to Sect. 12.3 is that the system of equations now includes also all of the constraints in the model.

I will proceed step-by-step to define the system of equations from the model in L.Alphard, shown in Fig. 13.1. The figure does not include constraints and I will introduce them in due time below.

1. I am interested in finding all complete and coherent outcomes of the model in Fig. 13.1, which include the following pick

$$P = \{ \langle x, \text{v.Satisfaction}, 1 \rangle \mid \forall x \in M \text{ s.t.}$$
$$x \in F \text{ and } \langle x, \text{v.Importance}, 1 \rangle$$
$$\text{and } \langle x, \text{v.ProgrStatus}, \textit{DesignApproved} \rangle \}.$$

2. Observe that the model in Fig. 13.1 has value assignments of four value types, v.Satisfaction, v.Importance, v.ImplTime, and v.ProgrStatus. It follows that the system of equations will be over four groups of variables, one per value type. Below is a sample member of each of these groups

> AmbArrIncLoc.v.Satisfaction,
> AmbArrIncLoc.v.Importance,
> DispSoftwRnkAmb.v.ImplTime,
> DispAmbRnk.v.ProgrStatus.

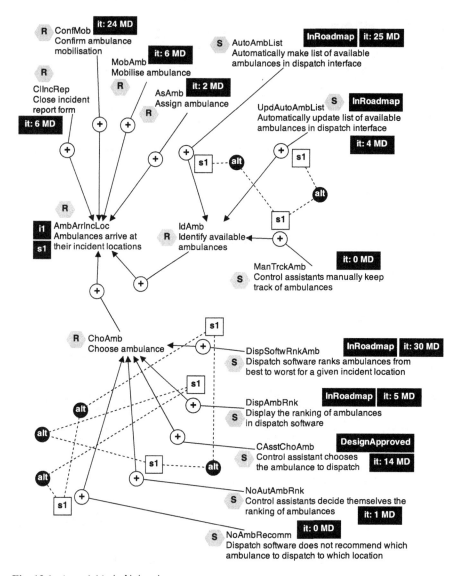

Fig. 13.1   A model in L.Alphard

I now define abbreviations for all variables in each group.

a. For each fragment x in M, I define a variable w_x as the variable which takes the v.Satisfaction value

$$w_x \equiv x.\text{v.Satisfaction}$$

and to further simplify notation, I have these equivalences

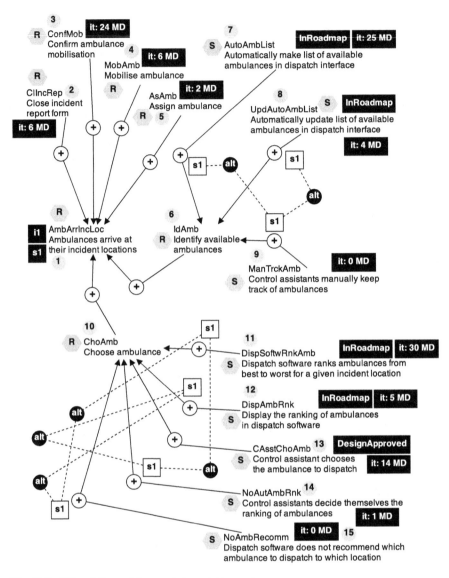

Fig. 13.2 Abbreviations of fragments in variable numbers

$$w_1 \equiv w_{\text{AmbArrIncLoc}}, \qquad w_2 \equiv w_{\text{ClIncRep}},$$
$$w_3 \equiv w_{\text{ConfMob}}, \qquad w_4 \equiv w_{\text{MobAmb}},$$
$$w_5 \equiv w_{\text{AsAmb}}, \qquad w_6 \equiv w_{\text{IdAmb}},$$
$$w_7 \equiv w_{\text{AutoAmbList}}, \qquad w_8 \equiv w_{\text{UpdAutoAmbList}},$$
$$w_9 \equiv w_{\text{ManTrckAmb}}, \qquad w_{10} \equiv w_{\text{ChoAmb}},$$
$$w_{11} \equiv w_{\text{DispSoftwRnkmb}}, \qquad w_{12} \equiv w_{\text{DispAmbRnk}},$$
$$w_{13} \equiv w_{\text{AsstChoAmb}}, \qquad w_{14} \equiv w_{\text{NoAutAmbRnk}},$$
$$w_{15} \equiv w_{\text{NoAmbRecomm}}.$$

b. I then define variables which take values of **v.Importance** for each fragment x in M, define a variable w_x as the variable which takes the **v.Satisfaction** value

$$p_x \equiv x.\text{v.Importance}$$

and I use these equivalences

$$p_1 \equiv p_{\text{AmbArrIncLoc}}, \qquad p_2 \equiv p_{\text{ClIncRep}},$$
$$p_3 \equiv p_{\text{ConfMob}}, \qquad p_4 \equiv p_{\text{MobAmb}},$$
$$p_5 \equiv p_{\text{AsAmb}}, \qquad p_6 \equiv p_{\text{IdAmb}},$$
$$p_7 \equiv p_{\text{AutoAmbList}}, \qquad p_8 \equiv p_{\text{UpdAutoAmbList}},$$
$$p_9 \equiv p_{\text{ManTrckAmb}}, \qquad p_{10} \equiv p_{\text{ChoAmb}},$$
$$p_{11} \equiv p_{\text{DispSoftwRnkmb}}, \qquad p_{12} \equiv p_{\text{DispAmbRnk}},$$
$$p_{13} \equiv p_{\text{AsstChoAmb}}, \qquad p_{14} \equiv p_{\text{NoAutAmbRnk}},$$
$$p_{15} \equiv p_{\text{NoAmbRecomm}}.$$

c. I now add equivalences for variables which take **v.ImplTime** values, and which have this format

$$t_x \equiv x.\text{v.ImplTime}$$

and I will use the following:

$$t_1 \equiv t_{\text{AmbArrIncLoc}}, \qquad t_2 \equiv t_{\text{ClIncRep}},$$
$$t_3 \equiv t_{\text{ConfMob}}, \qquad t_4 \equiv t_{\text{MobAmb}},$$
$$t_5 \equiv t_{\text{AsAmb}}, \qquad t_6 \equiv t_{\text{IdAmb}},$$
$$t_7 \equiv t_{\text{AutoAmbList}}, \qquad t_8 \equiv t_{\text{UpdAutoAmbList}},$$
$$t_9 \equiv t_{\text{ManTrckAmb}}, \qquad t_{10} \equiv t_{\text{ChoAmb}},$$
$$t_{11} \equiv t_{\text{DispSoftwRnkmb}}, \qquad t_{12} \equiv t_{\text{DispAmbRnk}},$$
$$t_{13} \equiv t_{\text{AsstChoAmb}}, \qquad t_{14} \equiv t_{\text{NoAutAmbRnk}},$$
$$t_{15} \equiv t_{\text{NoAmbRecomm}}.$$

d. Finally, as far as variables for fragments are concerned, there are variables that take v.ProgrStatus values

$$s_x \equiv x.\text{v.ImplTime}$$

and I will use the following:

$s_1 \equiv s_{\text{AmbArrIncLoc}},$ $s_2 \equiv s_{\text{ClIncRep}},$

$s_3 \equiv s_{\text{ConfMob}},$ $s_4 \equiv s_{\text{MobAmb}},$

$s_5 \equiv s_{\text{AsAmb}},$ $s_6 \equiv s_{\text{IdAmb}},$

$s_7 \equiv s_{\text{AutoAmbList}},$ $s_8 \equiv s_{\text{UpdAutoAmbList}},$

$s_9 \equiv s_{\text{ManTrckAmb}},$ $s_{10} \equiv s_{\text{ChoAmb}},$

$s_{11} \equiv s_{\text{DispSoftwRnkmb}},$ $s_{12} \equiv s_{\text{DispAmbRnk}},$

$s_{13} \equiv s_{\text{AsstChoAmb}},$ $s_{14} \equiv s_{\text{NoAutAmbRnk}},$

$s_{15} \equiv s_{\text{NoAmbRecomm}}.$

Figure 13.2 shows which number in a variable name corresponds to which fragment in the model in Fig. 13.1.

3. L.Alphard lets me assign v.Satisfaction values over relation instances, so that I need variables for all relation instances as well. They will have the following format, where x and y are fragments

$$w_{x.p.y} \equiv (x \text{ influences+ } y).\text{v.Satisfaction}.$$

Given the other abbreviations defined so far, I will have, for example

$$w_{2.p.1} \equiv (\text{ClIncRep influences+ AmbArrIncLoc}).\text{v.Satisfaction}.$$

I will not write all the other influence relation instances, as it should be clear what they are from the abbreviations above.

4. So far, I have defined the set of variables that will appear in the system of equations. Relation instances and functions for propagating satisfaction values give me a first set of equations. As there are only positive influences in Fig. 13.1, and each uses the rules from f.sat.inf.pos, the resulting equations are (same as in Sect. 12.3)

$$0 = w_2 - w_{2.p.1}, \qquad 0 = w_3 - w_{3.p.1},$$
$$0 = w_4 - w_{4.p.1}, \qquad 0 = w_5 - w_{5.p.1},$$
$$0 = w_6 - w_{6.p.1}, \qquad 0 = w_{10} - w_{10.p.1},$$
$$0 = w_7 - w_{7.p.6}, \qquad 0 = w_8 - w_{8.p.6},$$
$$0 = w_9 - w_{9.p.6},$$

$$0 = w_{11} - w_{11.p.10}, \qquad 0 = w_{12} - w_{12.p.10},$$
$$0 = w_{13} - w_{13.p.10}, \qquad 0 = w_{14} - w_{14.p.10},$$
$$0 = w_{15} - w_{15.p.10}.$$

5. r.alt.b instances also give equations and they are found the same way as in Sect. 12.3

$$1 = |w_{7.p.6} - w_{9.p.6}|,$$
$$1 = |w_{8.p.6} - w_{9.p.6}|,$$
$$1 = |w_{11.p.10} - w_{14.p.10}|,$$
$$1 = |w_{11.p.10} - w_{15.p.10}|,$$
$$1 = |w_{12.p.10} - w_{14.p.10}|,$$
$$1 = |w_{12.p.10} - w_{15.p.10}|,$$
$$w_1 = w_{2.p.1} \cdot w_{3.p.1} \cdot w_{4.p.1} \cdot w_{5.p.1} \cdot w_{6.p.1} \cdot w_{10.p.1},$$
$$w_6 = w_{7.p.6} \cdot w_{8.p.6} + w_{9.p.6},$$
$$w_{10} = w_{11.p.10} \cdot w_{12.p.10} \cdot w_{13.p.10}$$
$$+ w_{13.p.10} \cdot w_{14.p.10} \cdot w_{15.p.10}.$$

6. The first set of constraints reflects the value assignments to leaf fragments in Fig. 13.1. These constraints are as follows, for v.ImplTime value assignments

$t_2 = 6$,	$t_3 = 24$,	$t_4 = 6$,	$t_5 = 2$,
$t_7 = 25$,	$t_8 = 4$,	$t_9 = 0$,	
$t_{11} = 30$,	$t_{12} = 5$,	$t_{13} = 14$,	$t_{14} = 1$,
$t_{15} = 0$,			

and they are the following, for v.ProgrStatus

$$t_7 = InRoadmap, \qquad t_8 = InRoadmap,$$
$$t_{11} = InRoadmap, \qquad t_{12} = InRoadmap,$$
$$t_{13} = DesignApproved.$$

7. Observe that I did not define a specific relation which says how the implementation time of, say ChoAmb, depends on that of other fragments in the model. I do this with the following constraints:

$$t_1 = \sum_{i \in \{2,3,4,5,6,10\}} t_i * w_i,$$

$$t_6 = \sum_{i \in \{7,8,9\}} t_i * w_i,$$

$$t_{10} = \sum_{i \in \{11,12,13,14,15\}} t_i * w_i.$$

The constraints convey the idea that implementation time of a fragment x is the sum of the implementation times of all fragments which are satisfied, and which are positively influencing x.

8. I have no constraints for v.Importance value assignments other than the one in the pick, which is

$$p_1 = 1.$$

9. The pick gives two other constraints, namely

$$w_1 = 1,$$
$$s_1 = DesignApproved.$$

10. Recall from the definition of v.ProgrStatus that *DesignApproved* is the first progress status that can be assigned to a fragment, and following f.chkprogrstatus that it can be assigned only to fragments which have no other progress status value. Observe also that arithmetic operations are not defined over v.ProgrStatus, so that I need to introduce a coding of its values into, say, integers.

Since the pick requires AmbArrIncLoc to get the value *DesignApproved*, I introduce the following equivalences:

$$none \equiv 0,$$
$$DesignApproved \equiv 1,$$
$$EstimateDone \equiv 1,$$
$$InRoadmap \equiv 1,$$
$$TestReady \equiv 1,$$
$$ApprovedForRelease \equiv 1.$$

The above reflects the fact that design is approved on any fragment which either has *DesignApproved* value or has any v.ProgrStatus value which according to f.chi.progrstatus can be assigned after *DesignApproved*, that is, after the design has been approved.

Furthermore, I consider that if a fragment x is target of positive influence relation instances, then its progress status depends on the progress status of the fragments in which these positive influences originate. Therefore, I have the following constraints:

$$s_1 = \prod_{i \in \{2,3,4,5,6,10\}} s_i * w_i,$$

$$s_6 = \prod_{i \in \{7,8,9\}} s_i * w_i,$$

$$s_{10} = \prod_{i \in \{11,12,13,14,15\}} s_i * w_i.$$

11. I add the following as a final constraint

$$t_1 \leq 80.$$

12. At this point, I have equations that correspond to the pick, to all constraints resulting from the influence and r.alt.b relations in the model, and to all constraints I added in relation to v.ImplTime and v.ProgrStatus. All these equations constitute the system of equations to solve, in order to find one or more (if there are) outcomes which include the pick.

   Observe that such an outcome cannot satisfy both AutombList and DispSoftwRnkAmb, as this would violate the constraint that implementation time of AmbArrIncLoc is below 80 MD.

13.3 Summary on Constraints

This chapter illustrated how constraints over value assignments can be represented in models and how they can be taken into account when searching for outcomes. The discussion was limited to constraints defined over arithmetic operations only. I did not discuss the computational complexity of finding outcomes, and this remains outside the scope of this book.

An important idea in this chapter, and in part already illustrated in Chap. 12 is that a language may be such that its models can be rewritten as systems of equations. In other words, you can see such models as representations of the underlying systems of equations. This is relevant when you are interested in finding outcomes which include a specific pick which you defined. It also follows that you can see lànguages such as L.Alphard as tools to construct these systems of equations incrementally and iteratively.

Chapter 14
Preferences

When there are several outcomes, all of which include a pick you are interested in, which one of these outcomes do you choose? How do you choose it? Which one is the "best"? What tells you, in a model, if an outcome is "better" than another? This chapter focuses on how to enable languages to repsresent preferences and criteria, and then identify the best outcome. I discuss the following questions:

1. What are preferences and criteria? (Sect. 14.2)
2. How to represent preferences and criteria. (Sect. 14.3)
3. Where to find criteria in requirements. (Sect. 14.4)
4. How to use preferences to find the best outcomes in models. (Sect. 14.5)

14.1 Motivation

It may be more desirable to stakeholders that incident reports are managed via the dispatching software, than having it done via other software. Each of these, in turn, may be more desirable than to fill out and keep incident reports in paper format. Some outcomes will suggest to use dispatching software to manage incident reports, and will, with regard to how incident reports are managed, be more desirable to other outcomes, which recommend otherwise.

Choosing the "best" outcome can be done by indicating the relative desirability of value assignments, that is, *preferences*. Preferences can be associated with different criteria, such as cost, time to implement, ease of use, and so on. Given preferences and the criteria in a model, the aim is to somehow use them to compare outcomes. This involves various activities such as eliciting preferences, finding criteria, inferring missing preferences, and orders over outcomes.

You rarely have a total order over outcomes. There may be a number of value assignments, so it is not feasible to elicit all the comparisons needed to define the total order. It can also happen that you have none to elicit them from. Or you may, but perhaps you do not trust that these comparisons will remain unchanged. Stakeholders

© Springer International Publishing Switzerland 2015
I. Jureta, *The Design of Requirements Modelling Languages*,
DOI 10.1007/978-3-319-18821-8_14

need not know the values or outcome to prefer, especially if it is unclear how these values and outcomes translate to their specific context.

To define the total order, you can elicit pairwise comparisons of some value assignments and/or outcomes, and somehow deduce the remaining comparisons that you need to define the total order. In the worst case, you would need to elicit all possible comparisons among pairs of value assignments. Such comparisons are called *preferences*, each saying that some value assignment v_1 is more desirable than some other v_2.

Preferences are associated with criteria, such as "low cost," "short implementation time," "positive effect on the scalability of the system," and so on. For example, it may be more desirable that the average time to respond to incidents is 12 min than 16 min, and the criterion in this case may be called "lower average time to respond to an incident." However, it may be that achieving an average of 12 min is costlier (requires more ambulances, more personnel, and so on) than achieving an average of 16 min. The two value assignments are thus compared over two criteria, one being the average time to respond to an incident and the other the cost of the future system.

In short, the idea is that you would discover and elicit preferences incrementally and often partially. You may decide to stop when you have enough of them to approximate the total order over outcomes, and thereby highlight the best one.

This absence of information about preferences and its incremental discovery and elicitation are also major reasons to make languages that can represent preferences. As you elicit new preferences, you add them to a model and you can analyze how they relate to already existing preferences over the same criteria, or whether you need to add new criteria as well. You can evaluate if a given model includes enough information on preferences and criteria, to produce a partial or total order, over many criteria, over the outcomes.

14.2 Preferences and Criteria Basics

There is considerable research on preferences in philosophy [65, 116], economics [22, 86, 98, 103, 133, 137, 139, 145], operations research [47, 49, 57], and artificial intelligence [6, 42, 44]. In Sect. 14.2.1, I recall common ideas about two core preference relations, strict preference and indifference. In Sect. 14.2.2, I introduce the preference-related terminology specific to this book, and in Sect. 14.2.3 I introduce criteria and relate them to preferences.

14.2.1 Core Preference Relations

If you ask, of A and B, which is more desirable, you can expect any one of three answers. A, for example, may be more desirable than B, that is, better than B, or *vice versa*. In that case, there is the so-called *strict preference* for one over the other.

The second answer is that both *A* and *B* are equally desirable, that neither is better than the other. This is a case of being *indifferent* between *A* and *B*. Finally, *A* and *B* can be incomparable in terms of desirability, in which case there is no preference between them.

Strict preference and indifference are two core preference relations [66], and anything else is a derived preference relation. When I write "core preference relations," I refer to strict preference and indifference relations. When I want to be specific, I shall write "strict preference" or "indifference."

Strict preference is usually an irreflexive, antisymmetric, and transitive binary relation. Indifference is reflexive, symmetric, and transitive.

Core preference relations can, but need not be *complete* over a domain. A strict preference relation is complete for its domain iff there is an instance thereof between every pair of elements in that domain. This is different from the usual approach, where a preference relation can be complete if there is either strict preference *or indifference* between any pair of elements in the domain. I do this in order to simplify the discussion in this book.

Completeness is a desirable property when you want to establish a total order over outcomes. But as I said earlier, it can be difficult to find enough information to achieve it. There is considerable work on the elicitation of preferences [25], which I leave to you to explore.

All things in the domain of a preference relation are assumed to be *comparable*. This means that there are strict preference, or indifference, or both relation instances between any two pairs of things in the domain.

In addition to the above, it is also usually assumed that all things in the domain of a preference relation are mutually exclusive. That is, none is part of another, and none is compatible with another.

14.2.2 Domains of Preference Relations

In this book, preference relations are over value assignments. The domain of a preference relation includes only value assignments.

Fragments (and the same applies to relation instances), when taken independent of values, are not members of domains of preference relations. If I write that "fragment *x* is strictly preferred to fragment *y*" then it is not clear whether I am trying to say that "*satisfying* fragment *x* is strictly preferred to *satisfying* fragment *y*", or that "*including in the model the* fragment *x* is strictly preferred to *including in the model the* fragment *y*", or both, or none of these, but something else. Having only value assignments in preference domains allows me to be more precise, without losing the ability to say either of these. The statement "*satisfying* fragment *x* is strictly preferred to *satisfying* fragment *y*" is a preference over satisfaction values, while "*including in the model the* fragment *x* is strictly preferred to *including in the model the* fragment *y*" can be a preference over acceptability value assignments.

14.2.3 Criteria

In this book, a preference relation is always associated with a criterion. A criterion c, denoted crit.c, is a function over value assignments, such that if there is a preference relation instance

$$(\langle x_i, t_j, v_k \rangle, \langle x_l, t_p, v_q \rangle),$$

and it is associated with crit.c, then

$$\text{crit.c}(\langle x_i, t_j, v_k \rangle) > \text{crit.c}(\langle x_l, t_p, v_q \rangle)$$

A criterion is then a function that returns a greater value for more desirable alternatives.

Every criterion can have its own value type, which may, but need not be related in some way to other value types. Above, suppose that $\langle x_i, t_j, v_k \rangle$ is a cost value and $\langle x_l, t_p, v_q \rangle$ is an estimate of implementation time, the preference $(\langle x_i, t_j, v_k \rangle, \langle x_l, t_p, v_q \rangle)$ thus says that observing a specific cost is strictly more preferred than to observe a specific implementation time.

Criteria specialize preference relations, wherein there can be a preference relation specific to cost, another relation specific to implementation time, and so on. I write

$$(\langle x_i, t_j, v_k \rangle, \langle x_l, t_p, v_q \rangle) \in \text{r.Pref.c}$$

if $(\langle x_i, t_j, v_k \rangle, \langle x_l, t_p, v_q \rangle)$ is an instance of some preference relation called Pref, associated with the criterion C.

14.3 Representing Preferences

A preference relation instance compares two value assignments for desirability. To represent the core preference relations from Sect. 14.2, a language needs relations of two kinds, strict preference and indifference. There needs to be one strict preference relation and one indifference relation per criterion in the language.

Relation: pref.c

Strict Preference

Domain & Dimension

r.pref.c $\subseteq$ **V** $\times$ **V**, where c is a criterion, and **V** is a set of value assignments.

Properties

Irreflexive, antisymmetric, and transitive.

Reading

$(v, w) \in$ vr.pref.c reads "value assignment v is strictly more desirable than value assignment w on the criterion c."

Language services

- **s.IsPref**: Is value assignment v strictly preferred to value assignment w on crit.c? Yes, if $(v, w) \in$ vr.pref.c.

L.Bellartrix, the language defined below, adds vr.pref.c and criteria to L.Pollux. An additional change is that besides v.Satisfaction and v.Importance, the language has $n > 1$ additional value types. Each of these is the set of positive reals, $\mathbb{R}^+$. The language gives generic names to each of these value types, and you can define aliases for them, which are meaningful in the problem instance you are solving. I will illustrate this after the language definition.

Language: Bellatrix

Language modules
r.inf.pos, r.inf.neg, f.map.abrel.g, f.cat.ksr, vr.alt.b, vr.pref.c, f.sat.inf.pos, f.sat.inf.neg, f.sat.alt.b, f.sat.leaf, f.imp.asm

---

Domain

- The domain is made of a set of fragments **F**, relation instances **R** with a special subset **P** of preference relation instances, value types **T**, value assignments **V**, criteria **C**, and real numbers $\mathbb{R}$.
- Fragments have three partitions, namely requirements, domain knowledge, and specification fragments, $\mathbf{F} = $ c.r $\cup$ c.k $\cup$ c.s and c.r $\cap$ c.k $\cap$ c.s $= \emptyset$.
- Relation instances are over fragments or value assignments, $\mathbf{R} = (\mathbf{F} \times \mathbf{F}) \cup (\mathbf{V} \times \mathbf{V})$, and are partitioned as follows:

$$\mathbf{R} = \text{r.inf.pos} \cup \text{r.inf.neg} \cup \text{vr.alt.b} \cup \mathbf{P},$$

$$\emptyset = \text{r.inf.pos} \cap \text{r.inf.neg} \cap \text{vr.alt.b} \cap \mathbf{P},$$

where

$$P = \bigcup_{crit.c\in\mathbf{C}} vr.pref.c,$$

influences are over fragments, r.inf.pos $\subseteq \mathbf{F} \times \mathbf{F}$, r.inf.neg $\subseteq \mathbf{F} \times \mathbf{F}$, while mutual exclusion and preferences are over value assignments vr.alt.b $\cup\, \mathbf{P} \subseteq \mathbf{V} \times \mathbf{V}$.

- Value types are

$$\mathbf{T} = \{v.\text{Satisfaction}, v.\text{Importance}\} \cup \bigcup_{q=1}^{n>1} v.q.$$

v.Satisfaction and v.Importance are binary. Satisfaction value 1 reads "satisfied," and 0 "not satisfied." Importance value 1 reads "mandatory," 0 "not mandatory." Each of the $q = 1, \ldots, n$ value types v.q is the set of positive reals.

- Value assignments are ternary relations over fragments or relation instances, value types, and values of value types:

$$\mathbf{V} \subseteq (\mathbf{F} \cup \mathbf{R}) \times \mathbf{T} \times \bigcup_{v.t\in\mathbf{T}} v.t.$$

and has the following three partitions:

$$(\mathbf{F} \cup \mathbf{R}) \times \{v.\text{Satisfaction}\} \times \{1, 0\},$$
$$\mathbf{F} \times \{v.\text{Importance}\} \times \{1, 0\}, \text{ and}$$
$$\mathbf{F} \times \bigcup_{q=1}^{n>1} v.q \times \mathbb{R}^+.$$

Satisfaction values can be assigned to fragments and relation instances, while values of all other value types can be assigned only to fragments.

Syntax

A model M in the language is a set of symbols $M = \{Z_1, \ldots, Z_n\}$, where every ϕ is generated according to the following BNF rules:

$$A ::= x \mid y \mid z \mid \ldots$$
$$B ::= r(A) \mid k(A) \mid s(A)$$
$$C ::= B \text{ influences+ } B$$
$$D ::= B \text{ influences- } B$$
$$G ::= \langle A, E, F \rangle$$

$$H ::= G \text{ alternativeTo } G$$
$$I ::= G \text{ Pref.} J \, G$$
$$J ::= c_1 \mid c_2 \mid \ldots$$
$$Z ::= B \mid C \mid D \mid G \mid H \mid I$$

Mapping

Symbols map to domain elements as follows:

- A symbols denote fragments, $\mathscr{D}(A) \in$ **F**.
- B symbols are used to distinguish requirements, domain knowledge, and specification fragments, so that $\mathscr{D}(r(\alpha)) \in$ c.r, $\mathscr{D}(k(\alpha)) \in$ c.k, $\mathscr{D}(s(\alpha)) \in$ c.s.
- C and D symbols denote, respectively, positive and negative influence relations.
- E symbols denote value types, $\mathscr{D}(E) \in$ **T**.
- F symbols denote a value of a value type, and as there is one value type, $\mathscr{D}(F) \in$ v.Satisfaction.
- G symbols denote value assignments, $\mathscr{D}(G) \in$ **V**.
- H symbols denote alternatives, $\mathscr{D}(H) \in$ vr.alt.b.
- I symbols denote instances of preference relations, one per criterion c,

$$\mathscr{D}(I) \in \bigcup_{\text{crit.c} \in \mathbf{C}} \text{vr.pref.c.}$$

- J symbols denote criteria, $\mathscr{D}(J) \in$ **C**.

Language services

Those of relations and functions in the language.

Figure 14.1 is a visualization of 12 preference relation instances, over a model in L.Bellatrix. The model takes its contents from parts of the model in Fig. 13.2. The numbers used to abbreviate variables in Fig. 13.2 are the same as in Fig. 14.1.

Figure 14.1 shows two criteria, each associated with four preferences. crit.AdvDecSup says that the software should provide more advanced decision support. It follows that having the software automatically update the list of available ambulances, and having it make that list is strictly preferred to having control assistants perform this work manually. This is conveyed by the following preferences:

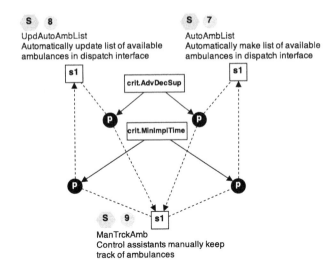

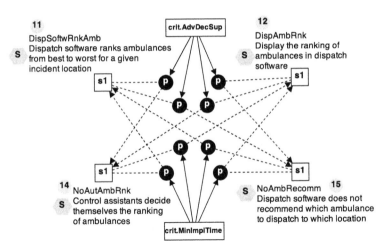

Fig. 14.1 Preferences and criteria in a model in L.Bellatrix

⟨UpdAutoAmbList, v.Satisfaction, 1⟩ Pref.AdvDecSup
⟨ManTrckAmb, v.Satisfaction, 1⟩ and
⟨AutoAmbList, v.Satisfaction, 1⟩ Pref.AdvDecSup
⟨ManTrckAmb, v.Satisfaction, 1⟩.

Following the same criterion, it is more desirable to have the software rank candidate ambulances for dispatching to an incident location and display the ranking, than not to assist control assistants in this way. This is represented with the following preferences:

⟨DispSoftwRnkAmb, v.Satisfaction, 1⟩ Pref.AdvDecSup
⟨NoAutAmbRnk, v.Satisfaction, 1⟩,
⟨DispSoftwRnkAmb, v.Satisfaction, 1⟩ Pref.AdvDecSup
⟨NoAmbRecomm, v.Satisfaction, 1⟩,
⟨DispAmbRnk, v.Satisfaction, 1⟩ Pref.AdvDecSup
⟨NoAutAmbRnk, v.Satisfaction, 1⟩, and
⟨DispAmbRnk, v.Satisfaction, 1⟩ Pref.AdvDecSup
⟨NoAmbRecomm, v.Satisfaction, 1⟩.

The second criterion in Fig. 14.1 is crit.MinImplTime, which says that lower implementation times, that is, lower values of v.ImplTime are strictly preferred to higher values of this value type. This gives the following preferences:

⟨ManTrckAmb, v.Satisfaction, 1⟩ Pref.MinImplTime
⟨UpdAutoAmbList, v.Satisfaction, 1⟩,
⟨ManTrckAmb, v.Satisfaction, 1⟩ Pref.MinImplTime
⟨AutoAmbList, v.Satisfaction, 1⟩,
⟨NoAutoAmbRnk, v.Satisfaction, 1⟩ Pref.MinImplTime
⟨DispSoftwRnkAmb, v.Satisfaction, 1⟩,

⟨NoAutoAmbRnk, v.Satisfaction, 1⟩ Pref.MinImplTime
⟨DispAmbRnk, v.Satisfaction, 1⟩,
⟨NoAmbRecomm, v.Satisfaction, 1⟩ Pref.MinImplTime
⟨DispSoftwRnkAmb, v.Satisfaction, 1⟩, and
⟨NoAmbRecomm, v.Satisfaction, 1⟩ Pref.MinImplTime
⟨DispAmbRnk, v.Satisfaction, 1⟩.

As a digression, note that all the preferences above can be written with variable abbreviations from Sect. 13.2. The following are two examples:

$(w_8 = 1)$ Pref.AdvDecSup $(w_9 = 1)$ and
$(w_7 = 1)$ Pref.AdvDecSup $(w_9 = 1)$.

All the preferences above are strict preferences over value assignments *of the same value type*, v.Satisfaction. There can also be preferences over value assignments over different value types, on the same or different fragments. Figure 14.2 shows examples.

The model part shown in Fig. 14.2 involves three new value types relative to Fig. 14.1. There is v.AvgIncArrTime, which is the average time for an ambulance

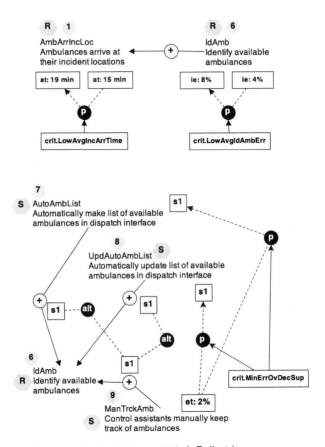

Fig. 14.2 More preferences and criteria in a model in L.Bellartrix

to arrive at an incident, from the moment the incident was reported. Ideally, this should be minimized, hence the criterion crit.LowAvgIncArrTime. The criterion gives the preference

⟨AmbArrIncLoc, v.LowAvgIncArrTime, 15⟩ Pref.LowAvgIdAmbErr

⟨AmbArrIncLoc, v.AvgIdAmbErr, 19⟩.

v.AvgIdAmbErr is the average percentage of ambulance identifications, in which the ambulance was identified as available, but in fact it was not. That is, this is the average proportion of erroneous identifications of available ambulances. Lower values are preferred so that there is crit.LowAvgIdAmbErr, which gives this strict preference over two assignments of v.AvgIdAmbErr

⟨IdAmb, v.AvgIdAmbErr, 0.04⟩ Pref.LowAvgIdAmbErr
⟨IdAmb, v.AvgIdAmbErr, 0.08⟩.

Both the above preferences are, each, over value assignments of values of one value type to one fragment.

There is also the value type v.AvgErrTrckAmb, which gives the percentage of errors when keeping track of ambulances manually, as in ManTrckAmb. There is the criterion crit.MinErrOvDecSup, which says that minimizing errors is preferred to giving more decision support to control assistants. Hence these two preferences, which are over value assignments of different value types, on different fragments are

⟨ManTrckAmb, v.AvgErrTrckAmb, 0.02⟩ Pref.MinErrOvDecSup
⟨AutoAmbList, v.Satisfaction, 1⟩, and
⟨ManTrckAmb, v.AvgErrTrckAmb, 0.02⟩ Pref.MinErrOvDecSup
⟨UpdAutoAmbList, v.Satisfaction, 1⟩.

Preferences, as in the examples above, suggest how to compare entire outcomes, depending on the value assignments in each. I consider this task in Sect. 14.5.

14.4 Finding Criteria

Fragments can include statements that suggest many preference relation instances. For example, suppose the stakeholders agree that they prefer lower to higher average times for ambulances to arrive at incidents, and that there is no lower limit to how short the average time can be. A stakeholder may say that she wants an ambulance to arrive as quickly as possible at an incident.

Statements such as "low incident response times," "less maintenance," and "low cost" have been studied in requirements engineering for several decades, and as non-functional requirements and critical for understanding and measuring system quality [16, 105].

I view these statements as suggesting criteria. For example, "ambulance quickly arrives at incident" gives a criterion, wherein if there are two alternatives in a model and they result in different values of a measure of how quickly ambulances arrive at incidents, then the one that gives a better value will be strictly preferred than the other on this criterion.

A statement such as "ambulance quickly arrives at incident" is not enough by itself to define a criterion. There should be a value type whose values measure how quickly ambulances arrive at incidents, and it is necessary to clarify what exactly these values measure.

The more general suggestion is to look for criteria in fragments that include gradable adjectives such as quick, slow, big, small, efficient, usable, easy to make, and so on. This is because such adjectives are applied presumably after comparison. Something is fast because it was compared to something else that seemed less fast. This also means that there is no universal threshold for a gradable adjective to truthfully apply always, everywhere, and in everyone's eyes. You may call car A fast because you are used to car B, which is not very fast. Another person may consider A as slow because she is used to car C, which is faster than A and so on.

Given a statement with a gradable adjective, such as "ambulance quickly arrives at incident," you can do the following.

1. In the model, identify the fragments such that value assignments on them can be characterized by the statement. These fragments will talk of things, situations, events, or otherwise and the value assignments will be assigning values that describe some properties of these things, situations, and events.

   For example, a fragment that says that an ambulance does or should arrive at an incident is about a process of the ambulance arriving at the incident.

2. Define a value type whose values can be used to describe some property of the situation, event, or object mentioned in fragments in the step above. The property should be such that the statement with the gradable adjective seems true for some of its values but not for all of them, and therefore, the value of that property can be used to compare different value assignments.

   Continuing the example, there can be a value type whose values describe the average time for an ambulance to arrive at an incident. If the statement with the gradable adjective is "ambulance quickly arrives at incident," then this statement will apply to some but not to all values of this value type. Perhaps 15 min average time for an ambulance to arrive at an incident is quick, but 30 min is not.

3. Make alternative value assignments of the value type defined above, and use the statement with the gradable adjective to define strict preferences over these value assignments.

   Continuing the example above, if there are two value assignments, 15 and 30 min, then there will necessarily be a strict preference for 15 min over that of 30 min.

Another way to understand the steps above, and using the terminology of the example, is that you are trying to a scale such that, when given any two different values on that scale, you or a stakeholder can say which of the two values describes ambulances arriving faster than the other. The solution in the example is to have a value type that gives the average time to arrive at an incident, so that when you have a value v and w of that value type, and $v \neq w$, then it is clear that if $v < w$ then v describes ambulances arriving faster than w.

I define crit.LowAvgIncArrTime below in such a way as to generate preference relation instances over value assignments when it is given a pair of v.AvgIncArrTime value assignments. The language module template for criteria is the same as for functions. The criterion takes a pair of value assignments and returns the preference relation over them. It works as a function. Nevertheless, I want to distinguish criteria from other kinds of functions, hence the dedicated template.

Criterion: LowAvgIncArrTime

Ambulance quickly arrives at incident

Input

A pair of value assignments

$$\langle x_1, \text{v.AvgIncArrTime}, v_1 \rangle, \text{ and}$$
$$\langle x_2, \text{v.AvgIncArrTime}, v_2 \rangle.$$

Do

Let v_i be the minimum and v_j the maximum in $\{v_1, v_2\}$.

Output

$$(\langle x_i, \text{v.AvgIncArrTime}, v_i \rangle, \langle x_j, \text{v.AvgIncArrTime}, v_j \rangle)$$
$$\in \text{vr.pref.LowAvgIncArrTime}.$$

Language services

- **s.WhLowAvgIncArrTime**: According to

  crit.LowAvgIncArrTime,

  which of the value assignments $\langle x_1, \text{v.AvgIncArrTime}, v_1 \rangle$
  and $\langle x_2, \text{v.AvgIncArrTime}, v_2 \rangle$ is strictly preferred to the other? : The one strictly preferred according to the output of this module.

You can define a more general criterion to use with value assignments where value types are real numbers, and the lowest or highest values are the most desirable. This criterion is given below.

Criterion: d.t

Prefer higher (or lower) v.t values

Input

- A value type t,
- a parameter d, which is either $d = low$ or $d = high$, and
- a pair of value assignments $\langle x_1, \text{v.t}, v_1 \rangle$ and $\langle x_2, \text{v.t}, v_2 \rangle$, such that v.t takes real values.

Do

Let v_i be the minimum and v_j the maximum in $\{v_1, v_2\}$, and

- if $d = Low$, then $w = (\langle x_i, \text{v.t}, v_i \rangle, \langle x_j, \text{v.t}, v_j \rangle) \in \text{vr.pref.d.t}$,
- if $d = High$, then $w = (\langle x_j, \text{v.t}, v_j \rangle, \langle x_i, \text{v.t}, v_i \rangle) \in \text{vr.pref.d.t}$.

Output

w.

Language services

- **s.WhPref.d.t**: According to crit.d.t, which of the value assignments $\langle x_1, t, v_1 \rangle$ and $\langle x_2, t, v_2 \rangle$ is strictly preferred to the other? : The one strictly preferred according to w which this module outputs.

If a model has no criteria that generate preference relations, then all individual preferences in the model need to come from some other approach to preference elicitation. Otherwise, if you have criteria that do generate preference relation instances, and there are value assignments which these criteria apply to, then you can automatically add preference relation instances.

Criteria can reflect more complicated preferences than crit.d.t. The following example is an illustration. It defines a criterion that is remotely related to a classical proposal in the field of multiple-criteria decision analysis.

Example 14.1 Suppose there is a value type v.ImplCost, and that you assign its values to fragments to indicate an estimate of the cost to implement what the fragment describes.

Moreover, suppose you have elicited the following statement, or concluded this from having elicited some other information from stakeholders: "The lowest implementation cost alternative is the best, unless it is not less than 20 % cheaper than the next lowest cost alternative, in which case the latter is better than the former."

This is inspired by the so-called Type V criterion in the PROMETHEE approach to multiple-criteria decision analysis [19], where the individual is assumed to be indifferent to value assignments until the difference between them reaches a certain value. Here, I adapt this idea to there being no indifference relation, and consider that there is a strict preference until the difference between the two assigned values goes above a threshold, which is some given percentage of the higher value. If the value goes above the threshold then the strict preference reverses. The following criterion captures these ideas.

Criterion: low.rev.h

Prefer lower of two v.t values, until their difference is more than h% of the higher

---

Input

- v.t, which must be a subset of real numbers,
- a percentage value $h\%$, and
- a pair of value assignments $\langle x_1, \text{v.t}, v_1\rangle$ and $\langle x_2, \text{v.t}, v_2\rangle$.

Do

Let v_i be the minimum and v_j the maximum in $\{v_1, v_2\}$ and if $|v_i - v_j|/v_j > h/100$, then

$$w = (\langle x_i, \text{v.t}, v_i\rangle, \langle x_j, \text{v.t}, v_j\rangle) \in \text{vr.pref.rev.d.t, else}$$
$$w = (\langle x_j, \text{v.t}, v_j\rangle, \langle x_i, \text{v.t}, v_i\rangle) \in \text{vr.pref.rev.d.t.}$$

Output

w.

Language services

- **s.WhPref.low.rev.h**: According to crit.low.rev.h, which of the value assignments $\langle x_1, \text{v.t}, v_1\rangle$ and $\langle x_2, \text{v.t}, v_2\rangle$ is strictly preferred to the other? : The one strictly preferred according to w which this module outputs.

•

The more general point is that preference relation instances can be automatically added to a model in case you have defined a criterion that suggests such preferences. There are many proposals for generic criteria that can be used in this way, especially in the field of multiple-criteria decision analysis [47, 100, 154]. The issue that remains unsolved is how to make sure that the criteria do correspond to stakeholders' preferences, an issue to be solved via elicitation, validation, and negotiation, rather than, unfortunately, language modules.

14.5 Better and Best Outcomes

Given a model that includes criteria and preference relation instances over fragments, how would you deliver the following language services?

- **s.BestOutcome**: Which is the best complete outcome of M?
- **s.BetterOutcome**: Which of the two outcomes o_i and o_j is better in model M?

Both are problems of preference aggregation, that is, of taking preference relation instances over value assignments in a model and deciding how to use them together in order to compare complete outcomes. Preference aggregation is a topic studied in various domains, including, for example, artificial intelligence [18], formal logic [110], multi-criteria decision making [47], and social choice [103].

I choose one approach to preference aggregation from artificial intelligence. Given a model M with value assignments, preference relations, and criteria, I want to deliver s.BestOutcome and s.BetterOutcome by mapping the value assignments and preferences to a Conditional Preference Network, CP-Net hereafter [18]. The language services s.BestOutcome and s.BetterOutcome are delivered by applying known algorithms to the resulting CP-net.

To reduce the number of preference relation instances that need to be elicited, CP-nets use the *conditional preference relation*.

A conditional preference is a pair (a, p), where p is a preference relation instance and $a = \langle x, \text{v.t}, v \rangle$ is a value assignment. The idea is that if the outcome includes a, then the preference p should be taken into account when computing answers to s.BestOutcome and s.BetterOutcome.

In order to map models to CP-nets, it should be possible to represent conditional preferences in models. This is done with the relation vr.pref.cond below.

Relation: pref.cond

Conditional preference

Domain & Dimension

r.pref.cond $\subseteq$ **V** $\times$ **P**, where **V** is a set of value assignments, and **P** is a set of vr.pref instances.

Properties

If the preference $p \in P$ should be taken into account when comparing outcomes, all of which include $\langle x, \text{v.t}, v \rangle$, then let

$$(\langle x, \text{v.t}, v \rangle, p) \in \text{vr.pref.cond}.$$

Reading

$(\langle x, \text{v.t}, v \rangle, p) \in \text{vr.pref.cond}$ reads "use the preference relation p when comparing outcomes, only if all these outcomes s include $\langle x, t, v \rangle$."

Language services

- **s.IsCondPref**: Should the preference p be used to compare outcomes in the set O? : Yes, if there is $(\langle x, \text{v.t}, v \rangle, p) \in \text{vr.pref.cond}$ and all outcomes in O include $\langle x, t, v \rangle$.

To illustrate how to make CP-nets from a model, I define below the language called L.Elnath, by adding vr.pref.cond to L.Bellartrix, and allowing manual assignment of binary v.Approval values on fragments.

Language: Elnath

Language modules
r.inf.pos, r.inf.neg, f.map.abrel.g, f.cat.ksr, vr.alt.b, vr.pref.c,
vr.pref.cond, f.sat.inf.pos, f.sat.inf.neg, f.sat.alt.b, f.sat.leaf,
f.imp.asm

Domain

- The domain is made of a set of fragments **F**, nonconditional relation instances **R** with a special subset **P** of preference relation instances, conditional relation instances **cP**, value types **T**, value assignments **V**, criteria **C** and real numbers $\mathbb{R}$.
- Fragments have three partitions, namely requirements, domain knowledge, and specification fragments, $\mathbf{F} = \text{c.r} \cup \text{c.k} \cup \text{c.s}$, and $\text{c.r} \cap \text{c.k} \cap \text{c.s} = \emptyset$.
- Relation instances are over fragments or value assignments, $\mathbf{R} = (\mathbf{F} \times \mathbf{F}) \cup (\mathbf{V} \times \mathbf{V})$, and are partitioned as follows:

$$\mathbf{R} = \text{r.inf.pos} \cup \text{r.inf.neg} \cup \text{vr.alt.b} \cup \mathbf{P},$$
$$\emptyset = \text{r.inf.pos} \cap \text{r.inf.neg} \cap \text{vr.alt.b} \cap \mathbf{P},$$

where

$$\mathbf{P} = \bigcup_{\text{crit.c} \in \mathbf{C}} \text{vr.pref.c},$$

influences are over fragments, $\text{r.inf.pos} \subseteq \mathbf{F} \times \mathbf{F}$, $\text{r.inf.neg} \subseteq \mathbf{F} \times \mathbf{F}$, while mutual exclusion and nonconditional preferences are over value assignments $\text{vr.alt.b} \cup \mathbf{P} \subseteq \mathbf{V} \times \mathbf{V}$.

- Conditional preference relation instances are over value assignments and nonconditional preference relation instances in **P**,

$$\mathbf{cP} = \text{vr.pref.cond},$$
$$\text{vr.pref.cond} \subseteq \mathbf{V} \times \mathbf{P}.$$

- Value types are

$$\mathbf{T} = \{\text{v.Satisfaction, v.Importance, v.Approval}\} \cup \bigcup_{q=1}^{n>1} \text{v.q}.$$

v.Satisfaction, v.Importance and v.Approval are binary. Satisfaction value 1 reads "satisfied" and 0 "not satisfied." Importance value 1 reads "mandatory," 0 "not mandatory." Approval value 1 reads "approved" and 0 reads "not approved." Each of the $q = 1, \ldots, n$ value types v.q is the set of positive reals.

- Value assignments are ternary relations over fragments or relation instances, value types, and values of value types:

$$\mathbf{V} \subseteq (\mathbf{F} \cup \mathbf{R}) \times \mathbf{T} \times \bigcup_{\text{v.t} \in \mathbf{T}} \text{v.t}.$$

and has the following three partitions:

$$(\mathbf{F} \cup \mathbf{R}) \times \{\text{v.Satisfaction}\} \times \{1, 0\},$$
$$\mathbf{F} \times \{\text{v.Importance}\} \times \{1, 0\}, \text{ and}$$
$$\mathbf{F} \times \bigcup_{q=1}^{n>1} \text{v.q} \times \mathbb{R}^+.$$

Satisfaction values can be assigned to fragments and relation instances, while values of all other value types can be assigned only to fragments.

Syntax

A model M in the language is a set of symbols $M = \{Z_1, \ldots, Z_n\}$, where every ϕ is generated according to the following BNF rules:

$$A ::= x \mid y \mid z \mid \ldots$$
$$B ::= r(A) \mid k(A) \mid s(A)$$
$$C ::= B \text{ influences+ } B$$
$$D ::= B \text{ influences− } B$$
$$G ::= \langle A, E, F \rangle$$

$$H ::= G \text{ alternativeTo } G$$
$$I ::= G \text{ Pref.} J \ G$$
$$J ::= c_1 \mid c_2 \mid \ldots$$
$$K ::= G \text{ CondFor } I$$
$$Z ::= B \mid C \mid D \mid G \mid H \mid I \mid K$$

Mapping

Symbols map to domain elements as follows:

- A symbols denote fragments, $\mathscr{D}(A) \in \mathbf{F}$.
- B symbols are used to distinguish requirements, domain knowledge, and specification fragments, so that $\mathscr{D}(r(\alpha)) \in$ c.r, $\mathscr{D}(k(\alpha)) \in$ c.k, $\mathscr{D}(s(\alpha)) \in$ c.s.
- C and D symbols denote, respectively, positive and negative influence relations.
- E symbols denote value types, $\mathscr{D}(E) \in \mathbf{T}$.
- F symbols denote a value of a value type, and as there is one value type, $\mathscr{D}(F) \in$ v.Satisfaction.
- G symbols denote value assignments, $\mathscr{D}(G) \in \mathbf{V}$.

- H symbols denote alternatives, $\mathscr{D}(H) \in$ vr.alt.b.
- I symbols denote instances of preference relations, one per criterion c,

$$\mathscr{D}(I) \in \bigcup_{\text{crit.c} \in \mathbf{C}} \text{vr.pref.c.}$$

- J symbols denote criteria, $\mathscr{D}(J) \in \mathbf{C}$.
- K symbols denote conditional preference relation instances,

$$\mathscr{D}(K) \in \text{vr.pref.cond.}$$

Language services

Those of relations and functions in the language.

Given a model M in L.Elnath, I need the following tuple from it:

$$(\mathbf{Vars}(M), \mathbf{V}, \text{vr.pref}, \text{vr.pref.cond})$$

where $\mathbf{Vars}(M)$ is the set of all variables in the model, $\mathbf{V}$ is a set of value assignments, and

$$\text{vr.pref.c} \subseteq \mathbf{V} \times \mathbf{V},$$
$$\text{vr.pref.cond} \subseteq \mathbf{V} \times \bigcup_{\text{crit.c} \in \mathbf{C}} \text{vr.pref.c.}$$

The following function takes the tuple above, and makes a CP-net from it.

Function: make.CPNet

Make a CPNet

Input

$(\mathbf{Vars}(M), \mathbf{V}, \text{vr.pref}, \text{vr.pref.cond})$.

Do

1. Let $\mathbf{G}(M)$ be a graph, in which $\mathbf{Vars}(M)$ is the set of nodes, and every node $x.t \in \mathbf{Vars}(M)$ is annotated with a so-called Conditional Preference Table (CPT), denoted $CPT(x.\text{v.t})$, where $x.\text{v.t}$ is the variable from $\mathbf{Vars}(M)$.

2. For every variable x.v.t $\in$ **Vars**(M), find all preference instances over that variable, let that set be $P(x$.v.t$)$ and find all conditional preferences to members of $P(x$.v.t$)$, and let that set be $C_P(x$.v.t$)$.
3. For every variable x.v.t $\in$ **Vars**(M), define its $CPT(x$.v.t$)$ by adding every preference $(\langle x, \text{v.t}, v_i \rangle, \langle x, \text{v.t}, v_j \rangle) \in P(x.t)$ and member of $C_P(x$.v.t$)$ to the relevant $CPT(x$.v.t$)$.
4. For each variable x.v.t $\in$ **Vars**(M), if its $CPT(x$.v.t$)$ is not complete, then elicit or otherwise find the missing preferences and vr.pref.cond instances, and add them to $CPT(x$.v.t$)$.

Output

The CP-Net $\mathbf{G}(M)$.

Language services

- s.BestOutcome: The best outcome is the outcome returned by an outcome optimization query [18] on the CP-net $\mathbf{G}(M)$.
- s.BetterOutcome: The better outcome is the one returned by a dominance query [18] on the CP-net $\mathbf{G}(M)$.

Figure 14.3 shows a model in L.Elnath. There are no value assignments in the figure. Each fragment in the figure is annotated with two preference relation instances. One gives the preference over satisfaction values, while the other is over approval values for that fragment.

There are four conditional preference relations in the figure. Two of them indicate that preference over satisfaction values of ChkDblLoc depends on the satisfaction value of IncCalRep. The other two say that preference over satisfaction values of DispSoftwChkDbl depends on the satisfaction value of ChkDblLoc.

Given these conditional preferences and all other preferences in the figure, what is the best complete outcome? That is, what are the best assignments of values to all fragments and relation instances in that model?

To answer this, the first step is to make a CP-net so as to find the best value assignmentto the fragments whose satisfaction values involve conditional preferences. The resulting CP-net is shown in Fig. 14.4. Next, running an outcome optimization query on the CP-net in Fig. 14.4 will result in the graph in Fig. 14.5, where each edge runs from a better to a worse combination of value assignments. The graph shows that the best combination assigns the satisfaction value 0 to IncCalRep, ChkDblLoc, and DispSoftwChkDbl.

While Fig. 14.5 does show the best combination of satisfaction values over three fragments, the best outcome will not necessarily include the best combination. The reason is that you still need to assign satisfaction and approval values to all other fragments and relation instances in the model, and in doing that, you need to take care about how satisfaction values propagate via f.sat.inf.pos, f.sat.inf.neg, f.sat, and f.sat.leaf.

The best approval outcome is easy to find. As the approval value of a fragmentor relation instance is independent of other assignments of approval values in the model, you can assign the preferred approval value to every fragment and relation instance. To keep the figures simple, I assume that the preferred approval value for every influence relation is 1. The best approval outcome is shown in Fig. 14.6.

Figure 14.7 shows an outcome that includes the best combination of satisfaction values of IncCalRep, ChkDblLoc, and DispSoftwChkDbl and the best assignment of satisfaction values to other fragments, which still satisfies propagation rules in f.sat.inf.pos, f.sat.inf.neg, f.sat, and f.sat.leaf. The obvious problem with the outcome is that AddRepEm is not satisfied.

You can repair AddRepEm by choosing an outcome that ignores the conditional relations. This outcome is shown in Fig. 14.8 where the red circles highlight the differences from the satisfaction values in Fig. 14.7. Another approach is to change the conditional preferences on DispSoftwChkDbl so that they are conditional on the satisfaction value of AddRepEm, rather than ChkDblLoc. Also, you could change the influence relations by removing the one from ChkDblLoc to AddRepEm.

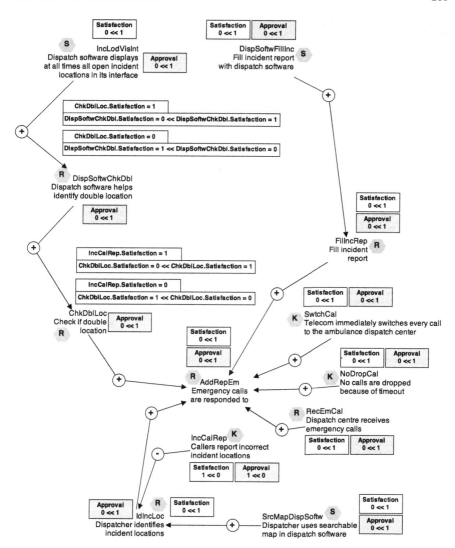

Fig. 14.3 Model in L.Elnath, with no value assignments

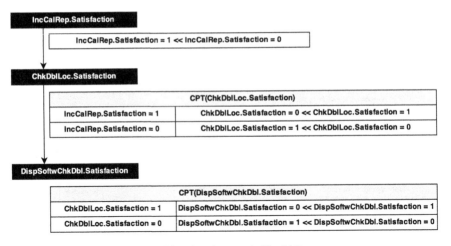

Fig. 14.4 CP-Net made from conditional preferences in Fig. 14.3

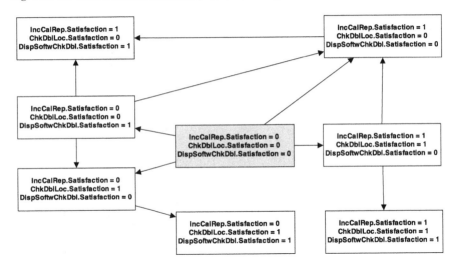

Fig. 14.5   Preference graph from the CP-net in Fig. 14.4

14.6 Summary on Preferences

I introduced binary preference relations, illustrated how to add them to languages and represent them in models, and finally, how to map models to CP-nets in order to use conditional preferences to find the best outcomes. Many open questions remain outside the scope of this book:

- How to represent that preferences are conflicting, that is, improvement over one leads to a decrease over another.

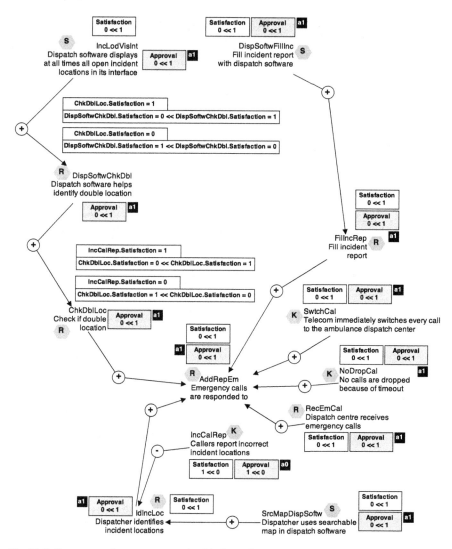

Fig. 14.6 Best approval outcome, assuming 1 is the preferred approval value on all relation instances

- How to represent acceptable tradeoffs between preferences, which are the allowed improvements over one preference and the acceptable decreases over others, which are in conflict with the first.
- How to use tradeoffs when searching for the best outcome

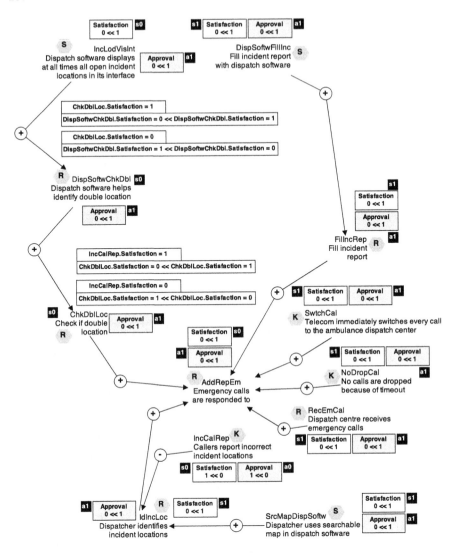

Fig. 14.7 Best outcome according to conditional preferences

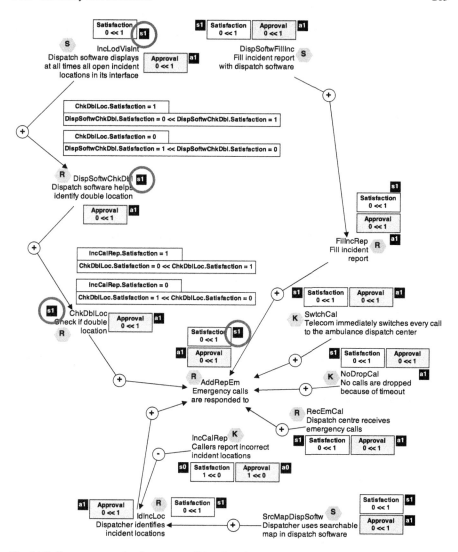

Fig. 14.8 Best outcome that ignores conditional preferences

Chapter 15
Links to Formal Logic

This chapter deals with how to relate languages in this book to formal logics. The convention in the chapter is that a formal theory, or simply a theory, is a name for a set of formulas with no free variables in some formal logic. So how can you map (parts of) models to theories, and why should we do so? Relationships between requirements modeling languages and formal logics are a recurrent topic in requirements engineering. In KAOS, theories in linear temporal first-order logic are themselves parts of models. The same in Tropos. The motivation is that you can take a model in a requirements modeling language and map (parts of) it to a theory in some formal logic, in order to answer questions that your requirements modeling language could not. I will look at two among many topics on the relationships between requirements modeling languages and formal logics. I restrict the discussion to one formal logic, namely classical propositional logic (CPL), and discuss the following.

1. How to map a model to a CPL theory, if every fragment equates to an atomic proposition. (Sect. 15.2)
2. How to map a model to CPL theory if every fragment maps to a conjunction of formulas of CPL. (Sect. 15.3)
3. What can be the risks of mapping models to theories. (Sect. 15.4)

15.1 Motivation

The overall aim of mapping models to theories is to deliver language services that the requirements modeling language could not deliver by itself. For example, I had no notion of consistency or inconsistency in languages that I introduced so far. To check if a model (part) is consistent, I need to have a notion of consistency in the language, that is, define the conditions that a model has to satisfy in order to be consistent. I can do this independently of any existing notion of consistency in another language, or a formal logic. Or, I can map my models to theories of a formal logic and consider my models as consistent in my language if the corresponding theories are consistent in

© Springer International Publishing Switzerland 2015
I. Jureta, *The Design of Requirements Modelling Languages*,
DOI 10.1007/978-3-319-18821-8_15

the formal logic. That is, I borrow a notion of consistency from an existing language or logic.

To be more concrete, recall that many languages defined so far can distinguish between fragments that are requirements, domain knowledge, or specifications. To represent instances of the DRP, a language also needs to be able to check if requirements, domain knowledge, and the specification are consistent and there is a proof of all requirements from the domain knowledge and the specification. This is summarized in the following language service.

Language service: DRPSol

Given a model M, which includes an instance P of DRP, is the part S of that model a solution to the problem instance?

---

s.DRPSol requires two capabilities, one related to proving requirements from domain knowledge and specifications, the other proving the absence of inconsistency. To avoid confusion about these, *Provability Condition* abbreviates hereafter the first condition in the DRP, and *Consistency Condition* the second condition.

To enable a language to deliver s.DRPSol, you need to define rules for constructing proofs, and in relation to these rules defining when inconsistency is the result of a proof.

A cautious approach to delivering s.DRPSol is to map the content of a requirements model to formulae in a formal logic, where the notions of proof and inconsistency are already well-defined. The clear benefit is that you are freed from the burden of inventing a new set of proof rules and justifying them. The risk is that you may be adopting the conventions of the formal logic, and they may be clashing with the conventions in the language you use. I return to this issue in Sect. 15.3.

The cautious approach has the effect that you do not need to add *new* relations to models. In other words, you will still be saying the same with your models, and you will use logic *only* to deliver s.DRPSol. The other way could have involved adding new relations to the language *because* of the ability of the formal logic to state such relations. In brief, I focus on mapping models to formulae of logic, and not the other way round. For the sake of simplicity, I will be mapping models to CPL theories [121].[1]

---

[1]Since I want to have a language that represents instances of the DRP, and not some other class of problems, a disclaimer is in order: The syntactic consequence relation in classical propositional logic is usually denoted ⊢, and this at least visually resembles the relation in DRP. I do not know exactly *which* logic the DRP takes that relation from, as the accompanying paper [153] does not say. I take classical propositional logic to be a conservative choice.

15.2 Models to Theories, Approach One

Suppose I have a model in a language that can represent fragments and positive and negative influence relations over fragments. As I am interested in the DRP, the language should also categorize all fragments into requirements, domain knowledge, and specifications. A simple language that has this is L.Rigel. Recall that L.Rigel also has v.Satisfaction and functions that propagate these values over relation instances and fragments.

Consider what you need to add to L.Rigel in order to map its models to propositional logic theories? Can the same model be mapped to different theories? If yes, then why would you map it to one of these theories and not another?

I start with the convention that the formal theory should have exactly one atomic proposition per fragment in a model. So a fragment is not rewritten into a sentence of CPL, but maps to an atomic proposition of CPL.

I will map positive influences to an implication from a conjunction, and negative influences to an implication to inconsistency. This is inspired by Techne. The following function does it.

Function: map.infl.impl

Map positive influences to implications, negative influences to inconsistency

---

Input

Model M.

Do

1. Let Δ be an empty set.
2. For every fragment x in M:

   a. Let $\{(p_1, x), \ldots, (p_n, x)\}$ be the set of all positive influences to x in M.

   b. Let $\{(q_1, x), \ldots, (q_m, x)\}$ be the set of all negative influences to x in M.

   c. Add the following sentences to Δ:

$$p_1 \wedge \ldots \wedge p_n \rightarrow x,$$
$$q_1 \wedge \ldots \wedge q_m \wedge x \rightarrow \bot.$$

Output

Set Δ of propositional logic sentences.

Language services

- **s.WhCPLTh**: What CPL theory corresponds to positive and negative influences over fragments in M? : Δ.

---

f.map.infl.impl sees positive influences as implications, because that roughly corresponds to the idea that if $p_1, \ldots, p_n$ are satisfied, then so should x. In contrast, it sees negative influences as logical inconsistencies, so that if $q_1, \ldots, q_m$ negatively influence x, then there can be no consistent model that includes all of them. Negative influences in this approach should not be tolerated in solutions.

If you add f.map.impl.infl to L.Rigel you have a language that can deliver s.DRPSol. It is called L.Sirius and is defined below. Delivering it involves finding in a model an instance of the Default problem and then being able to check if a submodel is a solution, that is, it satisfies the Provability Condition and the Consistency Condition.

The convention is that a model M' in some language is a submodel of a model M in the same, or another language, if M' can be obtained by only removing fragments and/or relation instances from M.

Language: Sirius

Language modules
r.inf.pos, r.inf.neg, f.map.abrel.g, f.cat.ksr, f.sat.inf.pos, f.sat.inf.neg, f.sat, f.sat.leaf, f.map.infl.impl

---

Domain

There is a set of fragments **F**, a singleton for value types

$$\mathbf{T} = \{\text{v.Satisfaction}\},$$

and a set of value assignments **V**. fragments have three partitions, namely requirements, domain knowledge, and specification fragments, $\mathbf{F} = \text{c.r} \cup \text{c.k} \cup \text{c.s}$ and $\text{c.r} \cap \text{c.k} \cap \text{c.s} = \emptyset$. Influences are over fragments, $\text{r.inf.pos} \subseteq \mathbf{F} \times \mathbf{F}$, $\text{r.inf.neg} \subseteq \mathbf{F} \times \mathbf{F}$. Value assignments are over fragments or relation instances, involve a value type, and a value, so that

$$\mathbf{V} \subseteq (\mathbf{F} \cup \text{r.inf.pos} \cup \text{r.inf.neg}) \times \mathbf{T} \times \text{v.Satisfaction.}$$

Satisfaction is binary, v.Satisfaction $= \{1, 0\}$.

Syntax

A model M in the language is a set of symbols $M = \{Z_1, \ldots, Z_n\}$, where every ϕ is generated according to the following BNF rules:

$$
\begin{aligned}
A &::= x \mid y \mid z \mid \ldots \\
B &::= r(A) \mid k(A) \mid s(A) \\
C &::= B \text{ influences+ } B \\
D &::= B \text{ influences- } B \\
G &::= \langle A, E, F \rangle \\
Z &::= B \mid C \mid D \mid G
\end{aligned}
$$

Mapping

A symbols denote fragments, $\mathscr{D}(A) \in \mathbf{F}$. B symbols are used to distinguish requirements, domain knowledge, and specification fragments, so that $\mathscr{D}(r(\alpha)) \in \text{c.r}$, $\mathscr{D}(k(\alpha)) \in \text{c.k}$, $\mathscr{D}(s(\alpha)) \in \text{c.s}$. C and D symbols denote, respectively, positive and negative influence relations. E symbols denote value types, $\mathscr{D}(E) \in \mathbf{T}$. F symbols denote a value of a value type, and as there is one value type, $\mathscr{D}(F) \in \text{v.Satisfaction}$. G symbols denote value assignments, $\mathscr{D}(G) \in \mathbf{V}$.

Language services

Those of relations and functions in the language, and
- s.DRPSol: Yes, S is the solution to the Default problem instance defined by the submodel P, if the following conditions are satisfied:

1. P and S are submodels of M,
2. If $\mathbf{F}_{\text{c.k}}$ is the set of atomic CPL propositions, one per domain knowledge fragment in M, $\mathbf{F}_{\text{c.s}}$ the set of atomic CPL propositions, one per specification fragment in M, $\mathbf{F}_{\text{c.r}}$ the set of atomic CPL propositions, one per requirement fragment in M and Δ the set of CPL sentences produced by applying f.map.imfl.impl to M, then
   a. $\mathbf{F}_{\text{c.k}}, \mathbf{F}_{\text{c.s}}, \Delta \vdash \mathbf{F}_{\text{c.r}}$, that is, the Provability Condition is satisfied,
   b. $\mathbf{F}_{\text{c.k}}, \mathbf{F}_{\text{c.s}}, \Delta \nvdash \bot$, that is, the Consistency Condition is satisfied,
3. S includes all fragments denoted by the atomic propositions in $\mathbf{F}_{\text{c.s}}$, and
4. P includes all fragments denoted by the atomic propositions in $\mathbf{F}_{\text{c.k}} \cup \mathbf{F}_{\text{c.r}}$.

Finding a default problem instance in a model in L.Rigel is simple. If the model has a set of requirements fragments and domain knowledge fragments, then it includes a default problem instance. There was no need for f.map.impl.infl to do this.

Recall that the Provability Condition consists of showing that $K, S \vdash R$. Let K be the set of all domain knowledge fragments in M, S of specification fragments, and R of requirements. You then need to have an atomic proposition for each fragment, so let $\mathbf{F}_{c.k}$ be the set of atomic CPL propositions, one per domain knowledge fragment in M, $\mathbf{F}_{c.s}$ the set of atomic CPL propositions, one per specification fragment in M, $\mathbf{F}_{c.r}$ the set of atomic CPL propositions, one per requirement fragment in M.

None of these sets includes influence relations, and it follows, cannot include Δ, the implications which correspond to the positive and negative influences in M. The revised Provability Condition is then to show that

$$\mathbf{F}_{c.k}, \mathbf{F}_{c.s}, \Delta \vdash \mathbf{F}_{c.r}.$$

The Consistency Condition becomes

$$\mathbf{F}_{c.k}, \mathbf{F}_{c.s}, \Delta \nvdash \bot.$$

In summary, if M gives the sets R, K, and S of propositions, and via f.map.infl.impl the set of implications Δ, and if it can be shown that the above two conditions are satisfied, then S is the solution to the Default problem in M.

Note that M may include other fragments and relations, but if only f.map.infl.impl is used, then M will be logically inconsistent if $F, \Delta \vdash \bot$, where F are all the fragments in M. It follows that M may be inconsistent, all the while $K, S, \Delta \vdash R$ and $K, S, \Delta \nvdash \bot$.

Suppose you are given the following CPL formulas:

$\mathbf{F}_{c.k} = \{$ SwtchCal, NoDropCal $\}$

$\mathbf{F}_{c.s} = \{$ SrcMap, IncLocVisSw, UpdOpIncLoc, FilSwIncRep $\}$

$\mathbf{F}_{c.r} = \{$ AddRepEm $\}$

$\Delta = \{$ FilIncRep $\wedge$ ChkDblLoc $\wedge$ IdIncLoc $\wedge$ RecEmCal
$\qquad \wedge$NoDropCal $\wedge$ SwtchCal $\rightarrow$ AddRepEm,
$\qquad$ SwtchCal $\wedge$ NoDropCal $\rightarrow$ RecEmCal,
$\qquad$ SrcMap $\rightarrow$ IdIncLoc,
$\qquad$ UpdOpIncLoc $\wedge$ IncLocVisSw $\rightarrow$ SwIdDuplCal,
$\qquad$ SwIdDuplCal $\rightarrow$ ChkDblLoc,
$\qquad$ FillSwIncRep $\rightarrow$ FillIncRep $\}$.

What fragments and relations are in a model M, if it is a model in L.Sirius, and which includes only the fragments that correspond to atomic propositions in $\mathbf{F}_{c.k}$, $\mathbf{F}_{c.s}$, and $\mathbf{F}_{c.r}$ above, and has influences which mapped to those in Δ above, via f.map.inf.impl?

Is there a default problem instance in M? Is S given above a solution to the Default problem instance in M? I leave this to you.

15.3 Models to Theories, Approach Two

Instead of mapping each fragment an atomic proposition, what would happen if you mapped a fragment to a CPL sentence?

Suppose, then, there is a function that takes a fragment and returns a sentence. Call it f.map.f.sntc. I have no suggestions on how to define this function other than that the modeler takes a fragment and writes a CPL sentence that best corresponds to the information in the fragment.

The effect of having f.map.f.sntc is that R, K, and S are now sets of sentences. You still need to map relations to sentences, and f.map.inf.impl can still be used, with the change that implications are now not necessarily only over atomic propositions, but over atomic propositions and/or sentences.

Changes to the problem are the same as in Sect. 15.2. Provability Condition is $K, S, \Delta \vdash R$ and the Consistency Condition is $K, S, \Delta \nvdash \bot$.

This has an effect on the complexity of checking the two conditions. The check could be done in linear time when the outputs are atomic propositions and implications in Sect. 15.2, since that output amounts to a set of propositional Horn clauses [43].

15.4 Risks of Mapping to Formal Theories

Suppose you have L.Rigel and f.map.inf.impl, and you map fragments to atomic propositions of CPL, as in Sect. 15.2.

Let x be a fragment, and an atomic proposition which is a requirement in a model M. You might want to check if

$$K, \Delta \vdash x,$$

and if yes, conclude that the requirement x is satisfied by the domain knowledge. More generally, you may want to check if $M' \vdash x$, where M' is the mapping of the model M to atomic propositions and implications.

There is nothing problematic with wanting to do this, but it can be misleading. The syntactic consequence relation $\vdash$ in CPL is reflexive, meaning that if $x \in M'$, then also $M' \vdash x$. So even if there are no implications from domain knowledge and specifications to x, and thus, no clear idea of how to satisfy the requirement x with M, it is the case that $M' \vdash x$. The danger is to conclude that x is a satisfied requirement according to M' and, therefore, M says how to satisfy x. This is incorrect.

A similarly misleading case is if $M' \vdash \bot$. When M' is inconsistent, then any atomic proposition and sentence is its conclusion in CPL. So any y, whether it is in

M or not, is such that $M' \vdash y$. If you were reading $M' \vdash x$ as indicating that M says how to satisfy the requirement x, then you would conclude anytime you have an inconsistent M', regardless of there being x in it, or not, or there being domain knowledge and specifications in M which say how to satisfy x.

The odd cases above happen not because there is a problem with the formal logic or with the requirements modeling language, but with the rules about how the two are related. For example, if M' can be inconsistent then it might be interesting to use a paraconsistent logic rather than CPL, to check if there is proof of x from M'. In short, the choice of a formal logic to map models to depends on exactly what you want to use this logic for, which consequently helps choose that formal logic.

15.5 Summary on Formal Theories

This section briefly mentioned several topics on how models in requirements modeling languages relate to theories in formal logics. The central idea and motivation is that (parts of) models can be mapped to theories of formal logic. It should then be possible to check properties of these theories, such as consistency, to draw conclusions that help change the original models. I leave many other questions outside the scope of this book:

- How does valuation in a language influence the choice of a formal logic to map its models to?
- Which properties of a language influence one's decision on what to map fragments and relations to, in a formal logic?
- When models can map to inconsistent theories, then which paraconsistent logic to map the models to, in order to do reasoning without repairing consistency first?

References

For the reader's convenience, the index includes the most important Language Modules, Language Services, and Requirements Modeling Languages, in order to help finding them quickly.

1. J.-R. Abrial, *The B-Book: Assigning Programs to Meanings* (Cambridge University Press, Cambridge, 2005)
2. A.V. Aho, M.R. Garey, J.D. Ullman, The transitive reduction of a directed graph. SIAM J. Comput. **1**(2), 131–137 (1972)
3. Anonymous. Report of the Inquiry Into The London Ambulance Service. Technical report, The Communications Directorate, South West Thames Regional Authority, 1993
4. C. Anumba, J.M. Kamara, A.-F. Cutting-Decelle, *Concurrent Engineering in Construction Projects* (Routledge, London, 2006)
5. K.J. Arrow, A. Sen, K. Suzumura, *Handbook of Social Choice and Welfare*, vol. 2 (Elsevier, Amsterdam, 2010)
6. F. Bacchus, A. Grove, Graphical models for preference and utility, in *Proceedings of the Eleventh Conference on Uncertainty in Artificial Intelligence* (Morgan Kaufmann Publishers Inc., San Francisco, 1995), pp. 3–10
7. J. Bang-Jensen, G. Gutin, *Digraphs: Theory, Algorithms and Applications* (Springer, Berlin, 2002)
8. H. Bekić, D. Bjørner, W. Henhapl, C.B. Jones, P. Lucas, A formal definition of a Pl/I subset, in *Programming Languages and Their Definition* (Springer, New York, 1984), pp. 107–155
9. T.J.M. Bench-Capon, P.E. Dunne, Argumentation in artificial intelligence. Artif. Intell. **171**(10), 619–641 (2007)
10. W.L. Benoit, D. Hample, *Readings in Argumentation*, vol. 11 (Walter de Gruyter, Netherlands, 1992)
11. P. Berander, A. Andrews, Requirements prioritization, in *Engineering and Managing Software Requirements* (Springer, Berlin, 2005), pp. 69–94
12. P. Beynon-Davies, Human error and information systems failure: the case of the London ambulance service computer-aided despatch system project. Interact. Comput. **11**(6), 699–720 (1999)
13. B. Boehm, P. Bose, E. Horowitz, M.J. Lee, Software requirements negotiation and renegotiation aids: a theory-w based spiral approach, in *17th International Conference on Software Engineering (ICSE)* (IEEE, 1995), pp. 243–243
14. B.W. Boehm, Software engineering economics. IEEE Trans. Softw. Eng. **10**(1), 4–21 (1984)
15. B.W. Boehm, A spiral model of software development and enhancement. Computer **21**(5), 61–72 (1988)

© Springer International Publishing Switzerland 2015

I. Jureta, *The Design of Requirements Modelling Languages*,

DOI 10.1007/978-3-319-18821-8

275

16. B.W. Boehm, J.R. Brown, M. Lipow, Quantitative evaluation of software quality, in *Proceedings of the 2nd International Conference on Software Engineering* (IEEE Computer Society Press, Los Alamitos, 1976), pp. 592–605

17. B.W. Boehm, R. Madachy, B. Steece, et al., *Software Cost Estimation with Cocomo II* (Prentice Hall PTR, Upper Saddle River, 2000)

18. C. Boutilier, R.I. Brafman, C. Domshlak, H.H. Hoos, D. Poole, CP-nets: a tool for representing and reasoning with conditional ceteris paribus preference statements. J. Artif. Intell. Res. (JAIR) **21**, 135–191 (2004)

19. J.-P. Brans, Ph. Vincke, Note: a preference ranking organisation method: (the promethee method for multiple criteria decision-making). Manag. Sci. **31**(6), 647–656 (1985)

20. Y. Brun, G. Di Marzo Serugendo, C. Gacek, H. Giese, H. Kienle, M. Litoiu, H. Müller, M. Pezzè, M. Shaw, Engineering self-adaptive systems through feedback loops, in *Software Engineering for Self-Adaptive Systems* (Springer, Berlin, 2009), pp. 48–70

21. R.E. Caflisch, Monte carlo and quasi-Monte Carlo methods. Acta Numer. **7**, 1–49 (1998)

22. C. Camerer, M. Weber, Recent developments in modeling preferences: uncertainty and ambiguity. J. Risk Uncertain. **5**(4), 325–370 (1992)

23. J. Castro, M. Kolp, J. Mylopoulos, Towards requirements-driven information systems engineering: the tropos project. Inf. Syst. **27**(6), 365–389 (2002)

24. E. Charniak, Bayesian networks without tears. AI Mag. **12**(4), 50 (1991)

25. L. Chen, P. Pu, Survey of preference elicitation methods, in *Ecole Politechnique Federale de Lausanne (EPFL), IC/2004/67* (2004)

26. B.H.C. Cheng, R. de Lemos, H. Giese, P. Inverardi, J. Magee, J. Andersson, B. Becker, N. Bencomo, Y. Brun, B. Cukic, et al., *Software Engineering for Self-adaptive Systems: A Research Roadmap* (Springer, Berlin, 2009)

27. C.I. Chesñevar, A.G. Maguitman, R.P. Loui, Logical models of argument. ACM Comput. Surv. (CSUR) **32**(4), 337–383 (2000)

28. Y. Chevaleyre, U. Endriss, J. Lang, N. Maudet, A short introduction to computational social choice, in *Proceedings of the 33rd Conference on Current Trends in Theory and Practice of Computer Science* (Springer, Berlin, 2007), pp. 51–69

29. L. Chung, J. Cesar Sampaio do Prado Leite, On non-functional requirements in software engineering, in *Conceptual Modeling: Foundations and Applications* (Springer, Berlin, 2009), pp. 363–379

30. E.M. Clarke, J.M. Wing, Formal methods: state of the art and future directions. ACM Comput. Surv. (CSUR) **28**(4), 626–643 (1996)

31. J. Cleland-Huang, R. Settimi, C. Duan, X. Zou, Utilizing supporting evidence to improve dynamic requirements traceability, in *Proceedings 13th IEEE International Conference on Requirements Engineering* (IEEE, 2005), pp. 135–144

32. J. Conklin, M.L. Begeman, gIBIS: a hypertext tool for exploratory policy discussion. ACM Trans. Inf. Syst. (TOIS) **6**(4), 303–331 (1988)

33. L. Conradt, C. List, Group decisions in humans and animals: a survey. Philos. Trans. R. Soc. B: Biol. Sci. **364**(1518), 719–742 (2009)

34. R. Cox, Representation construction, externalised cognition and individual differences. Learn. Instr. **9**(4), 343–363 (1999)

35. O. Creighton, M. Ott, B. Bruegge, Software cinema-video-based requirements engineering, in *14th IEEE International Conference on Requirements Engineering* (IEEE, 2006), pp. 109–118

36. A. Dardenne, A. Van Lamsweerde, S. Fickas, Goal-directed requirements acquisition. Sci. Comput. Program. **20**(1), 3–50 (1993)

37. R. Darimont, A. Van Lamsweerde, Formal refinement patterns for goal-driven requirements elaboration. ACM SIGSOFT Softw. Eng. Notes **21**(6), 179–190 (1996)

38. A. Davis, O. Dieste, A. Hickey, N. Juristo, A.M. Moreno, Effectiveness of requirements elicitation techniques: empirical results derived from a systematic review, in *14th IEEE International Conference on Requirements Engineering* (IEEE, 2006), pp. 179–188

39. V.A. de Carvalho, J.P.A. Almeida, G. Guizzardi, Using reference domain ontologies to define the real-world semantics of domain-specific languages, in *Advanced Information Systems Engineering* (Springer, Berlin, 2014), pp. 488–502

40. W.-P. de Roever, K. Engelhardt, K.-H. Buth, *Data Refinement: Model-oriented Proof Methods and their Comparison*, vol. 47 (Cambridge University Press, Cambridge, 1998)

41. E.W. Dijkstra, Chapter I: notes on structured programming, in *Structured Programming* (Academic Press Ltd., London, 1972), pp. 1–82

42. C. Domshlak, E. Hüllermeier, S. Kaci, H. Prade, Preferences in AI: an overview. Artif. Intell. **175**(7), 1037–1052 (2011)

43. W.F. Dowling, J.H. Gallier, Linear-time algorithms for testing the satisfiability of propositional horn formulae. J. Log. Program. **1**(3), 267–284 (1984)

44. D. Dubois, H. Prade, Possibility theory as a basis for qualitative decision theory. IJCAI **95**, 1924–1930 (1995)

45. P.M. Dung, On the acceptability of arguments and its fundamental role in nonmonotonic reasoning, logic programming and n-person games. Artif. Intell. **77**(2), 321–357 (1995)

46. N.A. Ernst, A. Borgida, I.J. Jureta, J. Mylopoulos, Agile requirements engineering via paraconsistent reasoning. Inf. Syst. **43**, 100–116 (2014)

47. J. Figueira, S. Greco, M. Ehrgott, *Multiple Criteria Decision Analysis: State of the Art Surveys*, vol. 78 (Springer, Berlin, 2005)

48. A.C.W. Finkelstein, D. Gabbay, A. Hunter, J. Kramer, B. Nuseibeh, Inconsistency handling in multiperspective specifications. IEEE Trans. Softw. Eng. **20**(8), 569–578 (1994)

49. J.C. Fodor, M.R. Roubens, *Fuzzy Preference Modelling and Multicriteria Decision Support*, vol. 14 (Springer, Berlin, 1994)

50. A. Fuxman, L. Liu, J. Mylopoulos, M. Pistore, M. Roveri, P. Traverso, Specifying and analyzing early requirements in Tropos. Requir. Eng. **9**(2), 132–150 (2004)

51. D. Gentner, S. Goldin-Meadow, *Language in Mind: Advances in the Study of Language and Thought* (MIT Press, Cambridge, 2003)

52. J. Ginzburg, Interrogatives: questions, facts and dialogue, in *The Handbook of Contemporary Semantic Theory* (Blackwell, Oxford, 1996)

53. P. Giorgini, J. Mylopoulos, E. Nicchiarelli, R. Sebastiani, Reasoning with goal models, in *Conceptual Modeling—ER 2002* (Springer, Berlin, 2003), pp. 167–181

54. L. Gleitman, A. Papafragou, Language and thought, in *Cambridge Handbook of Thinking and Reasoning* (2005), pp. 633–661

55. J.A. Goguen, C. Linde, Techniques for requirements elicitation, Requir. Eng. **93**, 152–164 (1993)

56. O.C.Z. Gotel, A.C.W. Finkelstein, An analysis of the requirements traceability problem, in *Proceedings of the First International Conference on Requirements Engineering* (IEEE, 1994), pp. 94–101

57. S. Greco, B. Matarazzo, R. Slowinski, Rough sets theory for multicriteria decision analysis. Eur. J. Oper. Res. **129**(1), 1–47 (2001)

58. S. Greenspan, J. Mylopoulos, A. Borgida, On formal requirements modeling languages: Rml revisited, in *Proceedings of the 16th International Conference on Software Engineering* (IEEE Computer Society Press, Los Alamitos, 1994), pp. 135–147

59. S.J. Greenspan, A. Borgida, J. Mylopoulos, A requirements modeling language and its logic. Inf. Syst. **11**(1), 9–23 (1986)

60. S.J. Greenspan, J. Mylopoulos, A. Borgida, Capturing more world knowledge in the requirements specification, in *Proceedings of the 6th International Conference on Software Engineering* (IEEE Computer Society Press, Tokyo, 1982), pp. 225–234

61. N. Guarino, Formal ontology, conceptual analysis and knowledge representation. Int. J. Hum. Comput. Stud. **43**(5), 625–640 (1995)

62. J.J. Gumperz, S.C. Levinson, *Rethinking Linguistic Relativity* (Cambridge University Press, Cambridge, 1996)

63. C.A. Gunter, E.L. Gunter, M. Jackson, P. Zave, A reference model for requirements and specifications, in *Proceedings 4th International Conference on Requirements Engineering* (IEEE, 2000), p. 189

64. S.J. Garland, K.D. Jones, A. Modet, J.M. Wing, Larch: languages and tools for formal specification, in *Texts and Monographs in Computer Science* (Citeseer, 1993)

65. S.O. Hansson, Preference logic, in *Handbook of Philosophical Logic* (Springer, Berlin, 2002), pp. 319–393
66. S.O. Hansson, T. Grne-Yanoff, Preferences, in *The Stanford Encyclopedia of Philosophy*, Winter 2012 edn., ed. by E.N. Zalta (2012), http://plato.stanford.edu/archives/win2012/entries/preferences/
67. D. Harel, B. Rumpe, Meaningful modeling: what's the semantics of "semantics"? Computer **37**(10), 64–72 (2004)
68. C.L. Heitmeyer, R.D. Jeffords, B.G. Labaw, Automated consistency checking of requirements specifications. ACM Trans. Softw. Eng. Methodol. (TOSEM) **5**(3), 231–261 (1996)
69. A. Herrmann, M. Daneva, Requirements prioritization based on benefit and cost prediction: an agenda for future research, in *16th IEEE International Requirements Engineering, RE'08* (IEEE, 2008), pp. 125–134
70. A.M. Hickey, A.M. Davis, A unified model of requirements elicitation. J. Manag. Inf. Syst. **20**(4), 65–84 (2004)
71. D. Hitchcock, Informal logic and the concept of argument. Philos. Log. **5**, 101–129 (2006)
72. C.A.R. Hoare, *Proof of correctness of data representations* (Springer, 2002)
73. J. Hopcroft, R. Tarjan, Algorithm 447: efficient algorithms for graph manipulation. Commun. ACM **16**(6), 372–378 (1973)
74. A. Hunter, B. Nuseibeh, Managing inconsistent specifications: reasoning, analysis, and action. ACM Trans. Softw. Eng. Methodol. (TOSEM) **7**(4), 335–367 (1998)
75. United Kingdom Hydrograph, United Kingdom Hydrographic Office, and U S Naval Observatory. *2010 Nautical Almanac: Commercial Edition*. Paradise Cay Publications (2009)
76. K.E. Iverson, Notation as a tool of thought. ACM SIGAPL APL Quote Quad **35**(1–2), 2–31 (2007)
77. D. Jackson, Alloy: a lightweight object modelling notation. ACM Trans. Softw. Eng. Methodol. (TOSEM) **11**(2), 256–290 (2002)
78. D. Jonassen, Using cognitive tools to represent problems. J. Res. Technol. Educ. **35**(3), 362–381 (2003)
79. D. Jonassen, J. Strobel, C.B. Lee, Everyday problem solving in engineering: lessons for engineering educators. J. Eng. Educ. **95**(2), 139–151 (2006)
80. I.J. Jureta, A. Borgida, N.A. Ernst, J. Mylopoulos, Techne: towards a new generation of requirements modeling languages with goals, preferences, and inconsistency handling, in *Requirements Engineering (RE)* (2010), pp. 115–124
81. I.J. Jureta, A. Borgida, N.A. Ernst, J. Mylopoulos, The requirements problem for adaptive systems. ACM Trans. Manag. Inf. Syst. (TMIS) **5**(3), 17 (2014)
82. I.J. Jureta, S. Faulkner, P.-Y. Schobbens, A more expressive softgoal conceptualization for quality requirements analysis, in *Conceptual Modeling-ER 2006* (Springer, 2006), pp. 281–295
83. I.J. Jureta, S. Faulkner, P.-Y. Schobbens, Clear justification of modeling decisions for goal-oriented requirements engineering. Requir. Eng. **13**(2), 87–115 (2008)
84. I.J. Jureta, J. Mylopoulos, S. Faulkner, Revisiting the core ontology and problem in requirements engineering, in *16th IEEE International Conference on Requirements Engineering, RE'08* (IEEE, 2008), pp. 71–80
85. I.J. Jureta, J. Mylopoulos, S. Faulkner, Analysis of multi-party agreement in requirements validation, in *17th IEEE International Conference on Requirements Engineering*, RE'09 (IEEE, 2009), pp. 57–66
86. D. Kahneman, A. Tversky, Prospect theory: an analysis of decision under risk. Econom. J. Econom. Soc. **47**, 263–291 (1979)
87. N. Karacapilidis, D. Papadias, Computer supported argumentation and collaborative decision making: the hermes system. Inf. Syst. **26**(4), 259–277 (2001)
88. J. Karlsson, C. Wohlin, B. Regnell, An evaluation of methods for prioritizing software requirements. Inf. Softw. Technol. **39**(14), 939–947 (1998)
89. P. Kay, W. Kempton, What is the Sapir-Whorf hypothesis? Am. Anthropol. **86**(1), 65–79 (1984)

90. J. Krogstie, O.I. Lindland, G. Sindre, Towards a deeper understanding of quality in requirements engineering, in *Advanced Information Systems Engineering* (Springer, Berlin, 1995), pp. 82–95

91. W. Kunz, H.W.J. Rittel, *Issues as Elements of Information Systems*, vol. 131 (Institute of Urban and Regional Development, University of California Berkeley, California, 1970)

92. B. Lawson, *How Designers Think: The Design Process Demystified* (Routledge, New York, 2006)

93. J. Lee, Extending the Potts and Bruns model for recording design rationale, in *Proceedings of the 13th International Conference on Software Engineering* (IEEE, 1991), pp. 114–125

94. J. Lee, K.-Y. Lai, What's in design rationale? Hum.-Comput. Interact. **6**(3–4), 251–280 (1991)

95. J.C. Sampaio do Prado Leite, P.A. Freeman, Requirements validation through viewpoint resolution. IEEE Trans. Softw. Eng. **17**(12), 1253–1269 (1991)

96. E. Letier, A. Van Lamsweerde, Reasoning about partial goal satisfaction for requirements and design engineering. ACM SIGSOFT Softw. Eng. Notes **29**, 53–62 (2004)

97. S. Liaskos, S.A. McIlraith, S. Sohrabi, J. Mylopoulos, Integrating preferences into goal models for requirements engineering. Requir. Eng. **10**, 135–144 (2010)

98. S. Lichtenstein, P. Slovic, *The Construction of Preference* (Cambridge University Press, Cambridge, 2006)

99. P. Louridas, P. Loucopoulos, A generic model for reflective design. ACM Trans. Softw. Eng. Methodol. (TOSEM) **9**(2), 199–237 (2000)

100. R.T. Marler, J.S. Arora, Survey of multi-objective optimization methods for engineering. Struct. Multidiscip. Optim. **26**(6), 369–395 (2004)

101. M. McGrath, Propositions, in *The Stanford Encyclopedia of Philosophy*, Spring 2014 edn., ed. by E.N. Zalta (2014), http://plato.stanford.edu/archives/spr2014/entries/propositions/

102. S. Modgil, M. Caminada, Proof theories and algorithms for abstract argumentation frameworks, in *Argumentation in Artificial Intelligence* (Springer, Berlin, 2009), pp. 105–129

103. D.C. Mueller, *Public Choice: An Introduction* (Springer, Berlin, 2004)

104. J. Mylopoulos, A. Borgida, M. Jarke, M. Koubarakis, Telos: representing knowledge about information systems. ACM Trans. Inf. Syst. (TOIS) **8**(4), 325–362 (1990)

105. J. Mylopoulos, L. Chung, B. Nixon, Representing and using nonfunctional requirements: a process-oriented approach. IEEE Trans. Softw. Eng. **18**(6), 483–497 (1992)

106. J. Neter, J. Wasserman, M.H. Kutner, *Applied Linear Regression Models* (Irwin Homewood, IL, 1989)

107. B. Nuseibeh, J. Kramer, A. Finkelstein, A framework for expressing the relationships between multiple views in requirements specification. IEEE Trans. Softw. Eng. **20**(10), 760–773 (1994)

108. J. Pearl, *Probabilistic Reasoning in Intelligent Systems: Networks of Plausible Inference* (Morgan Kaufmann, San Mateo, 1988)

109. E. Pederson, E. Danziger, D. Wilkins, S. Levinson, S. Kita, G. Senft, Semantic typology and spatial conceptualization. Language **74**, 557–589 (1998)

110. M.S. Pini, F. Rossi, K.B. Venable, T. Walsh, Aggregating partially ordered preferences. J. Log. Comput. **19**(3), 475–502 (2009)

111. J.L. Pollock, Defeasible reasoning. Cogn. Sci. **11**(4), 481–518 (1987)

112. F. Portoraro, Automated reasoning, in *The Stanford Encyclopedia of Philosophy*, Winter 2014 edn., ed. by E.N. Zalta (2014), http://plato.stanford.edu/archives/win2014/entries/reasoning-automated/

113. H. Prakken, G. Vreeswijk, Logics for defeasible argumentation, in *Handbook of Philosophical Logic* (Springer, Berlin, 2002), pp. 219–318

114. B. Ramesh, V. Dhar, Supporting systems development by capturing deliberations during requirements engineering. IEEE Trans. Softw. Eng. **18**(6), 498–510 (1992)

115. B. Ramesh, M. Jarke, Toward reference models for requirements traceability. IEEE Trans. Softw. Eng. **27**(1), 58–93 (2001)

116. N. Rescher, The logic of preference, in *Topics in Philosophical Logic* (Springer, New York, 1968), pp. 287–320

117. F. Ricca, G. Scanniello, M. Torchiano, G. Reggio, E. Astesiano, On the effectiveness of screen mockups in requirements engineering: results from an internal replication, in *Proceedings of the 2010 ACM-IEEE International Symposium on Empirical Software Engineering and Measurement* (ACM, 2010), p. 17

118. H.W.J. Rittel, M.M. Webber, Dilemmas in a general theory of planning. Policy Sci. **4**(2), 155–169 (1973)

119. W.N. Robinson, S.D. Pawlowski, V. Volkov, Requirements interaction management. ACM Comput. Surv. (CSUR) **35**(2), 132–190 (2003)

120. S. Russell, P. Norvig, Artificial intelligence. A modern approach. *Artificial Intelligence*, vol. 25 (Prentice-Hall, Egnlewood Cliffs, 1995)

121. S. Shapiro, Classical logic, in *The Stanford Encyclopedia of Philosophy*, Winter 2013 edn., ed. by Edward N. Zalta (2013), http://plato.stanford.edu/archives/win2013/entries/logic-classical/

122. M. Shaw, D. Garlan, *Software Architecture: Perspectives on an Emerging Discipline*, vol. 1 (Prentice Hall, Englewood Cliffs, 1996)

123. S.B. Shum, Design argumentation as design rationale. Encycl. Comput. Sci. Technol. **35**(20), 95–128 (1996)

124. S.B. Shum, N. Hammond, Argumentation-based design rationale: what use at what cost? Int. J. Hum. Comput. Stud. **40**(4), 603–652 (1994)

125. G. Simari, I. Rahwan, *Argumentation in Artificial Intelligence* (Springer, Heidelberg, 2009)

126. G.R. Simari, R.P. Loui, A mathematical treatment of defeasible reasoning and its implementation. Artif. Intell. **53**(2), 125–157 (1992)

127. H.A. Simon, The structure of ill-structured problems, in *Models of Discovery* (Springer, Berlin, 1977), pp. 304–325

128. G. Sindre, A.L. Opdahl, Eliciting security requirements with misuse cases. Requir. Eng. **10**(1), 34–44 (2005)

129. B. Smith, C. Welty, Ontology: towards a new synthesis, in *Formal Ontology in Information Systems* (ACM Press, USA, 2001), pp. 3–9 (pp. iii-x)

130. J.M. Spivey, J.R. Abrial, *The Z Notation* (Prentice Hall, Hemel Hempstead, 1992)

131. S. Staab, R. Studer, *Handbook on Ontologies* (Springer, Berlin, 2010)

132. M. Staples, Critical rationalism and engineering: ontology. Synthese **191**(10), 2255–2279 (2014)

133. C. Starmer, Developments in non-expected utility theory: the hunt for a descriptive theory of choice under risk. J. Econ. Lit. **38**, 332–382 (2000)

134. M. Suwa, J. Gero, T. Purcell, Unexpected discoveries and s-invention of design requirements: important vehicles for a design process. Des. Stud. **21**(6), 539–567 (2000)

135. B.G. Tabachnick, L.S. Fidell, et al., *Using Multivariate Statistics* (Allyn and Bacon Boston, 2001)

136. A. Tarski, The semantic conception of truth: and the foundations of semantics. Philos. Phenomenol. Res. **4**(3), 341–376 (1944)

137. Richard Thaler, Toward a positive theory of consumer choice. J. Econ. Behav. Organ. **1**(1), 39–60 (1980)

138. A. Tversky, D. Kahneman, Judgment under uncertainty: heuristics and biases. Science **185**(4157), 1124–1131 (1974)

139. A. Tversky, P. Slovic, D. Kahneman, The causes of preference reversal. Am. Econ. Rev. **80**, 204–217 (1990)

140. J.F.A.K. van Benthem, A. Ter Meulen. *Handbook of Logic and Language* (Elsevier, Amsterdam, 1996)

141. A. Van Lamsweerde, Goal-oriented requirements engineering: a guided tour, in *Proceedings of the Fifth IEEE International Symposium on Requirements Engineering* (IEEE, 2001), pp. 249–262

142. A. Van Lamsweerde, R. Darimont, E. Letier, Managing conflicts in goal-driven requirements engineering. IEEE Trans. Softw. Eng. **24**(11), 908–926 (1998)

143. A. Van Lamsweerde, E. Letier, Handling obstacles in goal-oriented requirements engineering. IEEE Trans. Softw. Eng. **26**(10), 978–1005 (2000)
144. D.N. Walton, *Informal Logic: A Handbook for Critical Argumentation* (Cambridge University Press, Cambridge, 1989)
145. P. Weil, Nonexpected utility in macroeconomics. Q. J. Econ. **105**, 29–42 (1990)
146. J. Whittle, P. Sawyer, N. Bencomo, B.H.C. Cheng, J.-M. Bruel, Relax: incorporating uncertainty into the specification of self-adaptive systems, in *17th IEEE International Conference on Requirements Engineering*, RE'09 (IEEE, 2009), pp. 79–88
147. J.M. Wing, A specifier's introduction to formal methods. Computer **23**(9), 8–22 (1990)
148. N. Wirth, Program development by stepwise refinement. Commun. ACM **14**(4), 221–227 (1971)
149. E.S.K. Yu, Modelling strategic relationships for process reengineering. Ph.D. thesis (University of Toronto, 1995)
150. E.S.K. Yu, Modeling organizations for information systems requirements engineering, in *Proceedings of IEEE International Symposium on Requirements Engineering* (IEEE, 1993), pp. 34–41
151. E.S.K. Yu, Towards modelling and reasoning support for early-phase requirements engineering, in *Proceedings of the Third IEEE International Symposium on Requirements Engineering* (IEEE, 1997), pp. 226–235
152. E.S.K. Yu, *Social Modeling for Requirements Engineering* (Mit Press, Cambridge, 2011)
153. P. Zave, M. Jackson, Four dark corners of requirements engineering. ACM Trans. Softw. Eng. Methodol. (TOSEM) **6**(1), 1–30 (1997)
154. M. Zeleny, J.L. Cochrane, *Multiple Criteria Decision Making*, vol. 25. (McGraw-Hill, New York, 1982)
155. J. Zhang, The nature of external representations in problem solving. Cogn. Sci. **21**(2), 179–217 (1997)

Index

For the reader's convenience, the index includes the most important Language Modules, Language Services, and Requirements Modeling Languages, in order to help finding them quickly.

© Springer International Publishing Switzerland 2015
I. Jureta, *The Design of Requirements Modelling Languages*,
DOI 10.1007/978-3-319-18821-8

Printed in the United States
By Bookmasters